Income Elasticity and Economic Development

Advanced Studies in Theoretical and Applied Econometrics

Volume 42

Managing Editor:
J. Marquez, *The Federal Reserve Board, Washington, D.C., U.S.A.*

Editorial Board:
F.G. Adams, *University of Pennsylvania, Philadelphia, U.S.A.*
P. Balestra, *University of Geneva, Switzerland*
M.G. Dagenais, *University of Montreal, Canada*
D. Kendrick, *University of Texas, Austin, U.S.A.*
J.H.P. Paelinck, *Netherlands Economic Institute, Rotterdam, The Netherlands*
R.S. Pindyck, *Sloane School of Management, M.I.T., U.S.A.*
W. Welfe, *University of Lodz, Poland*

The titles published in this series are listed at the end of this volume.

Income Elasticity and Economic Development

Methods and Applications

HB
139
H367
2005
WEB

by

M. Ohidul Haque

*Victoria University,
Footscray, Australia*

 Springer

A C.I.P. Catalogue record for this book is available from the Library of Congress.

ISBN-10 0-387-24292-9 (HB) Springer Dordrecht, Berlin, Heidelberg, New York
ISBN-10 0-387-24344-5 (e-book) Springer Dordrecht, Berlin, Heidelberg, New York
ISBN-13 978 0-387-24292-7 (HB) Springer Dordrecht, Berlin, Heidelberg, New York
ISBN-13 978 0-387-24344-3 (e-book) Springer Dordrecht, Berlin, Heidelberg, New York

Published by Springer,
P.O. Box 17, 3300 AA Dordrecht, The Netherlands.

Printed on acid-free paper

All Rights Reserved
© 2005 Springer
No part of this work may be reproduced, stored in a retrieval system, or transmitted
in any form or by any means, electronic, mechanical, photocopying, microfilming, recording
or otherwise, without written permission from the Publisher, with the exception
of any material supplied specifically for the purpose of being entered
and executed on a computer system, for exclusive use by the purchaser of the work.

Printed in the Netherlands.

TO MY PARENTS

CONTENTS

PREFACE

Consumer demand analysis attempts to explain variations in consumers' expenditure, using time-series and cross-sectional data on income, price, the distribution of income, the effects of the introduction of new commodities and changes in tastes and preferences. In most planning and forecasting situations, the error in forecasting of real income is likely to be less than that associated with relative prices. As a result, interest centres on the relationship between expenditure on a particular item and income, treating prices as fixed. Hence, it is of great interest to estimate income elasticity for various household expenditure items. This is because it gives the percentage change in expenditure on a commodity due to 1% rise in household income, which is very helpful for planning and forecasting purposes.

Any planned governmental investment would lead to economic growth, which is mainly measured by income elasticity, but the methods of estimating income elasticity is quite large, varying from traditional methods to sophisticated method based on concentration curves. The method of estimating income elasticity by various alternative methods is the subject matter of this book. The present book is mainly concerned with cross-sectional data in estimating income elasticity for various household expenditure items. It provides a number of new techniques for estimating income elasticity, which have distinct advantages over the traditional methods. For example, estimating income elasticity from the Box-Cox Engel function based on a non-linear multi-dimensional search technique is a new addition to our knowledge. A new method of computing Engel elasticity based on concentration curves is also presented in this book. Furthermore, a new method of estimating the change in consumer demand with respect to an increase in income and a change in income inequality from household expenditure survey data is also provided. Empirical illustrations are given with reference to Australian Household Expenditure Survey (HES) data.

The present book constitutes an investigation into the principles underlying the formulation and estimation of income elasticity by various techniques for the Australian HES data. Some basic observations on the Australian HES data collected by the Australian Bureau of Statistics (ABS) are provided in Chapter 2. The discrimination among the various forms of Engel curves has been made in Chapter 3, while various problems in computing Engel elasticity by the traditional Weighted Least Squares (WLS) method are dealt with in Chapter 4. Estimation of income elasticity based on the Box-Cox general Engel function is presented in chapter 5. A review of income distribution, and estimation of income elasticity based on concentration curves are presented in chapters 6 and 7 respectively. Chapter 8 is concerned with the estimation of increased consumer demand for various household consumption items with respect to changes in income and income inequality. Demands for some specific household consumption items such as food, transport and communication, and alcohol are presented in chapters 9, 10 and 11 respectively. Chapter 12 deals with a review of consumers' equivalence scales, which are important for an accurate estimation of income elasticity, while the final chapter provides some concluding remarks about the studies presented in this book.

This book provides good examples showing how to calculate income elasticity using a number of methods from widely available published grouped data. Some of the techniques presented here can be used in a wide range of policy areas in all developed, under developed and developing countries. Policy analysts, economists, business analysts and market researchers can find this book very useful.

M. O. HAQUE

ACKNOWLEDGMENTS

I wish to express my gratitude to Victoria University, where I spent more than seven years writing this book, which is heavily drawn from a number of published and forthcoming papers. Most importantly, I am grateful to an unknown referee, who read the entire manuscript several times and provided valuable comments to improve the manuscript. My appreciation is extended to Mr Li Weidong of Beijing Jiaotong University, who assisted me in typing a large portion of the book. I am also very grateful to Associate Professor Alan Morris, and Mr. Jesse Singh, who helped me to put the entire book into the publisher's prescribed formate. Of course, I gratefully acknowledge Mrs Herma Drees and Ms Deborah of Springer, who provided constant advice and help in preparing to the manuscript. Indeed I acknowledge Ms Margarita Kumnick of CSES of Victoria University who edited and proofread the final manuscript for publication.

At this stage, I gratefully acknowledge the publishers of *Metroeconomica, Journal of Economic Development, Sankhya, Indian journal of Quantitative economics, Drug and Alcohol Review, Transportation and Journal of Applied Statistics*, for permission to use my articles and notes already published in these journals.

Finally, I wish to express my appreciation to my wife, Nargis and my three children, Tariq, Sadira and Mahera. I missed many enjoyable moments with them due to my heavy workload in preparing this book.

ABOUT THE AUTHOR

Dr M. Ohidul Haque is an applied econometrician and a senior lecturer at Victoria University in Melbourne, Australia. He is a Fellow of the Royal Statistical Society (London), and completed his Ph.D from the University of Sydney in 1984.

Dr Haque was born in Bangladesh and earned his BSc. (Hons.) and M.Sc. degrees in Statistics in that country. He was awarded an Advanced Postgraduate Diploma in Econometrics and Planning from the Indian Statistical Institute, Calcutta.

Dr Haque came to Australia in 1977 as a Research Scholar to do his Ph.D at the University of Sydney. During his career he has been Chief Econometrician at the Australian Institute of Family Studies, Head of the Evaluation and Statistical Services Section of Vic Roads, and worked in many other organisations in various senior research and management positions in Australia and in overseas. He is a pioneer and one of the major exponents in inequality, social justice, and in road safety areas.

Dr Haque is the author of numerous journal articles, and research and technical reports which incorporate practical applications for business, public and social policy decision-making.

Currently Dr Haque is researching consumption inequality, which is sponsored by an Australian Research Council Discovery grant. He is now contemplating undertaking major studies on income inequalities for a number of countries in the world to see the effects of income inequality due to current economic growth and rapid economic development in recent years.

CHAPTER 1

INTRODUCTION

In this chapter, readers will find out what is contained in this book. A brief review on demand analysis and its properties are provided in this introductory chapter, because the book is concerned with income elasticity, which evolves from the theory of demand analysis. It also provides a brief review of literature on Engel curve analysis and its uses. A broad outline and contributions of the book are also presented here along with limitations and concluding remarks.

1. INTRODUCTION

A review of what is contained in this book is given in this introductory chapter. The book provides a number of alternative methods of estimating income elasticity based on the analysis of the Australian Household Expenditure Survey (HES) Data. The nature of the work is partly theoretical and partly empirical. In most of the chapters, methodological developments are provided first and then those theories are applied to the empirical data to estimate income elasticity. As this book is concerned with the estimation of income elasticity, which evolves from demand analysis, it is felt necessary to give a short review of demand analysis, which is presented in Section 2. Definitions, limitations and uses of Engel curve analysis are presented in Section 3, while an outline of the contributions of the book is given in Section 4. Some concluding remarks and limitations of the studies presented in this book are given in the final section.

2. A BRIEF DISCUSSION ON DEMAND ANALYSIS

Demand analysis attempts to explain variations in consumer expenditure, using time-series and cross-sectional data on income and prices. For a meaningful study, a model should be built in such a way that it can test *a priori* beliefs. These *a priori* beliefs may be taken on an *ad hoc* basis, or be deduced from the maintained hypothesis under some assumptions and postulates. Demand theory uses both the *ad hoc* specification and the derived theoretical specification. Most demand models are combinations of these two. However, a broad distinction can be made between two classes of models, which are known as '*ad hoc* models' and '*axiomatic* models'. The *ad hoc* models in demand theory can be constructed independently from utility theory, whereas the *axiomatic* models of demand have developed from the neoclassical utility theory.[1] As a result of the developments of utility theory, the empirical demand theorist can adopt as his maintained hypothesis a definite *axiomatic* structure, which yields substantial restrictions on the demand functions. Thus, it is clear that the estimates of the parameters of the '*axiomatic* model' are conditional. Moreover, empirical researchers can test the maintained hypothesis and test an *a priori* belief regarding the external factors.

On the empirical side, attention has been focused on the theory of demand and its relevance to applied demand analysis. In this connection, the theory is regarded as a tool of empirical investigation. Demand analysts are basically concerned with finding out the change in demand for a particular commodity due to a change in certain specified explanatory variables. In particular, we are interested to see the effects of changes in real income per person, the structure of relative prices, the distribution of income, the introduction of new commodities and changes in tastes and preferences. For example, per capita expenditure of a particular item may be expressed as a function of per capita income, the price of the goods relative to some overall price index, time, tastes and preferences, etc. In this regard, a functional form must be chosen for the demand equation before any analysis is carried out. Hence it is clear that the choice of the demand model itself has important implications.

Usually strong *a priori* beliefs are used to build demand models, which would interact with the data to yield reliable results. In this regard, some previously used functional form should serve as a basis for estimation. Moreover, even when the demand model is chosen, in most circumstances it is preferred to estimate only a few parameters for each consumption item. This is because in many planning and forecasting situations, the economist often has a much clearer idea about the future course of real income than relative prices. As a result, the interest centers on the relationship between expenditure on a particular item and income, treating prices as fixed. In 1857 Engel formulated empirical laws stating the relation between income and expenditure on a particular consumption item. More importantly, he established the proposition that 'the percentage of income spent on food decreased as the income increased'. This is popularly known as Engel's law. In this regard, some empirical illustrations are given below.

2.1 Literature on Applied Engel Curve Analysis

The collection of HES data is an old tradition, which stretches from the beginning of the nineteenth century to the present day. But, besides Engel's work, the subject did not attract much theoretical attention until Allen and Bowley (1935). They studied the British Family Budget data using a theoretical model and cross-sectional data. They used the linear functional form for their demand analysis. The

---

[1] For discussion of these works, see Marshall (1890), Cassel (1899, 1918), Moore (1914, 1922, 1925-26), Hicks and Allen (1934), Georgescu-Roegen (1936), Wold and Jureen (1953), Schumpeter (1954), Barten (1964, 1965, 1977), Bridge (1971), Brown and Deaton (1972), Ellis (1976), Blackorby, Boyce and Russell (1978), Deaton (1978, 1982, 1997), Muellbauer (1974, 1980), Deaton and Muellbauer (1980), Pollak and Wales (1978, 1979, 1981), Diewert and Wales (1987), Boyle (1996), David and Wales (1996), Banks, Blundell and Lewbel (1997), Brosig (1998, 2000)), and Huang and Lin (2000).

subject has further regained its importance, following the works of Nicholson (1949), Wold and Jureen (1953) and Stone (1954). After that, Prais and Houthakker (1955) conducted a pioneering work. They fitted five different forms of Engel functions, which can be listed as linear, semi-log, hyperbolic, double-log and log-inverse. They then concluded that the semi-log and the double-log Engel functions fitted best for food and non-food items respectively. They estimated the total expenditure elasticities for various food and non-food items on the basis of these functional forms.

Prais and Houthakker (1955) also incorporated household composition as a determinant of consumption patterns and rediscovered the concept of 'specific consumer scales' introduced by Sydenstricker and King (1921). In their analysis, individuals of different age and sex of a household were given different weights for different types of specific items. Unit weights were attached to the adult male members of the households for each specific commodity. They also introduced an overall 'income scale' by which individual consumers were weighted according to their shares in the total income of the household (HH). They used an iterative method to estimate these scales. Prais and Houthakker succeeded in estimating the specific coefficients because of the assumption of unit income coefficients over all types of family members at the outset of the analysis. This is an arbitrary assumption, which cannot be used in general for an Engel curve analysis. In this regard, Nicholson's (1949) method of estimating income scales may be used. He estimated the income coefficients of children by considering commodities for which the child's specific coefficients may be reasonably fixed at zero. Nicholson considered men's and women's clothing, tobacco and drinks for his analysis. His estimates were referred to as income differentials (or the 'cost of a child') rather than to income scales, because his Engel functions were not based on logarithmic transformations. However, the empirical results were disappointing although his principle seems to be sound. Forsyth (1960) made a thorough investigation on equivalent scales and concluded that the restrictions on the parameters of the Prais-Houthakker model, which incorporated specific and income effects could not be estimated simultaneously. Since then a number of authors such as Barten (1964), Singh and Nagar (1973), Muellbauer (1974, 1975, 1980), Bojer (1977, 1998), Kakwani (1977c), Hymans and Shapiro (1976), Kapteyn and Praag (1976), Ryan and Wales (1996, 1999), Ryan, Wales and Woodland (1982), and many other prominent authors have done research on this topic in different countries in the world, but none of them gained complete success. The problems of estimating 'consumers' *equivalence scales*' will be discussed extensively later in Chapter 12 of this book.

In 1957 Houthakker analysed 60 budget inquiries from 33 countries and concluded that expenditure elasticities varied from country to country. However, without any statistical tests, he has taken these elasticity estimates for different countries to be similar and established a few regularities, e. g.: (i) income elasticity of food is always less than unity (Engel's law); (ii) expenditure on housing also shows a similar pattern (Schwabe's law); and (iii) the elasticity of clothing is usually greater than unity. He used the double-log Engel function for this study. Later, Houthakker (1965) also used the double logarithmic functional form to combine time-series and cross-sectional data on expenditure of five groups of consumption items for the OECD countries and concluded that there were significant differences in the demand elasticities among various countries.

However, in the meantime Summers (1959) and Forsyth (1960) pointed out two major weaknesses of the traditional Engel curve analysis. Summers (1959) showed that the use of the Ordinary Least Squares (OLS) method to a single relationship with total expenditure as an independent variable produced inconsistent estimates of Engel parameters due to the fact that the statistical model underlying the study was really a set of simultaneous equations. Liviatan (1961) however, solved this problem by using the instrumental variable method, with family income as an instrument for total expenditure and obtained consistent estimates of Engel parameters for the double log and linear Engel functions.

The subject has also been developed in two other directions. First, Iyengar (1960a, 1964a) computed Engel elasticities for various Indian household consumption items from concentration curves, based on: (i) the double log Engel function; and (ii) the log-normal income (total expenditure) distribution function. Later, Kakwani (1977a, 1978) generalised this method and computed Engel elasticities from a special type of concentration curve. Second, Zarembka (1972, 1974) estimated total expenditure elasticities for Philippine food consumption items based on the Box-Cox type Engel function that contained many commonly used Engel functions. Bensu, Kmenta and Shapiro (1976) and Chang (1977) have also used the Box-Cox type Engel functions for their analyses.[2]

2.2 Properties of Demand Functions

A consumer's ordinary demand function gives the quantity of a commodity that a consumer will buy and can be expressed as a function of commodity prices (own price and prices of substitute, complementary and independent goods) and income (total expenditure) as follows.[3]

$$Y_i = f(P_1, P_2, ..., P_i, ..., P_n, X) \tag{1.1}$$

where Y_i = the quantity of the ith commodity, P_i = the price of the ith commodity and X = income (total expenditure).

The theory of consumer behaviour gives certain properties of individual demand from the constrained maximisation of a given individual utility function that is a

---

[2] Phlips (1974) showed how to analyse consumer behaviour of the households, using a dynamic demand system. While Lluch, Powell and Williams (1977) analysed the patterns of household demand and savings jointly for different countries of the world, using Lluch's (1973) extended linear expenditure system.

[3] This is because both total expenditure and prices of various goods and services play a major role in maintaining living standards. For example, the cost of living can vary significantly from region to region. In fact each region has its own price structure. Moreover, different people may pay different prices for the same commodity at a certain time in the same region, because of variation in prices among milk bars, Food Plus, Seven Eleven, 24 hour stores, super markets and items on sale, etc.

non-decreasing function of the quantities of all n commodities. However, if the above demand function is maximised subject to the budget constraints, then a complete demand model should satisfy the following restrictions.

(i) Budget restrictions:

$$\sum_i P_i \, Y_i \, (P,X) \;=\; X$$

(ii) Homogeneous of degree zero
in income and all prices, i.e.,

derivartives must satisfy:

$$X \frac{\partial Y_i}{\partial X} + \sum_j P_j \frac{\partial Y_i}{\partial P_j} \;=\; 0 \quad for\; i = 1,2,..\,n$$

(iii) Slutsky relations, i.e. the

substitution effect:

$$K_{ij} \;=\; \frac{\partial Y_i}{\partial P_j} + Y_j \frac{\partial Y_i}{\partial X}, \;\; \text{is symmetric, i.e}$$

K_{ij} for the ith item with

$$K_{ij} \;=\; K_{ji} \quad \text{for all i, j} = 1, 2,\ldots, \text{n and hence}$$

respect to the jth price:

$$\sum_i P_i K_{ij} \;=\; \sum_j P_j K_{ij} \;=\; 0.$$

These restrictions are the main content of the neoclassical theory of consumer demand. These are independent restrictions on a complete set of demand equations and are responsible for the considerable economy of parameterisation, which results when consumer behaviour is derived from certain axioms.

Applied consumption analysis is mainly concerned with the estimation of the parameters of one or all the equations in the system. Properties of these demand equations are obtained by utility maximisation. These properties will take the form of mathematical restrictions on the derivatives of the demand functions. The restrictions serve to reduce the dimensionality of the estimation problem and to deal with certain shortcomings of the available data. The analysis of demand can easily be conducted with reference to the traditional mathematical concept of 'slope' of the demand function, or the partial derivative. But usually it is historically analysed with reference to 'elasticity' or logarithmic partial derivatives. Thus the (Cournot) 'price elasticity of demand' for good i with respect to the price of the jth good is defined by

$$\eta_{ij} \;=\; \frac{\partial \, Log \, Y_i}{\partial \, Log \, P_j} \;=\; \frac{P_j}{Y_i} \frac{\partial \, Y_i}{\partial P_j} \tag{1.2}$$

If i = j, then η_{ij} is referred to as the 'own price elasticity' and otherwise 'cross-price elasticity'.

These (Cournot) price elasticities measure the percentage of uncompensated change in the demand for the ith good with respect to the percentage change in the price of the jth good. The alternative Slutsky's 'price elasticity of demand' is given by

$$S_{ij} = \left(\frac{P_j}{Y_i}\right) K_{ij} \tag{1.3}$$

where K_{ij} is defined earlier. It could easily be shown that S_{ij} measures the utility, maintaining income compensated percentage variation in the demand for the ith good, with respect to the percentage change in the jth price.

The 'Engel total expenditure (income) elasticity of demand' for the ith good is defined by

$$\eta_i = \frac{\partial \, Log \, Y_i}{\partial \, Log \, X} = \frac{X}{Y_i} \frac{\partial \, Y_i}{\partial \, X} \tag{1.4}$$

Here η_i measures the percentage change in demand with respect to percentage change in total expenditure (income).

Furthermore, the 'Budget share' of the ith good is defined by

$$W_i = \frac{P_i \, Y_i}{X} \tag{1.5}$$

which connects the Cournot and Slutsky price elasticities by the following relation.

$$S_{ij} = \eta_{ij} + W_j \, \eta_i \tag{1.6}$$

This relation is known as the Slutsky's relation. Finally the 'elasticity of substitution' between good i and j is defined by

$$d_{ij} = {S_{ij}}\big/{W_j} \tag{1.7}$$

With these concepts we can derive some important restrictions on a complete set of demand equations implied by utility theory, which can be listed as follows.

(a) Engel aggregation: $\Sigma W_i \, \eta_i = 1$

(b) Cournot aggregation: $\Sigma W_i \, \eta_{ij} = -W_j, (j = 1, 2, 3, \ldots \ n)$

(c) Symmetry condition: $W_i \, S_{ij} = W_j \, S_{ji}, \quad (i, j = 1, 2, 3, \ldots \ n)$

(d) Homogeneity: $\Sigma_j \eta_{ij} = -\eta_j \quad (i = 1, 2, \ \ldots \quad n)$

(e) Slutsky homogeneity: $\Sigma_j S_{ij} = 0, \quad (i = 1, 2, \ \ldots \quad n)$

(f)   Slutsky aggregation: $\sum_i W_i S_{ij} = 0, \quad (i = 1, 2, \quad \cdots \quad n)$

(g)   Slutskey's negative
        definite Hessian matrix: K is negative semi-definite, i.e.,

$$|K_{11}| < 0, \qquad \begin{vmatrix} K_{11} & K_{12} \\ K_{21} & K_{22} \end{vmatrix} \geq 0, \ \ldots \text{ etc.}$$

This is a familiar result that the principal minors of a negative definite matrix alternate in sign, beginning with the first minor being negative. These results are often relied upon in practice.

3. ENGEL CURVE ANALYSIS AND ITS USES

The theory of consumer behaviour is one of the most important sections of microeconomic theory. This is actually the theoretical basis of family budget analysis. This section of microeconomic theory is now regarded as a 'settled area of belief'. Hence theoretical models are well established. In this section, definitions, some problems and uses of Engel curve analysis are discussed. From the discussion in the previous section, we have seen that the demand equation of a particular item may be expressed as a function of consumers' income and market prices of all commodities. Now, if the prices are held constant, the demand for a particular item becomes a function of consumers' income only, which is popularly referred to as an Engel function.

Definition: An Engel curve is defined by the relationship between the expenditure on a particular commodity and total expenditure (disposable income). Thus, in general, the Engel curve is represented by

$$Y_i = f(X) \tag{1.8}$$

where Y_i represents the expenditure on the ith commodity and X is the consumer's total expenditure (disposable income). This is the starting point of the Engel curve analysis.

The estimation of the above Engel function (1.8) from HES data based on the assumption that on average, the differences in consumption patterns between high and low income households can be ascribed to their differences in current income (total expenditure). All other differences between consumption patterns of individual households are split into stochastic and non-stochastic components. The stochastic part is nicely described by a selected probability distribution, while non-stochastic differences are mainly due to differences of various socio-demographic characteristics of the households. Normally, the Engel curve analysis should be performed with homogeneous groups of households in which there is only a slight variation in factors that might have a significant effect on preferences. These factors are the educational and cultural background, occupation, age and sex composition of the households, and in particular the family size of the households. Moreover, this kind of study ignores prices, which means the budget data need to be collected over a short period of time and from regions where prices are more or less similar. In practice, these conditions are rarely satisfied, though a relaxation of some is made by certain techniques.

The concept of income and its statistical measurements are questionable. A household's wealth, both in total and in terms of its ownership of particular assets, could influence its current consumption pattern. The estimation of Engel curves without the separate influence of income and wealth is likely to be misleading if the relationship is used for prediction over time, because wealth and income are positively correlated in budget data. In such a situation, a sudden increase in income may not be matched by a similar increase in wealth. Dynamic specifications of demand functions are needed to solve this kind of problem. In a similar manner, the effects of the household's past income, consumption history and the effects of its expectations are ignored. By ignoring all these factors (which includes savings), the income variable can be treated as identical with total expenditure on consumer goods and services. Of all the factors other than income, household composition is the most important determinant of household consumption. Its effect on the expenditure pattern is also of considerable interest.

Households consist of individuals of different age, sex and family size. Their needs vary with these characteristics. There is no single natural measure of family size. Measurement of family size is a big problem in an Engel curve analysis. Counting the number of individuals in the household is one of the simplest measures of family size. Hence, a general formulation of the Engel curve is represented by

$$Y_{ij} = f_i(X_j, S_j) \tag{1.9}$$

where $Y_{ij}, X_j, and\ S_j$ are the expenditure on the ith item, household total expenditure (income) and household size of the jth household respectively. Application of the OLS method to this formulation (usually the widely used functional forms are linear, double log, semi-log, log-inverse and hyperbola) produces large standard errors of the estimated regression coefficients. This is because of the existence of a strong positive correlation between income and household size. In order to avoid this problem the function has often been formulated on a per capita basis as

$$\frac{Y_{ij}}{S_j} = f\left(\frac{X_j}{S_j}\right) \tag{1.10}$$

which is widely used in practice, but this has the disadvantage that in randomly selected samples $X_j \Big/ S_j$ tends to be negatively correlated with the number of children in the household.[4]

As a result of this, economies of scale prevail and hence for households with the same total expenditure (income) per person, the larger ones would enjoy a higher standard of living, in that they would have a larger expenditure per person on luxuries. Therefore, the family size measured by counting the number of persons in the household is not acceptable and hence both the above formulations are inadequate. Econometricians have tried to establish some measure for weighting the members of the household to transform them into a per unit consumer scale. For over a century, many attempts have been made by economists and statisticians to estimate the consumer unit scales. But, none of the attempts have been completely successful. An excellent review of the literature on *consumers' economics of scale* can be found in Woodbury (1944), Prais and Houthakker (1955), and Muellbauer (1980). The issue of measurement of *"consumer's unit scale"* will be discussed in details in Chapter 12 of this book.

Household expenditure surveys are concerned with the direct observation of the economic behaviour of households or of individuals of varying social and economic condition. Earlier, this kind of information was mainly used in making social policies, showing how poverty may affect certain sections of populations, what proportion of families live in various states of poverty, and how those proportions change through time. Household expenditure survey data can also be used for the purpose of providing weights for index numbers of the cost of living. Econometric investigations of family budgets are of great interest to academics for research purposes in understanding the demand structure of consumers and estimating income elasticities. This kind of data is also used to compare the living standard of households of different compositions.

Apart from the abovementioned uses, the demand functions derived from cross sectional data are of great interest and importance for production planning, policy making and for prediction purposes. Family budget analysis provides independent estimates of income elasticities in contrast to time series data, where both income and price elasticities can be estimated. Income elasticities estimated from time series data are not accurate because of the existence of serious multicollinearity between incomes and prices. But, the income elasticities derived from the cross-sectional data are quite good and hence these independent estimates are of great importance. Stone (1954) estimated price elasticities from time series data by using income elasticities derived from budget data as *a priori* information. Income elasticities derived from family budget data are also used in demand forecasting.

---

[4] A simple double logarithmic Engel curve for per capita expenditure on a particular item as a function of per capita income may avoid such a problem of multicollinearity.

4. OUTLINE AND CONTRIBUTIONS OF THIS BOOK

This book is mainly concerned with the estimation of income elasticity of demand for various Australian household expenditure items based on a number of Australian HESs data. These surveys were designed to investigate how the expenditure patterns of households varied according to various income levels and other characteristics (such as size and composition of the household, age, sex and occupational status of the household head, etc.). A rapid change of incomes and prices during several survey periods might have implications for interpreting changes in patterns of expenditure and income. This would not create a major problem for this study, because most of the present analyses are based on only one HES data, the 1975-76 Australian HES data, which are presented in a special form. Estimation of income elasticity by various alternative methods based on this data set is still quite valid and relevant even today for various developed, developing and under developed countries in the world. This is because even today most of the official HES data are published in grouped form due to the confidentiality nature of the data and for a number of other reasons.[5] Thus, income elasticity estimates by various methods based on this data can still be taken as relevant.

Estimating accurate income elasticity is important for making a number of proper social and economic development policies. This is because income elasticity of demand measures how much the quantity demanded of a good responds to a change in consumers' income. It is calculated as the percentage change in the quantity demanded divided by the percentage change in income. It allows us to analyse supply and demand with great precision. An accurate estimate of income elasticity is important, because, if elasticity lies between 0 and 1, the good is regarded as income inelastic, i.e., a necessary good implying that demand for it rises as income increases, but a smaller percentage of income is spent on these items. However, if the elasticity is greater than 1, the item is regarded as income elastic meaning a luxury item indicating that quantity demanded rises as income increases, and a larger percentage of income is spent on the item. Whereas, if the elasticity becomes negative then the item is considered inferior meaning that the demand for this kind of item decreases as income rises. Income elasticity of a certain item can indicate whether it is a luxury, necessary or inferior good depending on the level of income. Very high/low income elasticity suggests that when consumers' income goes up, consumers will buy more/less of that item. Thus, an accurate estimate of income elasticity of demand is very important and useful for proper policy implications, because it is used to see how sensitive the demand for income changes.

In addition to the above application of income elasticity, it is also commonly used in making proper demand forecasting. To estimate income elasticities one must specify and estimate demand relationships. This book constitutes an investigation into the principles underlying the formulation and estimation of income elasticity from the Australian HES data. Several methods of estimating income elasticity

---

[5] A number of HESs have been undertaken by the ABS since 1975-76, but none of them are appropriately presented to estimate income elasticity by the various methods used in this book.

based on the Australian HES data are presented in this book. The contents of each chapter of the book are discussed as follows.

Some basic observations on the Australian HESs data are provided in Chapter 2. The discrimination among the various forms of Engel curves has been made in chapters 3 and 5. We fitted several functional forms and found that a new functional form called the double semi-log (DSL) Engel function, which has never been used elsewhere, turns out to be the best functional form among several alternative functions on the basis of the distance function D^2-criterion and non-nested hypothesis testing procedure. This DSL function can also satisfy some important economic criteria viz.: (i) threshold; (ii) saturation; (iii) variable elasticity at different total expenditure levels; and (iv) the adding-up criteria. Finally, the elasticity estimates based on this DSL Engel function for different commodities show that the expenditure pattern of Australian households is very similar to those of other western developed countries.

A more general Engel function based on the Box-Cox transformation is presented in Chapter 5. A non-linear optimisation algorithm is applied to estimate the Box-Cox Engel function. A joint test on the different power transformations has been done by the likelihood ratio test and it turns out that the commonly used simple functional forms which are special cases of the general form, are not appropriate for the Australian HES data, although the double log function is not significantly different from the Box-Cox Engel function for five out of ten expenditure items. We thus, come to the crucial conclusion that the Box-Cox Engel function is the most appropriate to estimate income elasticity for various household expenditure items in Australia. However the estimated total expenditure elasticities for various food and non-food items obtained from the Box-Cox Engel function are not significantly different from those of commonly used Engel functions.

Chapter 4 is concerned with the problem of estimating non-linear Engel functions when estimated by the Generalized Least Squares (GLS) method for grouped data. It is argued here that in order to get unbiased estimates of Engel elasticities, the GLS method needs the within group geometric/harmonic means for the logarithmic/inverse Engel relationships. The Australian Bureau of Statistics (ABS) does not provide these within group geometric/harmonic means. We have estimated within group geometric/harmonic means by the indirect method based on concentration curves for any variable that is a function of per capita income.[6] These indirectly estimated within group geometric/harmonic means are then used to obtain Engel elasticities for the logarithmic/inverse relationships. The percentage differences of elasticity estimates computed by the GLS method using arithmetic means as the proxies for geometric/harmonic means, and estimated within group geometric/harmonic means based on concentration curves are then evaluated for the various non-linear Engel functions with reference to the Australian HES data. With regard to the direction of the difference of elasticity estimates of these two methods,

---

[6] Our results suggest that the estimation of within group geometric/harmonic means from concentration curve is not entirely satisfactory, since the indirectly estimated within group geometric/harmonic means sometimes exceeded the reported within group arithmetic means, which are calculated from sample values by the direct method.

in many cases our results contradict with the previous study made by Kakwani (1977b). In this chapter, we also extended the concept of the *average elasticity* of a variable elasticy Engel function for the multivariate case and some numerical results are then presented.

A review of the literature on personal income distribution is given in Chapter 6 to show how theoretical income density functions are developed. It also discusses the uses of income distribution in measuring income inequality and poverty for effective public policies, which may help to improve the economic well being of individuals and society as a whole. These concepts are then used to develop new theories to estimate income elasticities and increased consumer demands based on concentration curves, which are presented in the subsequent chapters.

A detailed discussion of the concentration curves, their constructions and specifications are provided in Chapter 7. We have also provided a new method of estimating income elasticity based on non-linear concentration curves. It is shown empirically, using the Australian HES data, that the proposed Engel curve is better than other commonly used well-known functional forms in two respects: goodness of fit, and the adding up criteria. The effects of family composition and *economies of scale* on total expenditure elasticities for the whole population are also provided. It should be pointed out that income elasticity estimates based on this new method can nicely describe the actual economic situation of the households of a nation at the time of economic growth and increasing inequality of income among individuals of a country. An alternative method of estimating increase in consumer demand from HES data is provided in Chapter 8. This is obtained by relaxing earlier assumptions about both the Engel function and the per capita total expenditure (income) distribution. The major contribution of this chapter is an evaluation of the effect of an increased income and changes in income inequality on consumer's demand of various commodities. Empirical results on an increase in consumers' demand for a number of functions are provided for the Australian HES data, and a few contradictory observations are made comparing these results to previous studies.

The natural sequence of the previous chapters is an extension of the analysis to specific commodities in detail instead of aggregate consumption of those commodities. In this respect, food, transport and communication, and alcohol expenditures are analysed separately in chapters 9, 10, and 11 respectively. Each of these items demands comprehensive study about the nature and composition of their expenditures. This is because food, and transport and communication are very important, since these are the largest and the second largest expenditure items respectively in Australian family budgets; while alcohol is an important part of Australian life and culture, and frequently used in religious, cultural and social ceremonies as well as business functions and recreational activities in Australia.

Demand for food is presented in Chapter 9 by disaggregating various food expenditure components, and per capita income levels and household compositions. Elasticities of various food items are computed based on the commonly used Engel functions along with the new method based on the implicit Engel function derived from concentration curves. It is demonstrated from our results that income elasticities of various food items are diminishing with the rising incomes, which is consistent with previously established theoretical and empirical evidence. More importantly, elasticity indices of various food items are provided in this chapter together with the contributions of each of the food items to the total food elasticity index. This will also show which food item contributes the highest or the lowest amount of inequality of food expenditure in Australia.

Demand for transportation and communication is provided in Chapter 10, which is based on the double semi-log Engel function, the best functional form on the basis of the distance function, D^2-criterion, and the non-nested hypothesis testing procedure. This function is then used to estimate total expenditure elasticity, and the percentage change in consumer demand due to changes in total expenditure and total expenditure inequalities; using the 1975-76 Australian Household Expenditure Survey data. The results of the analyses demonstrate that transport and communication is a necessary item in Australia on the basis of two criteria, viz., its elasticity is not significantly greater than unity, and the demand increases with the decrease of the total expenditure inequality, a criterion emphasized by Iyengar (1960b).

The demand for alcohol in Australia is presented in Chapter 11. Income elasticities for various alcohol items have been estimated from a new Engel function, which can be called the double semi-log Engel function. Beer had the lowest elasticity, whereas the elasticities for wine and spirits were much higher, placing them in the 'luxury' category. Elasticity indices of various alcohol items, including the contributions of different alcohol items to the total elasticity index are also provided in this chapter. The percentage changes in demand due to changes in total expenditure and total expenditure inequalities were also calculated. It is shown that the per capita changes in demand for beer and wine were inaccurate unless income distribution was considered. This technique can also be used to determine the level of consumption demand for various alcohol items.

An extensive review of literature on the measurement of consumers' equivalence scales is presented in Chapter 12, and discusses its usefulness in calculating income elasticity based on these scales due to varying needs of members of the household according to age and sex. Thus to find the consumers' unit scale, meaning exactly how many effective consumers there are in a household is important to accurately estimate income elasticity, which has wide ranging policy implications. Finally, some concluding remarks of the book are provided in Chapter 13.

5. LIMITATIONS AND CONCLUSIONS

This chapter briefly discusses demand analysis including Engel curve analysis and its properties. This is because income elasticity based on various alternative methods is presented in this book, which basically evolves from the theory of demand analysis. Major contributions of this book are also presented in this introductory chapter. The methods of estimating income elasticity presented in this book are highly relevant at present times when various countries are facing the problems of growing income inequality among its citizens due to emerging economic growth. Income elasticity estimates based on various methods presented in this book can nicely describe the actual economic situation of the households of a nation. This is because some of the methods can incorporate economic growth and income inequality nicely in calculating income elasticity. More importantly, we have presented a method, which is able to measure the effect of consumer's demand due to an increase in income and changes in income inequality. It is thus hoped that the contributions made by this book would help to solve some of the economic problems faced by various countries due to economic growth and income inequality.

Estimating income elasticity from a general survey is often problematic. More importantly, we have estimated income elasticity mainly based on household income and family size. We did not include other relevant socio-economic, environmental and geographical variables, which together might have a significant effect in estimating income elasticity. The income elasticity estimates presented in this book are based on the 1975-76 Australian HES data, which is quite dated. But it is still valid and relevant, because most of the elasticities are estimated based on grouped data, which are still valid and relevant since most of the official HES data are presented in grouped form due to the confidentiality nature of the data and for a number of other reasons. It can thus be argued that some of the new methods of estimating income elasticity based on grouped data, which are still widely produced by the data collecting authorities, are relevant even today more than any other time when various countries of the world are facing the problem of tackling the growing income inequality at a time of high economic growth.

CHAPTER 2

AUSTRALIAN HOUSEHOLD EXPENDITURE
SURVEYS

Readers will uncover how the Australian Bureau of Statistics (ABS) collects various versions of the Household Expenditure Survey (HES) data. They will also learn how these data are presented, their limitations and uses for academic and policy analyses, and how to improve the quality of the HES data for future social policy research.

1. INTRODUCTION

The Australian Household Expenditure Survey (HES) is a multi-purpose socio-economic enquiry of the nation conducted by the Australian Bureau of Statistics (ABS) in the form of successive 'series'. Each series took approximately a year for data collection. The enquiry on consumer expenditure has been a regular of all the HES series, beginning with the first series, which was conducted during July 1974 to June 1975 and confined to capital cities only. Later HESs covered the whole of Australia (except remote and sparsely populated areas).

These HESs were designed to find out how the expenditure patterns of private households vary according to different income levels and characteristics of households. Most of the information was collected from households on a recall basis with a particular reference period (which varied according to the type of expenditure) using interview techniques. In addition, all members of households aged 15 years and over were requested to record all 'payments made' over a two to four week period in a diary provided to each of them. The stratified multi-stage probability (proportional to the households and collector's districts) sampling procedure was followed for selecting the households, who were interviewed evenly throughout the survey year. Any expenditure made by members of the selected households for business purposes were not considered in these surveys. These surveys collected 'household expenditure', which included expenditures on those goods (both durable and non-durable) and services made by the members of the selected households for private consumption. Other components of household expenditure such as income tax, superannuation contributions, life insurance premiums, purchases of and deposits on dwellings and land are classified as 'other payments'.

Estimates for the broad (15 groups) and medium (120 major items) expenditure items were available from the beginning of the HES series by broad weekly household income and all households for the capital cities only. The estimates for urban and rural sectors were always distinguished and (see point 6 on page vii of the ABS catalogue No. 6516.0) became available from the 1975-76 HES in different broad income groups for different states and territories and for the whole of Australia. More importantly, the ABS began to release 'confidentialised' Unit Record Tapes for public use from the 1984 HES. Detailed tabulations covering various expenditure items can be found from the ABS publications for various versions of the HES. The concepts, definitions, and procedures remained more or less the same over the various versions of the HES, with some noticeable exceptions discussed in the following section.

Many important academic and policy research works are based on the HES data. Among many others, the following are some important and useful works based on these survey data.

* Studies on the functional forms of Engel curves by Haque (1988, 1989a, 1989b, 1996), Bewley (1982) and Hoa, Ironmonger and Manning (1983).
* Studies on income distribution by Yates (1991), Kakwani (1986), Houghton (1988), Harding (1984, 1995, 1997), Borland and Wilkins (1996), Borland (1998), Page and Simmons (2000) and NATSEM (1998, 2000).
* Studies on taxes and social welfare benefits on various classes of the population by Warren (1986, 1991), Dixon, Foster and Gallagher (1985), Agrawal (1989), Saunders (1987, 1992, 1994, 1997, 1998), Castles (1987), Australian Bureau of Statistics [ABS] (1987), and Mitchell, Harding and Gruen (1994).
* Studies on the cost of children by McDonald (1989, 1993), Bradbury (1989a) and Edgar (1989).
* Studies on patterns of household expenditure by Bradbury (1996), Haque (1984, 2000, 2001), Perkins (1991), Newell (1990), Whiteford (1991), Powles, Hage and Cosgrove (1990), and Newell, Ham and Coady (1987).

Despite many problems, researchers, planners and policy makers are using the HES data increasingly. It is necessary to continually examine the validity of the data and to take all possible steps for improving the usefulness of the data for planning and policy-making purposes at regional and national levels, and also for certain target groups such as aborigines and disadvantaged groups.

In this chapter, we make some observations on the limitations of HES data based on our experience, processing, tabulation and analysis of such data for various investigations. Among other things, we emphasise: (a) the need for field as well as technical studies, which examine the validity of the data being collected; (b) the need for studies on the inter-temporal comparability of the HES data from different versions; and (c) the need for timely release and/or publication of these data in a more meaningful way for some broad groups of consumption items.

2. CHANGES IN DATA COLLECTION PROCEDURES FOR VARIOUS VERSIONS

The basic data collection methodology remained approximately the same over the various versions of the HES. However, a few changes were made from time to time in the procedure of collecting HES data. Some important changes are mentioned below.

(1)   The geographical coverage of the 1974-75 HES was confined to the six state capital cities and Canberra only. However, the subsequent surveys covered the entire country (both urban and rural areas) except for remote and sparsely populated areas.

(2)   In the first series of the HES, any usual member of the household (including the head) absent at the time of interview and not returning within 7 days was excluded from the survey, whereas in the later series if the head of the household was absent at the time of interview and was expected to return after 7 days, but within 6 weeks of that date then the person was included as a member of the household. Income and expenditure data were collected for absent heads by a recall method without any diary information relating to the household head.

(3)   The diary-keeping period was 'two weeks' in the first series. During the second and third series the length of the diary-keeping period was two weeks for urban households and four weeks for rural households. But, in the 1988-89 HES the diary keeping period was two weeks for all households (both urban and rural).

(4)   In the first survey the value (retail price) of only free goods and services obtained from an employer was included in the 'income-in-kind' component. However, this concept was extended to cover goods and services provided by an employer at reduced prices and free of charge in the later surveys. In addition, from the second series, households were requested to keep records of all details of any product taken from their back yard and/or vegetable gardens in the supplied diary.

(5)   In the first series of HES any income earned by a member of the household aged less than 15 years was excluded from the family income. However, children's income was included in the family income from the second series.

(6)   The different treatment and incidence of non-monetary income commenced from the third series. Income in kind received from an employer is counted in the 1984 HES as both income and expenditure of the household concerned. However, the items are restricted in the income questionnaire to cars, housing, electricity and telephones, and to any goods obtained during the diary-keeping period. The respondent is asked for their current retail value (and the amount if any that they cost him). Unlike previous series only the last financial year's income from investment and/or self-employment is considered from the third series.

(7) Negative income (in the case of business loss) was collected to estimate the total household income from the 1988-89 HES. This income was treated as 'zero' in previous surveys.

(8) In order to estimate household expenditure, the first two series adopted a mixture of the 'payments (i.e. payments made during the reference period for goods and services, whether or not acquired or consumed during that period)' and 'acquisitions (i.e. the cost of those items acquired during the period, whether or not fully consumed or paid for)' approaches. However, only the acquisition approach was followed from the 1984 HES.

(9) Important changes in categorisation in the HES Commodity Code List (HESCCL) were made between the first two series and other series: separate identification of current housing costs for selected dwelling (item code 01); allocation of the principal component of mortgage payments to form part of 'other capital housing costs' (item code 16); and collapsing and splitting of previously established expenditure items. The number of expenditure items in different surveys is given in Table 2.1. This table shows that more detailed expenditure items are collected in recent HESs than earlier HESs, but major expenditure items remain approximately the same in various HESs except the 1998-99 HES when 609 detailed consumption items were collapsed into 123 major items; while total number of broad expenditure items remained same in Australia in various HESs.

Table 2.1. Number of expenditure items in various
HES in Australia: 1974-1975 to 1998-1999

Description	1974-75	1975-76	1984	1988-89	1993-94	1998-99
Detailed items	300	300	440	430	626	609
Major items	102	90	100	100	99	123
Broad items	15	17	17	17	17	17

Source: Australian Household Expenditure Surveys: 1974-1975 to 1998-1999.

(10) The Australian Standard Classification of Occupations (ASCO) has replaced the Classification and Classified List of Occupations (CCLO) since the 1988-1989 HES.

(11) A three-month recall period was used for some infrequently purchased items such as refrigerators, washing machines, etc., since the third series of the HES, while a two-week or four-week recall period was used for such items in earlier versions.

(12) Different sample sizes of households were used in different series of the HES. These are given in Table 2.2 below. This table shows that sample size of households vary from HES to HES.

Table 2.2. Number of households sampled in various HESs in
Australia: 1974-75 to 1998-1999

Year of survey	Sample size (number of households)
1974-75	9095
1975-76	5869
1984	9571
1988-89	7405
1993-94	8389
1998-99	6893

Source: Australian Household Expenditure Surveys: 1974-1975 to 1998-1999.

As a result, the estimates of the change in expenditure between different series of HESs are subject to various degrees of sampling and non-sampling errors. Standard errors for some variables can differ significantly from version to version.

(13) Financial years were chosen as a survey period for the first two series of the HES. However, a calendar year was chosen for the third series, 1984 HES. The data collection period for the fourth series was from July 1988 to July 1989.

(14) The main differences of the 1993-1994 HES from the previous HESs are as follows.

(a) The survey weighting process for the 1993-1994 HES used independent estimates of the number of households in Australia as benchmarks.

(b) The number of households contributing to the 1993-1994 HES (approximately 900) increased, replacing some missing items by its imputed values calculated on the basis of information reported for similar households.

(c) Estimated income tax was calculated for all households according to the taxation criteria for 1993-94, and using the income and other characteristics of household members, as reported in the survey.

(15) New techniques were introduced to collect the 1998-99 HES data. The main differences of the 1998-99 HES from that of the previous HESs are given below.

(a) A computer assisted interviewing (CAI) technique was used to collect data from households and individuals through a written diary.

(b) More household and individual estimates were used as the weighting process for the 1998-99 HES.

(c) Extra detail was collected for characteristics such as mobile phones, taxes, childcare, education, gambling, and income-in-kind through improved methods.

(d) New questions on financial stress and lump sum payments were included, and the definition of a dependent child changed. The new definition of a dependent child includes people 15 years and under, and full-time students aged between 15 and 24 years (instead of 15 to 20 years, as used previously), who have a parent in the household, but no child of their own.

(e) A Household Expenditure Classification was introduced instead of the HES Commodity Code List (HESCCL) as used previously.

These changes were made over various versions of the HES with a view to improve the quality of data. The idea behind all these changes was to obtain a more comprehensive picture of the economic activities of the households. However, there is a serious danger in interpreting and analysing such data, particularly for intertemporal comparisons among various versions of the HES data. Intertemporal comparability of household income and expenditure data is very important and useful to understand the performance of the economy, and the standard and quality of living of households. The continuing changes in the data collection procedures make it difficult to fulfill such objectives.

3. VALIDITY OF THE HES DATA

The HES data are based on recorded information in a diary (during a two to four weeks period depending on the series and locality of the responding households) as well as answers provided by a responding household to questions which were asked about their consumption of various goods and services during a certain period of time (using a recall period method). There could be random errors and biases in the data entries due to recall periods and wilful distortions. Also there is a possibility that the keeping of diaries results in behavioural change of the responding households. There is evidence that the respondents have a tendency to over-state some items of consumption and under-state the consumption of others. The diary keeping method is a good way of collecting day-to-day expenditure data. Yet, there is no way of getting over the response biases completely. Also, there is no evidence that a shorter reference period would necessarily ensure greater accuracy of the data.

From the third series, the ABS has adopted the acquisition approach which means the full cost of goods and services is recorded at the time of acquisition (not at the time of consumption) with a reference period of time, two weeks for diary keeping, and three months to two years for infrequent purchases depending on the item. Average weekly expenditures on various goods and services were then recorded on the basis of being evenly spread over the reference period. This creates a problem, because some households may not spend anything on certain items during the reference period or diary-keeping period at the time the survey was conducted. For example, the 1988-89 HES showed that 19% and 22% of households did not purchase anything on clothing and furniture respectively during the survey period. On the contrary, some households purchased more than usual during the survey period. As a result, in some cases their spending may well exceeding their income. The 1988-89 HES Unit Record Tape showed that 57% of households spent more than their net income over the reference period.

Experience suggests that as time passes, more and more Australian families are purchasing bulk household commodities including some food items such as flour, rice, meat, and seafood etc. As a result, they purchase household commodities at less frequent intervals. This could probably happen due to widespread use of cars, freezers etc., because of changing life-styles as well as to save time due to the greater participation rate in employment by couples. The Australian Institute of Family Studies (AIFS) Bulletin (no. 6, p. 17) shows that the employment participation for couples with children increased to 53.2% in July 1988 from 42.8% in July 1979; the corresponding figures for couples without children are 61.8% and 50.7% respectively.

The Australian Bureau of Statistics collects expenditure data with the main purpose of providing weights for the Consumer Price Index (CPI). However, data on quantity (in physical terms), which are very important for nutritional analysis, are not collected. Also, the availability of both quantity and expenditure information would provide a valuable crosscheck on the reliability of the information. By computing the price as a ratio of these two, it is possible to eliminate extreme observations due to errors of recording. It is thus hoped that the ABS will collect both quantity and expenditure information in future HESs.

Because quantities are not collected, it is not possible to estimate quality elasticity, an important indicator of the quality of living of the households. Quantity data can be obtained by dividing the expenditure estimates (value term) by consumer price indices. However, the consumer price indices available in the country produced by the ABS are often found to be inadequate for such purposes, as they relate to particular capital cities and to particular commodities. In addition, there is a problem of inter-temporal and inter-regional differentials in price variation. Hence, one should have different sets of consumer price indices for different income groups of the population. This is important for examining the expenditure pattern of households in real terms, because Haque (1991c) has shown that there is a clear time trend in average weekly household income and expenditure of the population in different income groups in different states.

We now come to the effect of seasonality on HES data. Spreading interviews evenly over the 12 months of the survey year eliminates the effect of seasonality almost completely as far as the averages of expenditures based on the entire survey year are concerned. However, as different households are interviewed at different points in time, seasonal variation is superimposed on the true variation between households, and the distribution of population by size-classes of household income exaggerates the true extent of the inequality. More seriously, seasonality may be distorting the estimates of the Engel functions and Engel elasticity based on the HES data.

Many analyses based on HES data assume that the biases (if any) in the data are uniform over time. This may not be true even under the most favourable situations, because the biases may change abruptly in some unusual situations, for example when prices change very sharply. Also, biases may fall or rise systematically through time. However, one might assume that estimates represent consumption expenditures obtained from large samples. But, in the case of the HES data, the situation was weakened by the changes in the data collection procedure mentioned in the preceding section.

One of the major weaknesses of HES data may be the 'unduly high' estimate of per capita intake of 'meals out and take-away food', and alcohol and non-alcohol beverages in the highest quintile income group, as the level of consumption of such items in physical terms is one of the better indicators of living standards in Australia. It is unfortunate that this problem has not been given the attention it deserves. Variations in consumption standards may be reflected more or less consistently over time and across regions. However, the absolute levels of these estimates are quite doubtful and should be checked more thoroughly. 'Ceremonial parties' may provide a partial explanation. The host households report the entire quantum of meals in hotels and restaurants, drinks and alcohol needed for the function in its budget, while most, if not all, of the invitees may forget that they had a meal outside when reporting for their respective households. The same difficulties arise when one is offered drinks or biscuits, etc., while visiting friend's or relative's houses on special occasions like Christmas Day or Mother's Day. Haque (1989a, 1989b) has observed that the Engel elasticity obtained for meals out and take-away food is high and sensitive.

Another criticism of the HES data may be the possible under-enumeration of the highest and lowest income bracket households. The HES excludes inmates of hospitals, jails, military cantonments, etc., and also is possibly under-enumerating the homeless and destitute people. Although, there is no clear evidence of such a claim, it is desirable to keep a systematic record of approximate characteristics of these households. It would be excellent if a representative sample of these casualty households could be pursued and covered for the consumer expenditure enquiry.

On the whole, the HES income data appear to agree fairly well with the corresponding figure derived from other household based surveys, such as the Survey of Employed Wage and Salary Earners, the Income Distribution Survey, the Housing Survey, etc. This agreement is quite remarkable considering the completely different data sets. However, when the HES and the Australian Taxation Office (ATO) data are compared, it appears that incomes have been significantly underestimated in the HES data. In a recent study, the Australian Bureau of Statistics (1991) has shown that the average annual per capita income for those individuals with taxable income over the tax threshold based on the 1988-89 HES was $20,007, compared to $24,374 based on the 1988-89 ATO estimates for those individuals who lodged tax returns. This obviously does not guarantee that the ATO income data are correct and should be preferred over HES income data. Substantial research work should be carried out to justify the superiority of the ATO income data over the HES income data.

As regards the pattern of household expenditure, the picture emerging from the HES differs systematically from that based on the private final consumption expenditure of the Australian National Accounts (ANA) estimates. These differences are quite reasonable on the grounds of the significant differences in scope, concepts, sources and methods used for these two data sets. The ANA estimate is designed to provide an aggregate of the diverse transactions in the economy, and the various components (viz. household sector) involved in those transactions. While, the HES deals with the levels of private expenditure of households in a narrowly defined population, one still does not know which of the two estimates approximates more closely to reality. By and large, the HES estimates are lower than the ANA estimates across commodity groups.

In view of the importance of the HES data, it is indeed surprising how little technical work has been done in the country to cross-examine the data to improve its quality. For example, there is no research to justify the 'accusation method' over the 'payment method', which has been adopted since the third version of the HES. It would be expected that a sample survey organisation would carry out various types of field studies before embarking on a regular large-scale survey and also to publish the results of such studies. This has hardly been done so far. As a result, there have been a very few field studies, which throw light on or justify the procedures followed in the HES. It is possible that sudden changes in the questionnaire and data collection procedures introduced a break in the time series of HES estimates and increased discrepancies between the HES estimates and the Official National Income and Expenditure estimates. In the absence of appropriate field trials, one cannot easily rule out this possibility. Similar observations may be made regarding the change in the method of imputation of consumption expenditure out of 'self-done jobs' and/or homegrown foods or vegetables. At this stage, we emphasise the need for systematic and continual verification of the HES data at the technical level with a view to solve the questions frequently raised by various users concerning the validity and the need for additional information for future HES data collection.

4. OTHER OBSERVATIONS ON THE HES DATA

One of the most obvious drawbacks of the HES data is the delay in the publication of results, although it has become quicker in the later series. Yet, it took about 15 months to get any usable data on income and expenditure from the HES from the completion of data collection. Further, the ABS failed to release any information on income and expenditure data for unemployed families at a time when the country was seriously discussing the 'problem of unemployment'. It is important to know the degree to which the community is suffering in terms of a fall in quality of living due to unemployment.

Household expenditure on different commodities and income data, have been published by weekly household gross income deciles, since the 1984 HES. However, the concept of income and its statistical measurement are questionable. Moreover, data on expenditure and income per family cannot give the real picture of the expenditure pattern of the commodity. This is because Cramer (1973a) has mentioned that

> large families tend to have high incomes, and conversely. This is not due to a direct causal link between the two variables (income and family size) but to fortuitous characteristics of our social structure.

Hence, there is a strong positive correlation between income and family size. For this reason, it is advisable to present the HES data for different per-equivalent adult (or at least per capita) total expenditure deciles instead of household gross income deciles. Literature in favour of total expenditure versus income is abundant [see Cramer (1973a), Friedman (1957), Prais and Houthakker (1955), Podder (1971), Vickrey (1947) and Haque (1984), Dayal, Gomulka, Milford, Southerland and Taylor (2000), Geoffrey and Ferraro (1996), and Thesia and Blanciforti (1994)].

Theoretically, one is interested in the relationship between expenditure on a particular item (Y) and income (X) and hence the same reference time interval (i.e., from July 1 to July 21; not some households in July, some in December, and some in March, etc.,) for all households. A moving two or three weeks reference period introduces transitory (seasonal) components in both X and Y. Successive transitory components are correlated. Under these circumstances, it is quite possible that the Engel elasticity for some luxury items may be over-estimated and those of some necessary items underestimated. This subtle problem has been relatively unnoticed in the literature [see Liviatan (1961)]. In this regard, the following steps are suggested to clarify the position.

(i)   Commodity type analysis may be undertaken by collecting budget data for the same reference year, through repeated visits. These data can be analysed to investigate the biases. If any bias is found in the currently collected HES data, a decision may then be taken for future data collection, to convert to a moving annual reference period for clothing and other categories of items where purchases are infrequent and marked by pronounced seasonality.

(ii)   The ABS may also collect data on infrequent purchases of two or three items such as clothing with respect to an annual reference period and the data be analysed to clarify the problem.

(iii) One may also obtain a better measure of consumption than per capita expenditure by excluding unusual purchases such as housing, cars, health or ceremonial expenses, and use these as explanatory variables in the Engel curve analysis. In this connection, it would be of interest to collect the data from those households who spent a large sum of money for housing, cars, health or ceremonial purposes, by asking how much the household normally spends on such items when they are not making the infrequent, large expenditures on those items. Those data would then be added with other expenditures to get the total expenditure, which can then be used as one of the explanatory variables in a regression model. Total expenditure elasticity for all the consumption items would then be accurately estimated.

Most researchers need some idea of the sampling errors of the ratios, indices or coefficients. Such needs cannot be met by computing the standard errors (S.Es) of a few global estimates. Even if S.Es are presented for every estimate appearing in the 'Tables with notes', the researchers may not be able to compute the S.Es of the ratios etc. In such situations, one may need sampling co-variances of various pairs of estimates. In this regard, one may consider the following list of statistics frequently estimated from HES data:

(1)   cumulative percentages of population living below specified levels of per capita expenditure (X);

(2)   shares in aggregate consumer expenditure enjoyed by various groups of the population;

(3)   Lorenz ratios for the distribution of population by size of (x);

(4)   the analogues of (2) and (3) for specified items of consumption like cereals, etc;

(5)   Engel elasticity of consumption for various items; and

(6)   indices of inter-regional variation (in consumer prices or the like) in average per capita household consumer expenditure.

Scrutiny of statistical data is an 'art' and it is difficult to put objective rules which would be acceptable to all experts. Scrutiny of filled-up HES 'consumer expenditure' questionnaires is essential; because some defects may arise from the failure to distinguish between purchase, expenditure and consumption. Without editing the raw data from the field, the technical section has problems with some absurd entries. The data for households can be scrutinised on a computer, using limits set up after preliminary examination of the data. A number of sample households can be rejected on the grounds of defective entries. A household can be rejected altogether if its per capita expenditure on some item, say for example consumption of cereals exceeds $30 or 10 kg per week, or the expenditure on cereals appears to be less than 50c or higher than $50 per kg. Similar rules can be applied to other items.

There are doubts about the utilization of multi-stage probability sampling techniques to measure and control non-sampling errors creeping in during the field work. It is really difficult to find biases that are common to both parties of investigators. However, the technique is extremely helpful in controlling errors entering at the processing and tabulation stages. Unfortunately, the importance of this is not clear to persons who do not have wide experience of survey data processing.

It is standard practice to publish mass individual household expenditure data in the form of cell means for a given classification of sample households. As a result, most analyses are based on grouped cell means, even though individual data are available. This is probably because of high variability in the individual data, which also fails to answer some basic questions such as what is the average expenditure on food made by the poor people of the community, is there any significant difference between the average expenditures on food by the poorer and richer sections of the community. Grouped cell means can answer these questions very accurately, if the distribution of expenditures on those commodities within groups is symmetrical.

Inspection of scatter diagrams of expenditures of different commodities by income groups of a number of individual households shows that the dispersion is so large that any Engel function will give an equally poor fit. A good fit of some specified form can emerge when the within group cell means are used. Cramer (1973a) has shown that the coefficient of determination (R^2) is usually low for individual data and a higher R^2 can be achieved by using the grouped data for the same phenomenon, leaving the properties of the regression estimates largely intact.

However, cell means are sometimes meaningless, since mean values are highly affected by the extreme values. In fact, the 1988-89 HES Unit Record Tape shows that the distribution of expenditure on some commodities, particularly infrequently purchased items, is highly skewed even within the gross income deciles. For some items there are multiple modes. In these circumstances, it is very difficult to accept cell means as the representative values for those groups. Moreover, cell means are dependent on the particular income class limits adopted. The choice of an optimal classification, which maintains homogeneity within each group, is a difficult task. The case of multiple regression grouping may well affect the correlation among the explanatory variables and hence lead to a serious multicollinearity problem, although this does not occur in the individual observations when the least squares method is used. Until now, very little attention has been paid to this problem. Prais and Aitchison (1954) mentioned that an investigation of optimal grouping in multiple regressions should begin from matrix algebra. We urge that the ABS should do some research work on the optimum classification and present the data accordingly instead of in gross income deciles. It is our feeling that the data would be better represented by fractile groupings [Vide, Mahalanobis (1960)], with households having continuous ranks when they were ranked in ascending order of income (say either gross or net). Then the group denoted by 0-5 per cent would comprise the bottom 5 per cent of the estimated number of households, the group represented by 5-10 per cent would comprise the next 5 per cent of the estimated number of households, and so on.

Currently, the ABS publishes the arithmetic cell means within each gross deciles income groups for different consumption items. Aitken's (1934) Generalised Least Squares (GLS) method can be used to obtain unbiased estimates of regression coefficients, using the within group arithmetic cell means if the linear function is chosen. However, Haque (1988, 1989b), Podder (1971), Bewley (1982) and many others have shown that the linear function is not superior over other functions for the Australian HES data. In fact, almost all published works are based on non-linear Engle functions such as semi-log, double-log, and log-log inverse. In such cases, Aitken's GLS method needs the within group geometric/harmonic means for the logarithmic/inverse functional forms, in order to estimate unbiased regression parameters and hence income elasticity. A bias is introduced when the within group arithmetic cell means are used as a proxy for the geometric/harmonic means in estimating non-linear Engel functions. Both Kakwani (1977b) and Haque (1990a) showed that these biases are significantly higher for some items, using the estimated within group geometric/harmonic means based on the concentration curves. It is thus urged that the ABS should produce at least one set of within group geometric/harmonic means for some broad groups of items. See more about the uses and validity of the HES data in the United Nations (1989), Taylor, Gomulka and Sutherland (2000), Sutherland, Taylor and Gomulka (2001) and Mario (1995).

5. RECOMMENDATION AND CONCLUDING REMARKS

Some recommendations and conclusions are made in this section. To examine the validity and to improve the quality of the HES data, the following recommendations are made.

Substantial technical work should be done by the ABS and elsewhere to verify the HES data both for internal consistency as well as against external evidence.

Fieldwork should be undertaken to investigate:

(a)   the effects of various changes made in the questionnaire over time in collecting the HES data;
(b)   the validity of the estimates for meals out and take-out food and drinks;
(c)   the effects of seasonality on the budget data;
(d)   the effects on data collection of the 'acquisition' method; and
(f)   the appropriateness of the month reference period for clothing and some other durable items.

Improved procedures of scrutinizing the field data should also be evolved and standardised.

· A systematic record of expenditures and incomes and other appropriate characteristics of the households at different income level particularly the lowest and the highest income groups should be kept.
. Expenditure, quantity as well as price information for various goods and regarding changes in the quality of living and in disparities of level of living in real terms cannot be answered satisfactorily with the present data. The HES data of various 'series' cannot be compared in the absence of appropriate Consumer Price Indexes for different income groups (deciles groups) of the population.
. It is important to publish estimates of consumption in quantity for a number of food items along with average prices. These are important for studies of nutrition. Also, Hofsten (1952) has shown that quality variations have an economically significant effect on the calculated value of the index number.

If the HES data have to meet the growing and varied needs of researchers and policy makers then the following recommendations should be given special considerations.

· All estimated statistics should be published promptly. They must include expenditure and quantity for detailed food items and other important groups of expenditure items.
· Statewide households and persons based data in different size-classes (deciles groups) of per capita expenditure data (if not per equivalent adult expenditure) should be published.

· A table for broad groups of items kept consistent for every 'series' should be published on the basis of per capita (if not per equivalent adult) fractile groupings of the total expenditure.
· It is also argued that the ABS should produce one set of within group geometric/harmonic means for broad groups of items based on per capita fractile groupings of the total expenditure.
· Estimates of standard errors and co-variances of some commonly estimated statistics mentioned in Section 4 should be published.
· The 'Unit Record Tape' should be released quickly to the users of the HES data.
· We finally would like to make a suggestion to the ABS to collect the same HES information repeatedly from version to version for some specified households (say 1500) who are socially disadvantaged such as aborigines, migrants and low income households (viz., single mothers, retired elderly people, etc., whose per capita annual income say is less than $10,000). This will help us to investigate how the living standards of those families are affected due to many changing situations such as economic recession, government interventions and changes in social and economic environments. Short and long term income elasticity of some consumption items using such **panel data** on households would be of great interest in making proper social policies. The demand for intake of nutrients such as Bhargava (1991), Strauss and Thomas (1998), and National Nutrition Surveys can also be analysed using time observations on individuals of households. It is hoped that these data will support the view that increases in household incomes will in turn improve the intakes of nutrients, which the Australian National Health and Medical Research Council (NHMRC) tries to establish for health reasons. This suggestion is quite consistent with an ABS Australian Statistician, Castles (1991), who wrote as:

Our mission is to assist and encourage informed decision-making, research and discussion within governments and the community by providing a high-quality, user-oriented and dynamic statistical service....

He also mentioned that in introducing the Australian Bureau of Statistics Bill 1975, the Honourable Minister L. F. Bowen, MP pointed out that:

There is no need for me to argue the virtues of statistical information in providing a generally informed society; in providing a firm basis for decision-making in providing a basis for the development of programs and a means of measuring their progress over time.

In conclusion, we would like to mention that the stratified multi-stage probability sampling procedure should be continued in the collection of HES data. In future, the data including tabulation and analyses of the HES as recommended in this study, should be supplied to the various researchers. It is important to bear in mind that the consumer expenditure enquiry over time for some specified households would be a major feature for future HES data collection. However, we may state that the risks of non-comparability of data from successive enquiries of the same nature would be minimised if the enquiries were carried out continuously. Also if one carries out budget enquiries at regular intervals, say once in every four or five years, the fluctuations in some consumption products may prevent us from examining gradual trends in levels of living. It appears to be wise to distribute the resources and effort over many medium-type enquiries to be carried out every year instead of conducting a large-survey at a regular interval of say every five years. Household Expenditure Survey data of this type is important for future development and social policies, and can be found in Carnegie and Walker (2001), Dasgupta (2001), Deaton (1997), Dolton (2002), and Lechner and Pfeiffer (2001).

CHAPTER 3

FUNCTIONAL FORMS FOR ENGEL CURVES

Readers will learn how to choose a best Engel function from various alternatives based on a number of statistical and economic criteria when estimating income elasticity. More importantly, they will find a new Engel function called the double semi-log (DSL) Engel function, which turns out to be the best functional form when compared with other widely used common functional forms based on the non-nested specification P_E-test, and the distance function, D^2-criterion. This DSL Engel function is quite flexible in that it gives rise to a wide range of shapes. It can also satisfy other economic criteria such as the adding-up criterion. More importantly, readers will find that the Weighted Least Squares (WLS) method produces inconsistent estimates of the parameters of a single relationship when total expenditure is used as one of the explanatory variables (which is usually the case). The Instrumental Matrix Approach is used to obtain consistent estimates of the Engel elasticities and their asymptotic standard errors, which are essential because of the simultaneous nature of the model. Both consistent and inconsistent income elasticities together with their standard errors are then calculated based on this DSL Engel function for various Australian household expenditure items, which are then used to conduct two separate one-tailed t-tests, taking 0 and 1 as the true elasticity to classify the necessary and luxury items respectively.

1. INTRODUCTION

The choice of the most appropriate functional form in an Engel curve analysis is an old econometric problem. There is no unique functional form and the choice depends mainly on the importance placed by the investigators on the various criteria they wish to satisfy. Many authors choose the best functional form from various alternatives on statistical grounds. Some emphasize the economic criteria (such as the adding up property).

The present study has two basic aims. First, we will find a best Engel function among various alternatives for different household expenditure items. Second, we estimate total expenditure elasticity for various consumption items on the basis of the best Engel function.

A new Engel function, which can be called the double semi-log (DSL) Engel function, is considered in this chapter. This function has the ability to satisfy various economic criteria (including the adding-up criterion), which will then be compared with other well-known Engel functions, using the non-nested hypothesis testing procedure, and the distance function criterion. The Australian 1975-76 Household Expenditure Survey (HES) data were used extensively for this purpose. The total expenditure elasticity was then computed for various Australian household expenditure items on the basis of the best Engel function.[7]

The outline of the chapter is as follows. The model for the Engel curve analysis is given in Section 2. Data used in the present study are described in Section 3. Section 4 is concerned with the choice of functional form; while empirical illustrations are given in Section 5. Conclusions with some comments and limitations of the study are given in Section 6.

2. THE MODEL

Under the homogeneity postulate, the expenditure per person can be written as a function of total expenditure/income per person. This does not allow for possible economies of scale, since it implies that expenditure on a particular item compared to total expenditure and household size, is homogeneous and of degree one. We have relaxed this rather restrictive assumption by including household size as a separate explanatory variable in the per capita model. Despite the many problems, which may be associated with this model, i.e., $Y/S = f(X/S, S)$, we will assume that it gives an adequate representation of the expenditure patterns for Australian households.

In the present chapter, household size is taken to be the number of persons in the household without regard to other characteristics such as age, sex, occupation, etc., which may have an important influence on the expenditure of particular commodities. Ignoring the effects of these characteristics can be justified because the analyses are based on averages of a number of households grouped by per capita income, but not grouped by *age* or sex, and hence the differential effects of variations in these characteristics are likely to average out between households.

---

[7] It should be noted that income and total expenditure are used alternatively throughout the book.

2.1 Specification of Functional Forms

The following forms of Engel curves have been considered for our investigation.

(i)	Linear	(L)	Y	=	$\alpha + \beta\ X + \gamma\ S$
(ii)	Semi – log	(SL)	Y	=	$\alpha + \beta\ \log\ X + \gamma\ \log\ S$
(iii)	Hyperbolic	(Hyp)	Y	=	$\alpha + \beta\ /\ X + \gamma\ /\ S$
(iv)	Double – log	(DL)	Log Y	=	$\alpha + \beta\ \log\ X + \gamma\ \log\ S$
(v)	Log – Inverse	(LI)	Log Y	=	$\alpha + \beta\ /\ X + \gamma\ /\ S$
(vi)	Log – log Inverse	(LLI)	Log Y	=	$\alpha + \beta\ \log\ X + \gamma\ /\ X + \delta\ \log\ S$
(vii)	Double Semi – log(	DSL)	Y	=	$\alpha + \beta X + \gamma\ \log\ X + \delta\ \log\ S$

where   Y = average per capita expenditure on a particular commodity made by households in a certain income group.

X = average per capita total expenditure of the households in that income group,

S = average family size of the households in that income group, and

α, β, γ and δ are parameters.

The first five functional forms are widely used by many authors, viz., Prais and Houthakker (1955), Podder (1971), Haque (1989a, 1990a, 1996), Wu, Li and Samuel (1995), Widjajanti and Li (1996), Tiffin and Tiffin (1999) and Werner (2000), to analyse household expenditure patterns around the world. The log log-inverse function is a direct generalisation of the double log model with the inverse of total expenditure term added to the explanatory variables. Goreux (1960) used this function for his larger FAO (Food and Agriculture Organisation of the United Nations) study. In a similar way, the semi-log model is generalised in the present study by adding a total expenditure term to the covariates to obtain the double semi-log (DSL) Engel function.

The justification for using the DSL functional form is that it covers widely varying situations because of the nature of the curve. It can also satisfy many economic criteria such as the adding-up property. It should be noted that we have also tried other functional forms including the Working model (1943), Generalized Working model due to Leser (1963), and the quadratic Engel curve due to Banks, Blundell and Lewebel (1997), Fry and Pashards (1992), Ryan and Wales (1999), Diewert and Wales (1987, 1988a, 1988b, 1993, 1995), Buse and Chan (2000) and many other functions given in Christine, Geoffery and Murray (1998), Fagiolo (2001), and Levedahl (1995). But these functions did not perform well compared to the DSL Engel function on the grounds of goodness of fit, when the simple relationship between per capita expenditure of various commodities and total expenditure was examined.

2.2 Complete Systems of Consumer Demand Equation

Engel curves may be estimated as a complete system of equations, rather than individually as proposed above. The systems approach takes account of contemporaneous covariance between disturbances in equations for different cross-equation parameter restrictions that arise from constrained utility maximisation. In general, the systems approach results in an efficiency gain when the Maximum Likelihood method or Zellner's (1962) procedures are followed.[8] However, these procedures are not more efficient than the single equation least squares estimation method if: (i) covariances are zero between equations and there are no cross-equation parameter restrictions; or (ii) all the regressors, i.e., independent variables in each equation, are the same and there are no cross equation parameter restrictions. Our Engel functions are not derived from the utility functions. Therefore, there are no cross-equation parameter restrictions. Moreover, all the independent variables in each of the equations are identical. Accordingly it is appropriate to use the Generalised Least Squares (GLS) method on each of the Engel functions to estimate elasticities for various items.

We will now discuss the adding up criterion, which asserts that the sum of expenditures on various commodities adds up to total expenditure. With the exception of the L and DSL forms, none of the functional forms considered in this chapter are capable of satisfying the adding up criterion at all potential data points. For the L and DSL forms, we can refer to Powell (1969) for the proof that the GLS method is appropriate and yields estimates that automatically satisfy the adding up criterion. For other functional forms this is clearly not the case, even though the adding up criterion can be approximated and verified empirically by Cramer's formula (1973a, p. 147). This states that the adding up criterion is approximately satisfied at a particular point if the Engel elasticity estimates weighted by the budget shares sum approximate to unity. If Cramer's adding up criterion is satisfied exactly at every point and the sum of expenditures on different commodities adds up to total expenditure at every point then Cramer's adding up criteria coincides with the general adding up criterion.

3. DATA

The Australian 1975-76 HES data obtained from a special tape prepared by the Australian Bureau of Statistics (ABS) is used for the present study. The data are divided into relatively homogeneous groups of 5,869 households in twofold cross-classified tables, namely 12 broad per capita (gross) income groups and 15 different household compositions. For each household composition, commodity-wise arithmetic mean expenditure, mean household disposable income, average number of persons in household and estimated number of households were available for the 12 per capita income groups. The absence of households in certain cells leaves 120 observations in all.

[8] A number of authors such as Conniffe (2001), Park, Holcomb, Raper and Capps (1996), and Frohberg and Winter (2001) have undertaken a systems approach to study various household expenditure items.

In this chapter only 10 broad expenditure items are considered for our investigation. These items are: (1) all food; (2) current housing costs; (3) fuel and power; (4) all alcohol and tobacco; (5) clothing and footwear; (6) household equipment and operation; (7) medical care and health expenses; (8) transport and communication; (9) recreation and education; and (10) miscellaneous goods and services. These groups are mutually exclusive and exhaustive.

4. THE CHOICE OF FUNCTIONAL FORM

The main objective of the present investigation is to examine the suitability of different algebraic forms of Engel curves. Quite often researchers have uncritically used only one form for estimating Engel elasticity. But the choice of the functional form for the relationship between the expenditure on a particular item and total expenditure (income) is a matter of great concern. Bhattacharya (1973), Kakwani (1977b), Leser (1963), Prais (1953a), and Prais and Houthakker (1955), Miles, Pereyra and Rossi (2000), Beatty and LaFrance (2001), and Dong, Shonkwiler and Capps (1998), Brosig (1998, 2000), and Elsner (1999) have shown that the calculated Engel elasticities depend appreciably on the algebraic form used. Having this fact in mind, we tried to find the best functional form among seven different Engel curves, which are listed earlier in Section 2.1.

It is desirable that the functional form should be simple and should satisfy the following properties:

(i)   the possibility for threshold and saturation levels;
(ii)   the adding up criterion. i.e. the sum of all expenditures is equal to total expenditure at all levels; and
(iii) it is supposed to give the best representation of the data on statistical grounds.

In general, none of the well-known Engel functions satisfy all these properties simultaneously. Therefore, options are given to econometricians for their personal judgments in choosing the functional form for Engel curve analysis. Criterion (i) was considered by Iyengar (1967), and Prais and Houthakker (1955); while Barten (1965), Leser (1961), Nicholson (1949) and Theil (1965) emphasised; (ii) and finally, Jain and Tendulkar (1973), Kakwani (1977b), Podder (1971), Ray (1973), Singh (1973), Levedahl (1995), and Didukh (2001) based their choice of functional form on goodness of fit. In fact most authors such as Miles, Pereyra and Rossi (2000), Ryan and Wales (1999), Diewert and Wales (1987, 1988a 1988b, 1993, 1995), Hanrahan (2002), Shahabi-Azad (2001) and Huang and Lin (2000) used the latter criterion. In this study, we select the form of the Engel function, which satisfies most criteria.[9]

In the present chapter, a non-nested hypothesis testing procedure is used to discriminate various Engel functions on statistical grounds. This is because Pesaran

---

[9] See Ramsay and Silverman (2002) for more on functional data analysis.

(1974) argued that the widely used R^2 as a model selection criterion among nested models is not appropriate and misleading. However he mentioned that R^2 could be used as a selection criterion, only when the models are not nested. This alone is not sufficient, and does not guarantee against high probability of choosing a 'non-true model'. On the other hand, the parametric test on the power parameters of the Box-Cox type Engel function [See Zarembka (1972), Bensu, Kmenta and Shapiro (1976), Davidson and MacKinnon (1985), Godfrey, McAleer and McKenzie (1988), Linnet (1988) etc.] cannot be done, since the seven functional forms are not nested under one super-model.

4.1 Non-nested Hypothesis Testing

A non-nested test is used to find a best Engel function. Non-nested procedures are called for because the standard Neyman-Pearson theory of hypothesis testing applies only when the null hypothesis Ho and the alternative hypothesis H_1 belong to the same family of distributions. This theory fails when they belong to separate families, which is the case for the Engel curves considered in this study.[10] The idea of testing for separate families of hypothesis was introduced by Cox (1961, 1962). In recent years, non-nested hypothesis testing has received considerable attention and some important contributions are made by Peasran (1974), Pesaran and Deaton (1978), Evans and Deaton (1980), Davidson and Mackinnon (1981), Mackinnon, White and Davidson (1983), Aguirre-Torres and Gallant (1983), Mizon and Richard (1982) and many others. An excellent review of the literature on model specification against non-nested alternatives is given in Mackinnon (1983).

We have applied the procedure due to Mackinnon, White and Davidson (1983) to test our Engel functions against each other, because their procedure is very easy computationally and has a very clear intuitive explanation. This test is now outlined.

Suppose that the model to be tested is

$$H_0 : \ Y_t = f_t (X_t, \beta) + \mu_{0t}, \qquad \mu_{0t} \sim NID(0, \sigma_0^2 I) \text{ and the alternative is}$$
$$H_1 : \ h_t (Y_t) = g_t (Z_t, \gamma) + \mu_{1t}, \qquad \mu_{1t} \sim NID(0, \sigma_1^2 I)$$

where $h_t (\ . \ )$ is a monotonic, continuously differentiable function, e.g., $\log Y_t$, $\exp Y_t$, and $Y_t^{1/2}$, which does not depend on parameters.

Z_t and X_t are vectors of exogenous variables, β and γ are parameter vectors, and the u_{it} ($i = 0, 1$) are random disturbances. The Mackinnon et al. (1983) test procedure for this situation is based upon the artificial regression

$$Y_t - \hat{f}_t \ = \ \alpha \left(\hat{g}_t - h_t (\hat{f}_t)\right) + \hat{F}_t b + u_t \qquad (3.1)$$

---

[10] Two probability density functions (p.d.f.) $f_1(Y, \theta_1)$ and $f_2(Y, \theta_2)$ are said to be of separate families, if for an arbitrary parameter value θ_{10} the p.d.f of $f_1(Y, \theta_{10})$ cannot be approximated closely by $f_2(Y, \theta_2)$ for any θ_2.

where $\hat{F}_t$ is the row vector of derivatives of $f_t(X_t, \beta)$ with respect to β evaluated at $\beta = \hat{\beta}$, $\hat{\beta}$ is the nonlinear least squares estimates of β, and b is a vector of regression coefficients. The procedure then is to test $\alpha = 0$ in Equation (3.1), i.e., whether the model under the null hypothesis H_0 is true.

The test is plausible, because if the model under the null hypothesis (H_0) is true then $\alpha = 0$ in Equation (3.1), whereas $\alpha = \dfrac{1}{h'_t}$ if the model under the alternative hypothesis (H_1) is true and the power of the alternative hypothesis (H_1) decreases as h'_t increases, where h'_t is the derivative of h_t. This can be shown as follows.

$$\text{Under } H_1: Y_t = h_t^{-1}[g_t(Z_t, \gamma) + u_{1t}].$$

So the estimation of u_{0t} in H_0 is that of

$$h_t^{-1}[g_t(Z_t, \gamma) + u_{1t}] = f_t(X_t, \beta) + u_{0t.}$$

or

$$g_t(Z_t, \gamma) + u_{1t} = h_t[f_t(X_t, \beta) + u_{0t}]$$

$$\approx \quad h_t[f_t(X_t, \beta) + h'_t(\xi) u_{0t}] \quad \text{(By Taylor's series expansion)}$$

$$u_{0t} = \frac{[g_t(Z_t, \gamma) - h_t\{f_t(X_t, \beta)\} + u_{1t}]}{h'_t(\xi)}$$

$\therefore Y_t$ in H_0 when alternative hypothesis (H_1) is true, is given by

$$Y_t = f_t(X_t, \beta) + 1/h'_t[g_t(Z_t, \gamma) - h_t\{f_t(X_t, \beta)\} + u_{1t}]$$

Hence $\alpha = 1/h'_t \neq 0$.

The t-statistic on α from Equation (3.1) is given by

$$\frac{(Y - \hat{f})' \hat{M}_0 (\hat{g} - \hat{f})}{\hat{\sigma}\left[(\hat{g} - \hat{f})' \hat{M}_0 (\hat{g} - \hat{f})\right]^{1/2}} \tag{3.2}$$

where Y, $\hat{f}$ and $\hat{g}$ are vectors whose t^{th} components are Y_t, $\hat{f}_t$ and $\hat{g}_t$ respectively, and $'$ denotes the transpose, σ is the estimated standard error, based on the nonlinear least squares from (3.1) and

$$\hat{M}_0 = I - \hat{F}\left(\hat{F}'\hat{F}\right)^{-1}\hat{F}'\ ; \text{ where } \hat{F} \text{ is the matrix whose } t^{th} \text{ row is } \hat{F}_t.$$

Mackinnon, White and Davidson (1983, pp. 57-59) show that under certain assumptions, the null distribution of (3.2) tends in probability to

$$u_0'M_0(g - f) / \sigma_0 [(g - f)'M_0(g - f)]^{1/2} \tag{3.3}$$

which is N (0, 1). The quantities without hats in this last expression are evaluated at β_0, the true value of β, or at γ_0, the plim of $\hat{\gamma}$ under H_0. The principal merit of this test procedure is its simplicity. It can readily be applied in empirical research.

Moreover, Mackinnon *el al.* claimed that their experience with the test suggests that:

> ... it often has plenty of power in applied situations, so that its theoretical deficiencies may be of small consequence to applied workers who find its simplicity appealing.

5. EMPIRICAL APPLICATION

The Mackinnon, White and Davidson (1983) model specification test against non-nested alternatives has been used to compare different Engel functions. This test has been applied on a pair-wise basis for five Engel functions (viz., L, HYP, LI, LLI and DSL), and the values of the t-statistics for ten different expenditure items are presented in Table 3.1.[11]

It should be noted that the DL and SL functions are excluded from the non-nested hypotheses testing procedure. This is because the DL and SL are nested within the LLI and DSL Engel functions respectively.

Significant values at the (asymptotic) 5% level are indicated by #. Many interesting and important observations can be made from Table 3.1. First, in many two-way comparisons, both functional forms are rejected. For example, for transport and communication the linear form is rejected when tested against the log-inverse form, and similarly the log-inverse form is also rejected against the linear form. Second, the LLI form is accepted against one another and all other forms treating

---

[11] Although the tests are pair-wise tests of one functional form against another, the overall choice of functional form is based upon an evaluation of results for all pair-wise tests on all commodities. As is well known, the procedure leads to difficulties in establishing an appropriate significance level for the overall decision regarding the best functional forms. For example, a joint hypothesis is to be rejected if either of two single hypotheses is rejected. It has long been recognized that if several t-tests have been performed jointly, the probability that at least one of these is significant and is much greater than 0.05 [see Cochran and Cox (1957, pp. 756-76]. For example, if the t-tests are independent then this probability is 0.04 for ten tests. This is an undeveloped area in statistics.

each of the forms as H_1 for all the commodities. The DSL Engel function is also accepted against all functions for all commodities, with the single exception against the LLI form for current housing costs. The hyperbolic Engel function is rejected against most of the other functions for almost all commodities.

Therefore, the non-nested hypothesis testing procedure based on Mackinnon, *et al.* P_E test shows that the LLI and DSL Engel functions are consistently accepted against each other and against all the other functions. This shows that the LLI and DSL are two competing functions and their P_E test is not able to discriminate between two rival models.

Now, we come to a conclusion that there are some 'true models' in the Engel functions under investigations. If this conclusion is taken as correct and if all the properties of the classical regression models hold for the 'true models' then there is no harm in choosing the best model between two non-nested 'truly specified' rival models on the grounds of goodness of fit.

In order to choose the best functional form on the grounds of goodness of fit between the LLI and DSL Engel functions, we have regressed the per capita expenditure (Y) of a particular item on per capita total expenditure (X) and the household size (S) by the Weighted Least Squares (WLS) method, taking the proportion of the estimated population in each income class as weights.[12]

The LLI and DSL Engel functions are then compared on the basis of the distance function, D^2-criterion. We have defined the distance function criterion for choosing curve type c_o by

$$D^2 c_o = \text{Min } c_o \ [\ \{\ \Sigma\ \theta_i\ e^2_{ij,c}\} \ / \ (g-k)] \tag{3.4}$$

where c_o is the curve type which attains the minimum mean residual sum of squares, and $e^2_{ij,c}$ is the residual in predicting per capita expenditure on the ith commodity in the jth observation with curve type c_o, and θ_i is the estimated sample proportion of the population in the jth cell, g is the number of groups and k is the number of parameters to be estimated for a specified Engel function under consideration. The smaller the value of D^2-statistic the better the functional form. Jain and Tendulkar (1973), Kakwani (1977b) and Haque (1989b, 1992, 1996) also used this criterion to choose a best Engel function from various alternatives.

The values of the distance function, D^2-statistic for the DSL and LLI Engel functions for various commodities are presented in Table 3.2. The values of the D^2-statistic from Table 3.2 show that the DSL Engel function performs better than the LLI form in 9 out of 10 cases, while the LLI fits better than the DSL function only in one case. This implies that the DSL Engel function fits well for most of the

---

[12] In the family budget study, total expenditure is commonly used rather than income as an independent variable, because of the unreliability of income data. Thus, it is used to avoid the errors in the income variable. Literature in favour of total expenditure versus income is abundant [Cramer (1973a), Friedman (1957), Prais and Houthakker (1955), Podder (1971) and Vickrey (1947)].

Australian expenditure items, which would be able to describe the overall Australian household expenditure pattern more accurately than other functions.

Table 3.1. The values of test-statistics for various Engel functions under non-nested alternatives

Functional forms in null hypothesis (H_0)	Consumption items	Functional forms as alternative hypothesis (H_1)				
		L	LI	HYP	LLI	DSL
Linear (L)	(1) All foods		0.54	0.35	0.56	0.74
	(2) Current housing costs		*	-0.48	*	2.38#
	(3) Fuel and power		2.82#	3.32#	0.44#	2.92#
	(4) All alcohol & tobacco		-1.05	-1.43	-0.48	-1.34
	(5) Clothing & footwear		1.20	1.46	1.51	1.92
	(6) Household equipment & operation		-0.65	-0.75	0.17	0.95
	(7) Medical care & health expenses		1.33	1.36	1.35	1.34
	(8) Transport & communication		2.22#	2.53#	2.06#	1.89
	(9) Recreation & education		0.86	-0.61	1.49	2.32#
	(10) Miscellaneous goods		-0.17	0.48	-0.31	-0.58
Hyperbola (Hyp.)	(1) All foods	8.31#	4.03#		5.60#	8.45#
	(2) Current housing costs	5.99#	*		*	6.03#
	(3) Fuel & power	2.18#	0.08		1.91	2.56#
	(4) All alcohol & tobacco	6.93#	*		*	6.90#
	(5) Clothing & footwear	3.72#	*		*	4.01#
	(6) Household equipment & operation	4.66#	*		*	4.65#
	(7) Medical care & health expenses	2.10#	*		*	1.94
	(8) Transport & communication	6.67#	*		*	6.58#
	(9) Recreation & education	6.32#	*		*	6.54#
	(10) Miscellaneous goods	4.27#	*		*	4.26#

* Indicates that comparisons could not be made, because the log of negative values.
# Significant at (asymptotic) 5% level.

Source: The 1975-1976 Australian Household Expenditure Survey data obtained from a special tape supplied by the Australian Bureau of Statistics.

(Table 3.1. Continued)

	(1) All foods	$4.74^{#}$		$3.90^{#}$	$4.62^{#}$	$4.67^{#}$
	(2) Current housing costs	$2.34^{#}$		$2.33^{#}$	$2.70^{#}$	$2.23^{#}$
	(3) Fuel & power	$2.72^{#}$		$2.39^{#}$	$3.52^{#}$	0.99
	(4) All alcohol & tobacco	$3.15^{#}$		$2.60^{#}$	$3.05^{#}$	$3.14^{#}$
	(5) Clothing & footwear	1.78		$1.98^{#}$	1.86	1.94
	(6) Household equipment & operation	1.55		$1.34^{#}$	1.59	1.55
Log-inverse (LI)	(7) Medical care & health expenses	0.78		$0.36^{#}$	0.56	0.51
	(8) Transport & communication	$2.37^{#}$		1.64	$2.94^{#}$	$2.29^{#}$
	(9) Recreation & education	$6.25^{#}$		$5.22^{#}$	$6.22^{#}$	$6.15^{#}$
	(10) Miscellaneous goods	$3.38^{#}$		$3.43^{#}$	$3.44^{#}$	$3.37^{#}$
	(1) All foods	0.76	0.48	0.56		0.71
	(2) Current housing costs	-0.26	-0.19	-0.12		-0.28
	(3) Fuel & power	1.77	-0.60	-0.50		0.21
	(4) All alcohol & tobacco	0.50	0.19	0.38		0.50
	(5) Clothing & footwear	-0.75	0.43	-0.52		-0.51
Log log-inverse (LLI)	(6) Household equipment & operation	0.61	-0.66	0.62		0.62
	(7) Medical care & health expenses	0.90	0.23	-0.62		-0.78
	(8) Transport & communication	-0.79	-1.72	-1.92		-1.17
	(9) Recreation & education	0.52	0.01	-0.51		0.49
	(10) Miscellaneous goods	-0.45	0.65	-0.23		-0.43
	(1) All foods	-0.28	0.53	0.72	-0.12	
	(2) Current housing costs	-1.61	1.29	0.90	$2.25^{#}$	
	(3) Fuel & power	-0.74	1.41	1.24	1.62	
	(4) All alcohol & tobacco	-0.91	-0.06	0.36	-0.51	
Double semi-log (DSL)	(5) Clothing & footwear	-0.48	*	-1.12	*	
	(6) Household equipment & operation	-0.91	0.19	0.24	0.29	
	(7) Medical care & health expenses	0.66	-0.41	0.18	-0.38	
	(8) Transport & communication	1.57	-0.03	0.60	0.06	
	(9) Recreation & education	-1.46	1.80	0.87	1.90	
	(10) Miscellaneous goods	-0.20	-0.72	-0.75	0.02	

We have drawn the estimated double semi-log Engel curves for some selected commodities for two-member households in Figure 3.1. It is apparent from this figure that the DSL is quite flexible in that it gives rise to a wide range of shapes. Food, fuel, and medical care, and health expenses approach some saturation levels within a certain range of total expenditure. These are quite expected from Australian households, because the bulk of medical care and health expenses are covered by

Medicare, while expenditures on fuel are more or less the same for all types of households, because of a generous government subsidy for poor income households. Expenditure on total food generally continues to rise and attends a situation level at some income level probably because of consumption of better quality of food as income increases, which is expected from the expenditure pattern of households with growing income without violating Engel's law. Engel's law suggests that the share of expenditures on food decreases as income increases. On the other hand, Figure 3.1 shows that expenditures on current housing costs, clothing and miscellaneous goods and services grow as the total expenditure increases. This is quite expected from the Australian society, because Australian households are very fond of spending money for better housing, clothing, cosmetics and other luxury items.

Thus, the analysis so far suggests that the DSL Engel function is the most appropriate functional form for the Australian 1975-76 HES data, based on both statistical and economic criteria.

5.1   Computation of Engel Elasticity

One of the primary aims of the present chapter is to estimate total expenditure elasticities for various commodities. We have estimated the total expenditure elasticities for all the commodities, based on seven Engle functions. However, we only present the elasticities for the DSL Engel function, since this function dominates the other functions on the basis of the specification tests and goodness of fit criterion as indicated in the previous section. The calculated expenditure elasticities together with the estimates of their standard errors are presented in parentheses in Table 3.3.[13]

We also present the consistent estimates of elasticities and their asymptotic standard errors obtained by the instrumental matrix approach in Table 3.3.[14] This approach is used because the use of the Weighter Least Squares (WLS) method in estimating single relationships, taking total expenditure as one of the independent variables, produces inconsistent estimates of the Engel parameters due to the simultaneity of the model as pointed out by Summers (1959). In this chapter three instrumental variables are used to form an instrumental matrix Q for the data matrix

---

[13] Calculation of standard error for elasticity estimate is based on Cramer (1946), which is given in Appendix 3A.

[14] Liviatan (1961) also used the instrumental variable approach in order to solve the simultaneity problem of the single equation relationship between expenditure of an item and total expenditure.

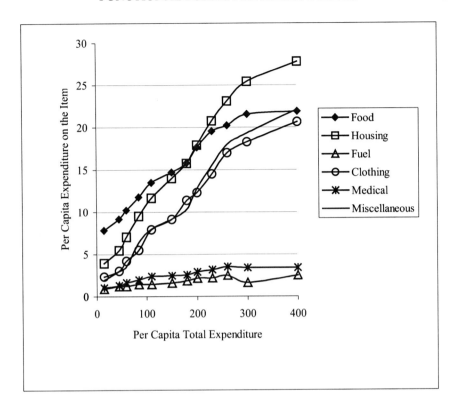

Figure 3.1. Double semi-log Engel curves for some selected items of two person households.

Table 3.2.   The value of the distance function, D^2-criteria, for the log-log inverse and the double-semi log Engel functions

Commodities	Distance function statistics	
	LLI	DSL
(1) All food	0.0134	0.0129
(2) Current housing costs	0.0876	0.0866
(3) Fuel and power	0.0004	0.0003
(4) All alcohol and tobacco	0.0109	0.0097
(5) Clothing and footwear	0.0244	0;.0235
(6) Household equipment & operation	0.1393	0.1242
(7) Medical care & health expenses	0.0019	0.0019
(8) Transport and communication	0.0665	0.0543
(9) Recreation and education	0.0535	0.0556
(10) Miscellaneous goods	0.0481	0.0476

Source: The 1975-1976 Australian Household Expenditure Survey data obtained from a special tape supplied by the Australian Bureau of Statistics.

X of the same order. The three instrumental variables are measured household income (I), the log of household income (Log I), and the log of family size (Log S). Note that the last variable serves as its own instrument.

The estimates of the instrumental variable coefficients β^* of various variables can be obtained by

$$\beta^* = [Q'\,(GG')^{-1}\,X]'\,[Q'(GG')^{-1}\,Y \qquad (3.5)$$

where $(GG')^{-1}$ is a diagonal matrix with the estimated proportion of households in different per capita income classes as diagonals, Y is a vector of the per capita expenditure and Q' stands for the transposition of Q.

It can easily be shown that these parameter estimates are consistent if there exists a high correlation both between total expenditure (X) and income (I), and between the log of total expenditure (log X) and the log of income (log I).

5.2 Classification of Items

Consumer goods can be classified on the basis of their Engel elasticities into three major categories, viz., luxury, necessary and inferior, on the basis of Engel elasticities according as $\eta > 1$, $0 \leq \eta \leq 1$ and $\eta < 0$ respectively.

On the basis of the above criteria, estimates of the expenditure elasticities from Table 3.3 indicate that all food, fuel and power, clothing and footwear, and medical care and health expenses are classified as necessary goods. All other items seem to be luxuries.

The conventional one-tailed t-test at the 5% level of significance is now applied to the estimated elasticities for the classification of different expenditure items. Two separate one-tailed t-tests are carried out for each necessary item, taking 0 and 1 as the true elasticity in two separate null hypotheses. Luxury items are tested by a one-tailed t-test, taking 1 as the elasticity in the null hypothesis.[15]

The outcomes of these statistical tests are presented in Table 3.3 by putting N or L for necessary or luxury items respectively. The tests for classification of items confirm that all expenditure items are necessaries, except all alcohol and tobacco.

The value of the elasticity of the DSL form depends on the parameter estimates and on total expenditure. The rate at which the proportional expenditure on the ith commodity changes with total expenditure is given by

$$\frac{d\left(y_i / x\right)}{dx} = \left\{\frac{\dfrac{d\,y_i}{d\,x}.x - y_i}{x^2}\right\} = \left\{\frac{y_i\,(\eta_i - 1)}{x^2}\right\} \qquad (3.6)$$

---

[15] It is noted here that an item is classified as necessary if its elasticity is neither significantly greater than 1 nor significantly less than 0, whereas the item is considered as luxury if the elasticity is significantly greater than 1.

This shows that the proportional expenditure on the ith commodity increases or decreases depending on whether the commodity is or is not a luxury good.

The results of the present analyses contradict previous findings made by many authors such as Podder (1971), Williams (1976b), McRae (1980), Bewley (1982) and Hoa (1986), who found that many of the above commodities were luxuries in Australia. This might have happened due to the use of different functional forms and data sets together with differences in item definition. Thus, the use of the 1975-76 cross-classified (120 observations) HES data and an appropriate Engel functional form could change the previous estimates, and demonstrate that the various household expenditure items in Australia are necessary items. Despite many problems in interpreting the results of various studies, one can clearly observe that the elasticity estimates for various commodities vary widely over time. This may be explained by structural changes in the economy as shown by Williams (1978c).

Table 3.3. Estimates of total expenditure elasticities at mean values of X and S*

Commodities	Elasticity estimates for the DSL Engel function based on	
	Single equation	Simultaneous equation
(1) All food	0.49N (0.10)	0.53N (0.11)
(2) Current housing costs	1.20N (0.41)	1.17N (0.43)
(3) Fuel and power	0.18N (0.15)	0.25N (0.17)
(4) All alcohol and tobacco	1.51L (0.25)	1.54L (0.26)
(5) Clothing and footwear	0.96N (0.27)	0.86N ((0.30)
(6) Household equipment & operation	1.19N (0.59)	1.83N (0.60)
(7) Medical care & health expenses	0.72N (0.21)	0.84N (0.25)
(8) Transport and communication	1.16N (0.18)	1.13N (0.19)
(9) Recreation and education	1.28N (0.44)	1.32N (0.49)
(10) Miscellaneous goods	1.19N (0.42)	1.29N (0.44)

*Estimated standard errors are presented in parentheses ( ). The classification of items based on the DSL Engel function is represented by N or L for necessary or luxury items respectively.

Source: The 1975-1976 Australian Household Expenditure Survey data obtained from a special tape supplied by the Australian Bureau of Statistics.

6. LIMITATIONS AND CONCLUSIONS

This section discusses some of the limitations and conclusions of the present study. First, it should be pointed out that some disadvantages arise from the nature of the data itself such as the grouping of observations on the basis of income rather than total expenditure. Second, the data used for the study are grouped means instead of individual household data and therefore the estimated coefficients based on grouped data (reduced data point) have reduced efficiency due to loss of observations, hence the estimated elasticity also has a lower efficiency. Third, in this study within group arithmetic means are used as the proxies for the within group geometric and harmonic means of expenditures of various expenditure items, total expenditure and family size for different per capita income classes when logarithmic and/or inverse relationships are estimated. But, it can be demonstrated that the use of such within group arithmetic means as the proxies for geometric and harmonic means produces biased regression coefficients when logarithmic and/or inverse relationships are estimated by the Aitken's Generalized Least Squares (GLS) method. This is because, in order to obtain unbiased estimates of logarithmic and/or inverse relationships when within group individual values of various variables are transformed into logarithms and/or inverses, the within group geometric and/or harmonic means are needed in order to obtain unbiased regression coefficients for the logarithmic and/or inverse relationships. This problem of estimating non-linear Engel functions in the absence of appropriate grouped means will be dealt with in the next chapter. Fourth, the survey did not collect data on the quantities of the commodities purchased by the households; as a result it was not possible to estimate quality elasticity. Also, we did not consider other economic, demographic and geographical factors, which might affect our calculated elasticities. Finally, no attention has been paid to the household composition in terms of *consumer's equivalent units*, which would have been a truer representation of reality. This problem will be discussed further in Chapter 12.

The main conclusions of the present study are as follows. First, the Mackinnon *et al.* (1983) P_E test is used to discriminate different Engel functions, which has not been applied for Engel curve analysis in Australia. Second, both the DSL and LLI Engel functions are accepted against each other and against all other functions under study for all items except in one case, against the LLI form when the non-nested hypothesis tenting procedure was carried out. This makes it difficult to find a best Engel function, because the P_E test is not able to discriminate between the LLI and DSL rival models. In order to choose the best Engel function between these two rival non-nested models (DSL and LLI), we have used the distance function criterion, which shows that the DSL Engel function is better than the LLI function for most of the expenditure items for our data set.

Our preference between these two functions is for the DSL Engel function. This is because the DSL Engel function performs better than all other functions for most items on statistical grounds. It also satisfies some important economic criteria viz.; (i) threshold; (ii) saturation; (iii) variable elasticity at different total expenditure levels; and (iv) the adding-up criterion. The elasticity estimates and their standard errors can be taken directly from the standard regression results.

Finally, the elasticity estimates for different commodities show that the expenditure pattern of Australian households is very similar to that of other Western developed countries, which can be found in Fousekis and Revell (2001), Kalwij, Alessie and Fontein (1997), Lariviere, Laure and Chalfant (2000) and Blake and Nied (1997).

APPENDIX 3A: APPROXIMATE STANDARD ERRORS OF ELASTICITY ESTIMATES[16]

Let f be a function of r parameters $\vec{\theta} = \{\theta_1, \theta_2, \quad \cdots \quad \theta_r\}'$ for the expenditure elasticity η, i.e.,

$$\eta = f\{\theta_1, \theta_2, \ldots \theta_r\}$$

Then the estimate of η may be written as

$$\hat{\eta} = f\{\hat{\theta}_1, \hat{\theta}_2, \cdots \hat{\theta}_r\}$$

where the $\hat{\theta}_i$'s are the least squares estimates of the θ_i's; $i = 1, 2, \ldots, r$.

The function $f\{\hat{\theta}_1, \hat{\theta}_2, \cdots \hat{\theta}_r\}$ can be expanded around the true parameters $\theta_1, \theta_2, \ldots \theta_r$ in a Taylor series and the variance of

$$\hat{\eta} = f\{\hat{\theta}_1, \hat{\theta}_2, \cdots \hat{\theta}_r\}$$

can be approximated by

$$Var(\hat{\eta}) = \sum_{i=1}^{r} \sum_{j=1}^{r} \left(\frac{\partial f}{\partial \theta_i}\right)_{\hat{\theta}} \left(\frac{\partial f}{\partial \theta_j}\right)_{\hat{\theta}} Cov(\theta_i, \theta_j)$$

$$\therefore S.e(\hat{\eta}) = \sqrt{Var(\hat{\eta})}$$

The numerical estimated values of variances and co-variances can be taken from the output of any regression program.

---

[16] For detailed proof see Cramer (1946, pp. 353-54) and Klein (1953, p. 259).

CHAPTER 4

PROBLEMS IN NON-LINEAR ENGEL FUNCTIONS

The readers will discover how the widely reported within-group arithmetic means (AMs) introduce biases when the parameters of various non-linear Engel functions are estimated by the Aitken's Generalised Least Square (GLS) method. This is because within-group geometric means (GMs) and harmonic means (HMs) are needed to get unbiased estimates of the parameters for various logarithmic and inverse Engel functions. It is shown here how the reported AMs can be used to estimate appropriate grouped means (for instance GMs or HMs) for a number of variables based on a general type of concentration curve, which can then be used to obtain unbiased estimates of the parameters for various non-linear Engel functions. These unbiased estimates of the parameters can be used to estimate unbiased Engel elasticities for various non-linear Engel functions. These unbiased elasticities are different from those obtained from various logarithmic and inverse Engel functions when AMs are used as proxies for GMs and HMs. It is also demonstrated here that the average elasticity of a variable elasticity Engel function is more meaningful than the traditional elasticity estimates computed at some representative values for some variable elasticity Engel functions. Empirical illustrations are provided for the Australian HES data[17].

1. INTRODUCTION

Engel curve analysis relates household expenditure on a particular commodity or a group of commodities to total expenditure (income) and other socio-demographic variables. If the relationship is $Y = f(X, S)$, then the elasticity of Y with respect to X is $\{\partial Y / \partial X\} \cdot (X/Y)$, i.e. $\{\partial \log Y / \partial \log X\}$. In general, the elasticity varies with X and S, and conventionally the elasticity is calculated at its arithmetic means. The algebraic form of the relationship is often not specified by universally accepted economic theory, although some theoretical analysis can point to some particular forms.

This chapter deals with some specific problems of Engel curve analysis for grouped data. First, we will consider some of the statistical questions that arise in estimating regression parameters of non-linear Engel functions (EFs) that are still linear in parameters, but non-linear in their variables. In a pioneering work, Prais and Aitchison (1954) demonstrated that Aitken's GLS method could produce

---

[17] Materials presented here were earlier published in the *Journal of Applied Statistics* [see Haque (1993)].

unbiased estimates of regression parameters when grouped arithmetic means are used. It can be shown that their inference is correct only for linear functions. Thus, this method fails to produce unbiased estimates of the coefficients for non-linear EFs. In fact, to get unbiased estimates of the parameters for the logarithmic/inverse EFs, the GLS method needs the geometric mean (GM)/harmonic mean (HM) within each income group. Because of the nature of some questionnaires of the HES, and the confidentiality of the various socio-economic data, grouped arithmetic means (AMs) are usually published in tabular forms. A bias is introduced when these AMs data are used to estimate the parameters of the non-linear EFs. However, unbiased estimates of parameters from grouped data for the class of functions to be considered here would be possible if one uses the unbiased estimates of within-group appropriate means (for instance GMs or HMs) for logarithmic and inverse functional forms.

We have estimated the within-group GMs/HMs from a general type of concentration curve (CC) for a number of variables that are functions of per capita income. One of the purposes of this chapter is to investigate whether the method of estimation of within-group GMs/HMs based on the CC is reliable and valid for the Australian HES data.[18] Another contribution of this chapter is that we have extended Bhattacharya's (1973) definition of the average elasticity of variable elasticity EFs for more than one variable, which is different from the conventionally estimated elasticities at the arithmetic means of the explanatory variables. Empirical illustrations are given with reference to the 1975-76 Australian HES data.

This chapter is organized as follows. Section 2 considers methodological issues in estimating within-group GMs/HMs from the CCs and the average elasticity of variable elasticity EFs. Numerical illustrations are given in Section 3, while some comments are made in the final section.

2. METHODOLOGICAL ISSUES

2.1 Estimation of Engel Functions from Grouped Means

The specification of EFs is an important issue in an Engel curve analysis. A huge body of literature is available for the specification of an appropriate EF. Many authors such as Banks, Blundell and Lewbel (1997), Bates and Watts (1988), Carrol, Ruppert and Stefanski (1995), Fry and Pashardes (1992), Hausman, Newey and Powell (1995), Kneip and Engel (1995), Tiffin and Tiffin (1999) and Zweimuller (1998), have discussed the specification of the functional form of the Engel curve, and estimated income elasticity for various household consumption items.

Six non-linear Engel functions (ii) – (vii), specified in Section 2.1 of Chapter 3 are considered here to show how the estimated unbiased income elasticity for

---

[18] Kakwani (1977b) also estimated the within-group GMs/HMs from the Kakwani-Podder (1976) Lorenz curve for various non-linear Engel functions to estimate unbiased elasticity for various Indonesian household consumption items.

different expenditure items based on the estimated within group GMs and HMs differs from those elasticities when estimated by using the AMs as the proxies for the GMs/HMs for various logarithmic and/or inverse Engel functions. It is worth noting that all these functions have the common property that they can be estimated by Aitken's GLS method after appropriate transformation from grouped data.

We have estimated each of the equations (ii) – (vii) given in Section 2.1 of Chapter 3 separately by the GLS method, using the directly estimated within group AMs obtained from observed sample values. Henceforth, the elasticity estimate based on this method will be referred to as method A. This method A is the simplest and most conventional method of getting elasticities.[19]

It should be noted that expenditure on commodity (Y) can be zero for individual households, and hence functions featuring logY must necessarily be fitted to non-zero values, and thus average values are preferred rather than data on individual households. However, Keen (1986) has shown how to deal with zero observations when estimating Engel elasticities. To obtain unbiased estimates of the logarithmic/inverse EFs, the GLS method requires within group AMs of the transformed variables like the within group means of log X or (1/X). This follows from the fact that here, the variables are aggregated (integrated) over a number of households within a group. For example, if the Engel relation $Y = \alpha + \beta \log X + \gamma \log S$ holds good for each individual household, then the Engel relation for a group of households can be obtained by

$$\iint Y f(X,S)\,dX\,dY \ = \ \iint (\alpha + \beta \log X + \gamma \log S)\, f(X,S)\,dX\,dY$$

where $f(X, S)$ is the joint density function of X and S. After integrating (or summing in the case of integer variables such as S), over the range of X and S for a particular group, the above expression can be written as

$$\bar{Y} \ = \ \alpha + \beta \log \bar{X}_G \ + \gamma \log \bar{S}_G$$

where $\bar{X}_G$, $\bar{S}_G$ stand for the within-group GMs of the variables X and S. Similarly, the estimated within-group GMs/HMs of each Y, X and S are needed, depending on the various functional form to be estimated.

The within-group sample GMs/HMs for Y, X and S in each income classes are not provided by the Australian Bureau of Statistics (ABS). However, we have estimated the within-group GMs/HMs of Y, X and S indirectly from the equation of the CCs, which is discussed below.

---

[19] Many authors such as Brosig (1998), Buse (1994), Lyssiotos, Pashardes and Stengos (1999), Meenakshi and Ray (1999), Michelini (1997), Pashardes (1995b), Pashardes and Fry (1994), Perali (2001), Tiffin and Tiffin (1999), and Yatchew (1999), have used the reported within-group AMs as the proxies for the GMs and HMs to estimate income elasticities from various non-linear Engel functions.

2.2 Estimation of Within Group Geometric and Harmonic Means from Concentration Curves

The concentration curve is the generalized version of the Lorenz curve. A detailed discussion of the properties of these curves will be provided later in Chapter 7.

Let X is the per capita income (total expenditure) of a family, and also a random variable with mean μ and density function $f(X)$. Now let the probability distribution function and the proportion of income (total expenditure) attributable to families with an income (total expenditure) not exceeding x are respectively defined by $P(x)$ and $Q(x)$. The relationship between $P(x)$ and $Q(x)$, defined implicitly via x, is known as the Lorenz curve for per capita income (total expenditure). Analogous to $Q(x)$, one could define $Q_i\{W_i(x)\}$ to be the proportion of expenditure on the ith commodity made by families with a per capita income (total expenditure) not exceeding x. The relationship between $P(x)$ and $Q_i\{W_i(x)\}$, again implicitly defined via x, is known as the concentration curve for the ith commodity. For the Engel function $W_i(x)$, $Q_i\{W_i(x)\}$ can be expressed as follows

$$Q_i\{W_i(x)\} = \frac{\int_0^x W_i(x) f(x) dx}{\int_0^\infty W_i(x) f(x) dx} \tag{4.1}$$

Further, for any function $S(x)$, one may define

$$Q_i\{S(x)\} = \frac{\int_0^x S(x) f(x) dx}{\int_0^\infty S(x) f(x) dx} \tag{4.2}$$

and the relationship between $Q_i\{S(x)\}$ and $P(x)$ is the CC for $S(x)$. We shall later make use of the particular function $S(x)$, being the family size at income (total expenditure) x.

Suppose the CC is expressed by $Q(x) = g\{P(x)\}$. This expression can be used to derive within-group GMs/HMs. This requires the assumption that the density function $f(x)$ is continuous and

$$\frac{dP}{dX} = f(X); \qquad\qquad \frac{dQ}{dX} = \frac{X f(X)}{\mu}$$

exist. Under these assumptions, it can be shown that X is related to these curves by

$$X = \mu \frac{dQ}{dP} \tag{4.3}$$

Therefore, the log of the GM and the inverse of the HM for any arbitrary group k can be obtained by the following relations

$$\log(GM)_k = \frac{\int_{P_{k-1}}^{P_k} \log\left(\mu \frac{dQ}{dP}\right) dP}{\int_{P_{k-1}}^{P_k} dP} \tag{4.4}$$

$$\frac{1}{(HM)_k} = \frac{\int_{P_{k-1}}^{P_k} \left[1 \Big/ \left(\mu \frac{dQ}{dP}\right) \right] dP}{\int_{P_{k-1}}^{P_k} dP} \tag{4.5}$$

where dQ/dP can be obtained from any implicitly specified CC. Any estimates of the GMs and HMs based on the equations (4.4) and (4.5) will be called the indirect estimates of the GMs and HMs respectively.

The indirect estimates of within-group GMs and HMs for different variables are then used to obtain estimates of the regression coefficients for logarithmic and inverse relationships. In fact, these functions are estimated exactly in the same way as method A by replacing indirectly estimated GMs and HMs of various logarithmic and inverse variables in the appropriate places. This will now be called method B.

2.3 Average Elasticity of a Variable Elasticity Engel Curve

The elasticity of an EF [except the constant elasticity EF (iv) of Section 2.1 of Chapter 3] should vary with different values of explanatory variables. In order to obtain the variability of the elasticity of EFs, econometricians often fit variable elasticity EFs to HES data. Elasticities of these curves are usually computed at some representative values. Usually these are the mean values, but occasionally the median values [see Prais and Houthakker (1955), Iyengar (1964a), Sinha (1966), etc.] are also used. The weighted average of the elasticities at all the points of the Engel curve may be looked upon as the market elasticity if per capita income changes in the same proportion for all the consumers. In most situations, it is a better measure than the elasticity at the mean values, which does not have any particular significance.

Bhattacharya (1973) introduced the notion of an average elasticity of a variable elasticity EF. He took the shares of the different income classes in the aggregate expenditure of the item under consideration as weights instead of the weighted average of the Engel elasticities at all the points of the EF. This is actually an application of Stone's (1954) formula for getting the macro-elasticity from the micro-level. Here, we have extended Bhattacharya's definition of the average elasticity of a variable elasticity EF. In our analysis, a multivariate type of EF is considered.

2.3.1 *Definition*

Let the variable elasticity Engel curve be denoted by $Y = \psi(X, S)$, where Y is the per capita household expenditure of a commodity, and X and S are the per capita household total expenditure and family size respectively.

Let $h(X, S)$ be the joint density function of X and S and if $\psi(X, S) = E(Y / X, S)$, the conditional expectation of Y given X and S, then the total expenditure elasticity with respect to X is given by

$$\eta_x = \frac{\delta \log[\psi(X, S)]}{\delta \log X}$$

The average elasticity of the function $E(Y / X, S)$ for the entire range of X and S is defined below.

$$\overline{\eta_x} = \frac{\displaystyle\int_0^\infty \int_0^\infty h(X, S)\, E(Y / X, S)\, \eta_x(X, S)\, dX\, dS}{\displaystyle\int_0^\infty \int_0^\infty h(X, S)\, E(Y / X, S)\, dX\, dS}$$

$$= \frac{\displaystyle\int_0^\infty \int_0^\infty h(X, S)\, E(Y / X, S)\, \eta_x(X, S)\, dX\, dS}{E(Y)} \qquad (4.6)$$

For convenience, we will drop the subscript X from the elasticity formula η throughout the remainder of the chapter.[20]

This is, in fact, the market elasticity if all X-values change in an equiproportional manner. It will not be appropriate for other types of shifts in the X-distribution. It depends on the form of the EF and the joint distribution of X and S, and hence the marginal distribution of X and S.

It is important to observe that for the DL Engel function, $\overline{\eta}$ coincides with the constant value of the Engel elasticity. Furthermore, $\overline{\eta}$ is more meaningful than η ($\overline{X}, \overline{S}$) for a variable elasticity EF, since the elasticity of such a function varies with the values of explanatory variables.

The above equation may be written as

$$\overline{\eta} \;=\; \int_0^\infty \int_0^\infty p\,(\mathrm{X,S})\,\eta\;(X,S)\,dX\;dS \tag{4.7}$$

where
$$p(X,S) \;=\; \frac{h(X,S)\,E\,(Y/X,S)}{E(Y)}$$

This $p(X, S)$ has all the characteristics of a joint density function and hence

$$\overline{\eta} \;=\; E_p\{\eta(X,S)\} \tag{4.8}$$

where E_p stands for the expectation taken with respect to $p(X, S)$.

Engel functions are often such that η (X, S) is a convex or concave function of (X, S). Then, by Jensen's inequality, we have

$$\overline{\eta} \;=\; E_p\{\eta\,(X,S)\} \;>=<\; \eta\,\{E_p\,(X,S)\} \tag{4.9}$$

according as η (X, S) is a convex, linear or concave function of X and S. The formulae of the average elasticity ($\overline{\eta}$) for some variable elasticity EFs are given below.

---

[20] Note that the symbol '/' stands for conditional.

(i)   Linear (L)   : $\overline{\eta} = \left(\beta \overline{X}\right)/\left(\alpha + \beta \overline{X} + \gamma \overline{S}\right)$

(ii) Semi-log (SL)   : $\overline{\eta} = \beta / \left(\alpha + \beta \log X_G + \gamma \log S_G\right)$

(iii) Hyperbolic (HYP)   : $\overline{\eta} = \left(\beta / X_H\right)/\left(\alpha - \beta / X_H - \gamma / S_H\right)$

(iv) Log-Inverse (LI)   : $\overline{\eta} = -\beta \, E\left(Y / X\right)/ E\left(Y\right)$

(v)   Log Log-inverse(LLI)   : $\overline{\eta} = \beta - \gamma \, E\left(Y / X\right)/ E\left(Y\right)$

(vi) Double Semi-log (DSL) : $\overline{\eta} = \left(\beta \, \overline{X} + \gamma\right)/\left(\alpha + \beta \overline{X} + \gamma \log X_G + \delta \log S_G\right)$

where the overbar and the subscripts G and H stand for the arithmetic, geometric and harmonic means of the respective variables. We refer to the average elasticity of various Engel functions obtained by the above formulae as method C.

It is mentioned here that for the linear EF the average elasticity and the elasticity at mean values ($\overline{X}, \overline{S}$) are exactly the same. But for other Engel functions (ii) - (vi) of Section 2.1 of Chapter 3, the average elasticity and the elasticity at mean values will be different because of the need of within group E (Y/X), GMs and HMs as shown by the above formulae. In case of the LI and the LLI, we need to estimate within group expected value of (Y/X) [i.e., E (Y/X)] for all the households in the population. In the absence of such figures, it may however be approximated by taking the weighted average of the ratios $\left(\overline{Y}_{kl} / \overline{X}_{kl}\right)$ for all the kxl cells, where k and l are the number of classifications of the per capita total expenditure and family size respectively, and $\overline{Y}_{kl}$ and $\overline{X}_{kl}$ are the average expenditure on the commodities and the per capita total expenditure in the $(k, l)^{th}$ cell. Further, we need to know within group GMs and HMs for the per capita total expenditure to compute the average elasticity for some logarithmic and inverse EFs. In order to estimate within group GMs and HMs of total expenditure and family size, we fitted the following Lorenz equation (4.10) for both the per capita total expenditure and family size to their marginal distributions obtained from the cross-classified 1975-76 HES data.[21]

3. NUMERICAL ILLUSTRATIONS

The theoretical considerations discussed in Section 2 are now applied to the Australian 1975-76 HES data. Commodity wise weekly AMs of household expenditure on various commodities, total expenditure, income, number of persons, etc., per household and the estimated number of households were available in ascending order for twelve average weekly per capita (gross) income groups of households in Australia.[22]

---

[21] In order to estimate the concentration curve for household size, we first arranged the household size in ascending order (out of household composition) and then found the frequency for each household size.

[22] Twelve groups classified by average weekly per capita income are given by: (i) less than $30; (ii) $30-$50; (iii) $50-$70: (iv) $70-$100; (v) $100-$130; (vi) $130-$160; (vii) $160-$190; (viii) $190 -$220; (ix) $220-$250; (x) $250-$280; (xi) $280-$310; (xii) $310; and more.

These data are used to estimate within group GMs/HMs of Y, X and S by the following concentration curve

$$Q_i = P_i - a_i \, P_i^{\alpha}{}_i \, (1 - P_i)^{\beta}{}_i \tag{4.10}$$

where a_i, α_i and β_i are the parameters of the CC for the ith item, and all are greater than zero. A sufficient condition for Q_i to be a convex function of P_i in the unit interval is that $0 < \alpha, \beta < 1$, although this is not a necessary condition. Note that Kakwani (1980a) used this Lorenz curve to describe the poverty measure. We use this CC to obtain within-group GMs and HMs.

The implicit Lorenz function derived from its properties was introduced by Kakwani and Podder (1973). The CC given in Equation (4.10) is constructed from the properties of a CC that should satisfy the following: (i) $Q = 0$ if $P = 0$; (ii) $Q = 1$ if $P = 1$; (iii) $Q \leq P$, for $0 < P < 1$; (iv) $dQ/dP \geq 0$; (v) $d^2 \, Q/ \, dP^2 \geq 0$, for $0 < P < 1$; and (vi) $0 \leq \int_0^1 g(P) \, dP \leq 1/2$. Equation (4.10) satisfies all these properties except (iv) and (v), which do not give positive values in many cases. This is why many of the fitted values of α are required to be greater than 1 for the eligibility of Equation (4.10) to be a concentration curve. It should be pointed out that unlike the Lorenz curve derived from the well-known income distribution, viz., the log-normal distribution, Equation (4.10) is not symmetrical unless $\alpha = \beta$. This is quite understandable, since this curve is based on its fitting performance to the real data.

Equation (4.10) is estimated by the non-linear least squares method [the ordinary least squares method can also be used to estimate the parameters taking logs on both sides after rewriting Equation (4.10) as $P_i - Q_i = a_i \, P_i^{\alpha}{}_i \, (1 - P_i)^{\beta}{}_i$]. The estimated parameters and the values of the residual sum of squares for different expenditure items, total expenditure and family sizes are presented in Table 4.1. Table 4.1 shows that the residual sums of squares for most of the items are very small, indicating that the Equation (4.10) fits well to the data. After estimating the parameters of Equation (4.10) and finding dQ/dP, the GMs/HMs for different expenditure items, total expenditure and family size in each income classes have been estimated by the relations (4.4) and (4.5) respectively, which are presented in Table 4.2. Simpson's numerical integration technique is used for this purpose.

The familiar inequality AM $\geq$ GM $\geq$ HM must hold. This inequality holds good for our various estimated means based on the indirect method of estimation from CCs. For example, the indirect estimates of the AMs $\geq$ GMs for cereals and dairy products in different income classes, which are shown in Table 4.3.

However, figures from Table 4.2 show that the indirectly estimated GMs exceed the reported AMs obtained directly from the sample for about half of the per capita income classes for almost all items. Our results appear to contravene the well-known inequality that AM $\geq$ GM. Since the AM has been correctly calculated, it follows that the indirect estimates of the GM and HM ought here to be rejected in many cases. Thus, our finding questions the reliability of Kakwani's (1977b) method of estimation of within-group GMs/HMs from the CC. The explanation for this may be that these means are in fact not calculated from the same set of numbers. The income distribution within any income group implied by the fitted CC will invariably differ somewhat from the sample observations, which are used to calculate the within group AMs. Thus, the use of the restrictive functional form of the CC might be the cause of such results.

Table 4.1. Parameter estimates of the concentration curves for different commodities

Commodity groups	A	α	β	Residual sum of squares
(1) Bread, cakes, cereals, dairy products, oils & fats	0.070646	0.844887	0.981122	0.000020
(2) Meals in restaurants & hotels	1.252357	1.251027	0.646148	0.000755
(3) All foods	0.332769	1.031065	0.755593	0.000015
(4) Alcohol & tobacco	0.817956	1.214220	0.839964	0.000215
(5) Current housing costs	0.794079	1.384408	0.679038	0.000170
(6) Fuel & power	0.224401	0.905444	0.634756	0.000159
(7) Clothing & footwear	0.767346	1.156576	0.932109	0.000146
(8) Household equipment & operation	0.517776	0.902163	0.507240	0.000682
(9) Medical care & health expenses	0.434448	0.946921	0.796430	0.000104
(10) Transport & communication	0.742749	1.075145	0.847491	0.000045
(11) All recreation & education	0.832697	1.180547	0.818986	0.000205
(12) Miscellaneous goods & services	0.866451	1.193864	0.785701	0.000319
(13) Total expenditure	0.614966	1.090035	0.736060	0.000038
(14) Family size	0.201084	0.825278	0.681528	0.000839

Source: The 1975-1976 Australian HES data based on the 12 weekly per capita income groups supplied by the ABS.

*Table 4.2.   Within-group GMs estimated indirectly from concentration curve**

Per capita income groups	Commodity groups						
	All food	All alcohol & tobacco	Current housing costs	Fuel & power	Clothing & footwear	Household equipment & operation	Medical care & health expenses
< $30	8.12 (7.84)	1.99 (1.77)	6.04 (3.94)	0.99 (0.91)	2.60 (2.33)	2.26 (2.95)	0.98 (1.01)
$30–50	8.94 (9.14)	1.96 (2.06)	4.88 (5.45)	1.13 (1.19)	2.87 (3.03)	3.67 (3.44)	1.30 (1.30)
$50–70	10.37 (10.23)	2.79 (2.93)	5.75 (6.85)	1.27 (1.21)	4.18 (4.20)	4.93 (4.60)	1.65 (1.63)
$70–100	11.83 (11.77)	3.86 (3.52)	7.86 (7.03)	1.39 (1.43)	5.59 (5.48)	6.15 (6.90)	1.97 (1.97)
$100–130	13.30 (13.45)	4.96 (5.22)	10.64 (9.32)	1.51 (1.45)	6.88 (6.86)	7.54 (6.98)	2.26 (2.37)
$130–160	14.64 (14.68)	5.90 (6.11)	13.60 (13.95)	1.64 (1.59)	7.86 (7.92)	9.13 (9.66)	2.51 (2.46)
$160–190	15.87 (15.77)	6.69 (6.81)	16.58 (18.76)	1.77 (1.84)	8.55 (8.48)	10.99 (12.47)	2.72 (2.55)
$190–220	16.90 (17.62)	7.26 (6.67)	19.23 (21.97)	1.90 (2.16)	8.99 (10.37)	12.95 (7.51)	2.90 (3.17)
$220–250	17.91 (15.99)	7.77 (7.57)	21.96 (26.48)	2.04 (2.19)	9.32 (9.65)	15.30 (14.23)	3.06 (2.23)
$250–280	19.01 (21.42)	8.28 (8.11)	25.08 (26.81)	2.20 (2.51)	9.60 (8.74)	18.35 (22.58)	3.24 (3.18)
$280–310	19.91 (19.36)	8.66 (12.53)	27.74 (19.31)	2.35 (1.62)	9.79 (18.27)	21.25 (24.12)	3.38 (2.92)
≥ $310	23.03 (22.41)	9.81 (9.18)	37.16 (29.31)	2.94 (2.51)	10.26 (6.51)	33.57 (43.77)	3.84 (4.77)
Over the entire range	11.91 (12.93)	2.14 (2.32)	8.22 (8.91)	1.48 (1.61)	3.43 (3.72)	5.83 (6.33)	1.96 (2.13)

* Arithmetic means estimated directly from the sample values are presented in parentheses, while the harmonic means of total expenditure and family size estimated indirectly from concentration curves, are given in curly braces.

Source: The 1975-1976 Australian HES data based on the 12 weekly per capita income groups supplied by the ABS.

Table 4.2. (Continued)

	Commodity groups				
Per capita income groups	Transport & communi-cation	All recreation & education	Miscellaneous goods & services	Total expenditure	Family size
< $30	5.08 (5.16)	2.82 (2.40)	2.58 (1.94)	32.72 (30.26) {32.69}	3.98 (4.54) {3.98}
$30 – 50	6.49 (6.44)	2.90 (3.22)	2.56 (2.99)	36.83 (38.27) {36.68}	3.54 (3.13) {3.54}
$50 – 70	9.79 (10.12)	4.28 (4.01)	3.82 (3.56)	49.24 (49.34) {49.11}	3.23 (3.53) {3.23}
$70 – 100	13.14 (12.92)	6.00 (5.96)	5.46 (5.38)	63.32 (62.38) {63.16}	2.98 (3.15) {2.98}
$100-130	16.32 (16.23)	7.76 (8.14)	7.21 (7.58)	78.14 (77.62) {78.04}	2.74 (2.69) {2.73}
$130-160	18.95 (19.18)	9.30 (9.09)	8.81 (8.45)	92.10 (93.11) {92.01}	2.50 (2.17) {2.50}
$160-190	21.08 (22.46)	10.61 (11.40)	10.22 (10.34)	105.21 (110.89) {105.16}	2.27 (1.95) {2.26}
$190-220	22.66 (21.37)	11.61 (11.02)	11.34 (12.80)	116.33 (114.69) {116.29}	2.05 (1.99) {2.05}
$220-250	24.05 (22.97)	12.51 (10.83)	12.40 (10.50)	127.41 (122.72) {127.37}	1.82 (1.80) {1.82}
$250-280	25.43 (22.66)	13.43 (10.49)	13.52 (14.97)	139.66 (141.58) {139.61}	1.55 (1.71) {1.55}
$280-310	26.49 (21.82)	14.15 (27.21)	14.41 (26.75)	149.84 (154.29) {149.83}	1.33 (1.85) {1.33}
≥ $310	29.62 (33.23)	16.35 (16.74)	17.24 (13.50)	184.69 (182.01) {180.77}	1.23 (1.54) {0.99}
Over the entire range	11.02 (11.96)	5.58 (6.06)	4.50 (4.88)	56.08 (60.85) {51.37}	2.64 (3.09) {2.22}

Table 4.3. Estimated arithmetic and geometric means for cereals and dairy products based on concentration curves

Various income classes[*]	Various estimated means	
	Arithmetic means	Geometric means
< $30	2.65	2.64
$ 30–50	2.80	2.80
$ 50–70	2.91	2.91
$ 70–100	2.99	2.99
$ 100–130	3.05	3.04
$130–160	3.08	3.07
$160–190	3.11	3.10
$190–220	3.12	3.12
$220–250	3.13	3.13
$ 250–280	3.14	3.13
$ 280–310	3.14	3.14
≥ $ 310	3.15	3.14

[*] These income classes are defined in Footnote 22.

Source: The 1975-1976 Australian HES data based on the 12 weekly per capita income groups supplied by the ABS.

The greater the discrepancy between the implied income distribution within any income group and the actual distribution of the group, the less likely it is that the inequality between the GMs and HMs will be preserved. An inspection of goodness of fit reveals that the poor GM estimates arise precisely from commodities like current housing costs, whose goodness of fit is eight times worse than that of cereals. This suggests that for the indirect method to be a success, a high degree of accuracy is needed in fitting the CC. This is unlikely to be attainable for practical data sets. Thus, we come to the conclusion that Kakwani's method of estimating within group GMs and HMs based on the CC is not reliable in all cases, certainly not for our data set. However, the overall indirectly estimated GMs based on CCs show that these means are lower than the overall directly estimated AMs for the entire sample (see total expenditure and family size in Table 4.2), but not within the groups.

3.1 Comparisons of Elasticities

Engel elasticities for various expenditure items of different non-linear, and variable elasticity EFs have been estimated to show the effects of using the estimated within group GMs/ HMs based on the CC, and to show how the average elasticity of variable elasticity EF differs from those elasticity estimated at the mean values of the various independent variables. Elasticity estimates of various expenditure items based on methods A, B and C are presented in Table 4.4. It is interesting to note that the elasticity estimates for some items based on method A, are similar to the estimates of method B, although elasticity estimates based on these two methods A and B are different for some expenditure items. For example, the elasticity for total food based on the SL function is estimated to be only 0.24 when the indirectly estimated within group GMs of per capita total expenditure and family size are used, compared to 0.48 when directly estimated within group AMs are used as the proxies for the GMs of these variables. But none of the estimates are unreasonable. Some different results are also observed for other functional forms of various items. The extent of the difference of elasticity estimates based on methods A and B varies considerably from function to function and from commodity to commodity.

The difference between the estimates of Engel elasticity calculated at mean values of the explanatory variables and the average elasticity of a variable elasticity EF is often very large and hence important. For example, elasticity estimates calculated at mean values of the explanatory variables for the hyperbolic function are often below one for some common luxuries such as recreation and education, miscellaneous goods and services, etc. But the average elasticity of the hyperbolic form correctly indicates that these items are luxuries. It is reasonable to suppose that a commodity is a luxury for low spenders but a necessity for higher spenders. In particular, a commodity may well have elasticity greater (less) than one at the means, but an average elasticity less (greater) than one overall. This casts doubt on the validity of a single elasticity statistic. Thus, average elasticity of a variable elasticity EF is more meaningful than the elasticity computed at the mean values for the variable elasticity EFs, which vary with the values of explanatory variables. Larger discrepancies are also frequently noted for the SL form. For most of the items $\overline{\eta}$ is highest for the SL form. For the LI and LLI the two estimates are often very close. For the DSL Engel function, the two estimates are very similar except in two cases.

Table 4.4. Estimation of Engel elasticities by methods A, B, and C

Various consumption items	Method A Elasticity at 'AMs' for various Engel functions							Method B Elasticity at 'GMs and HMs' for various Engel functions							Method C Average elasticity for different variable elasticity Engel functions						
	L	SL	HYP	DL	LI	LLI	DSL	L	SL	HYP	DL	LI	LLI	DSL	L	SL	HYP	DL	LI	LLI	DSL
Current housing cost	1.20	0.63	0.39	0.71	0.43	0.80	0.95	1.20	0.62	0.35	0.75	0.57	1.86	0.74	1.20	0.71	0.53	0.71	0.64	1.00	1.00
Fuel & power	0.35	0.28	0.17	0.28	0.23	0.26	0.32	0.35	0.05	0.21	19	0.27	0.12	0.05	0.35	0.21	0.19	0.28	0.25	0.21	0.15
Food	0.50	0.48	0.29	0.52	0.37	0.48	0.49	0.50	0.24	0.31	0.47	0.40	0.46	0.45	0.50	0.50	0.38	0.52	0.41	0.48	0.48
All alcohol & tobacco	1.04	0.96	0.55	1.22	0.85	1.22	1.08	1.04	0.71	0.65	1.45	0.92	1.66	1.50	1.04	0.81	0.71	1.22	0.78	1.18	0.75
Clothing & footwear	0.75	0.94	0.65	1.17	0.94	1.03	0.91	0.75	1.07	0.77	1.53	0.96	1.32	1.15	0.75	1.08	0.97	1.17	0.98	1.01	1.09
Housing equipment & operation	1.77	1.01	0.82	1.21	0.76	1.28	1.73	1.77	1.49	0.10	0.59	0.77	1.30	0.40	1.77	1.20	1.28	1.21	1.12	1.18	1.17
Medical care & health expenses	0.69	0.75	0.48	0.85	0.66	0.77	0.81	0.69	0.48	0.43	0.81	0.65	0.36	0.66	0.69	0.78	0.67	0.85	0.77	0.79	0.79
Transport & communication	1.03	1.06	0.65	1.41	1.05	1.32	1.14	1.03	0.91	0.69	1.52	1.04	1.06	1.54	1.03	1.29	1.04	1.41	1.06	1.33	1.26
Recreation & education	1.10	1.00	0.57	1.20	0.89	1.16	1.15	1.10	0.61	0.63	1.53	1.00	1.62	1.53	1.10	1.25	1.12	1.20	1.09	1.18	1.22
Miscellaneous goods & services	1.13	0.98	0.56	1.15	0.90	1.08	1.14	1.13	0.44	0.67	1.55	1.02	1.77	1.09	1.13	1.14	1.09	1.15	1.11	1.12	1.17

Source: The 1975-1976 Australian HES data based on the twelve weekly per capita income groups (these groups are given in Footnote 22) supplied by the ABS.

4. CONCLUSIONS

We have investigated Kakwani's method of estimating of within-group GMs and HMs for various consumption items, family size and total expenditure in various per capita income classes for the 1975-76 Australian HES data. Our results suggest that Kakwani's method of estimation of within group GMs/HMs is not valid for our data set, because in some cases the within-group GMs exceeded the correctly estimated AMs directly obtained from sample observation, which is contradictory to the familiar inequality AM ≥ GM ≥ HM for any set of data. Thus, we come to a crucial conclusion that Kakwani's method of estimation of within-group GMs and HMs is not reliable for all data sets. Hence, we urge researchers to investigate the estimated within-group GMs and HMs based on Kakwani's method by verifying the usual inequality AM ≥ GM ≥ HM before using such means for any estimation of the parameters of the logarithmic/inverse relationships.

Thus, in the absence of actual within-group GMs/HMs, Kakwani's method of estimating within-group GMs/HMs based on CCs can be used if these means satisfy the usual inequality, i.e. AM ≥ GM ≥ HM. If it fails to satisfy the usual inequality, investigators are advised to find a suitable CC, which can give a high degree of precision to the fitted data that hopefully can estimate the appropriate within-group means, which satisfy the usual inequality.

In this study, the average elasticity of a variable elasticity EF has also been taken into consideration. The average elasticity for variable elasticity EFs has been computed and the results show that the average elasticities for the HYP and SL functions are higher than the elasticilies computed at the mean values. As a result, some luxury items are correctly classified even for the HYP function, which cannot be achieved if elasticity estimates are correctly computed at mean values. Therefore, our average elasticity estimates for variable elasticity EFs are more meaningful than the traditional elasticity estimates calculated from mean values.

Thus, we recommend that investigators should give more importance to specify the EF correctly and if a variable elasticity EF is found to be more satisfactory than other alternatives for a certain data set, average elasticity of that data set be estimated by our method, using the correctly estimated within-group appropriate means based on the method described in this chapter.

Our average elasticity estimates show that the Lorenz ratio may approximate many types of EFs. A new type of Lorenz equation is used to estimate the GMs and HMs instead of using some common income distribution function. Finally, it should be pointed out that our study shows how the Engel elasticilies for various non-linear EFs and average elasticity of a variable elasticity EF can be obtained for more than one independent variable (for example, per capita total expenditure and family size) when the appropriate within-group means are not available. Thus, our method can be used to estimate appropriate within-group means for other types of independent variables for the multivariate Engel curve analysis. The generalizations of our methods are straightforward.

CHAPTER 5

THE BOX-COX ENGEL FUNCTION

Readers will find out how a general type of Engel function, the Box-Cox Engel function, is developed using the Box-Cox transformation. This function encompasses many commonly used Engel functions, and it is shown here that each of the many commonly used Engel functions can become special cases of the Box-Cox Engel function. This function is also used to discriminate among the commonly used Engel functions, by performing a parametric test on the power parameters. A joint test on the different power transformations has been done by the likelihood ratio test, and it turns out that none of the commonly used Engel functions is appropriate for the 1975-76 Australian HES data, although the double log Engel function is not significantly different from the Box-Cox Engel function for five out of ten expenditure items. The Maximum Likelihood (ML) method is used to estimate the parameters of the Box-Cox Engel function, which are then used to estimate income elasticities for food and various non-food items.[23]

1. INTRODUCTION

In estimating income elasticities for various household expenditure items, one needs to specify the form of the Engel function. This is important, because the calculated elasticities depend appreciably on the algebraic form used. To find an appropriate Engel function is a difficult task and no solution appears to have found general acceptance even in recent times. However, the works of Box and Cox (1964), Zarembka (1974), Poirier (1978), Hamilton and Wyckoff (1991), Wooldridge (1992), Berndt, Showalter and Wooldridge (1993), Ornelas, Shumway and Ozuna (1994), Buchinsky (1995), Jones and Yen (2000), Machado and Mata (2000), and Koebel, Martin and Francois (2001) on the transformation of variables facilitate the use of a more general functional form to estimate the relationship between the dependent and explanatory variables for which many commonly used Engel functions become special cases.

---

[23] Materials presented here were published earlier in *Metroeconomica* [see Haque (1988)].

The purpose of this chapter is to develop a general type of Engel function, which we will call the Box-Cox Engel function, and to show how some of the commonly used Engel functions such as (i) to (v) of Section 2.1 of Chapter 3, become special cases to this Box-Cox Engel function. The maximum likelihood (ML) method is used to estimate the parameters of this Box-Cox Engel function, using grouped HES data.[24] These estimated parameters are then used to estimate Engel elasticities for total food and various non-food items. Moreover, the Box-Cox Engel function is used here to discriminate among the commonly used Engel functions, by performing a parametric test on the power parameters.[25]

The outline of this chapter is as follows. The model and the specification of the Engel functions are given in Section 2. The Engel function derived from the Box-Cox transformation is discussed in Section 3. The derivation of the elasticity formula, and estimation procedures of the Box-Cox Engel function are given in Section 4. The empirical results are presented in Section 5. A statistical test in discriminating among commonly used Engel functions, which are special cases of the Box-Cox Engel function, is performed and presented in Section 6, while some comments and limitations of the study are given in Section 7.

2. THE MODEL SPECIFICATION OF THE ENGEL FUNCTIONS

2.1 Specification of Functional Forms

The following Box-Cox (BC) Engel function is developed and used for our investigation.

$$\text{Box-Cox (BC):}\quad \frac{(Y^{\lambda}-1)}{\lambda} = \alpha + \beta\,\frac{(X^{\mu}-1)}{\mu} + \gamma\,\frac{(S^{\nu}-1)}{\nu} \qquad (5.1)$$

where, Y, X and S were defined earlier in chapter 3, and α, β, γ, λ, μ and ν are parameters.

---

[24] In order to derive the Box-Cox Engel function, separate Box-Cox transforming parameters are used for dependent and the various independent variables. This does not seem to have been tried elsewhere. Bensu, Kmenta and Shapiro (1976) used different power transformations for dependent and independent variables, but they used the same transformation on different independent variables. Moreover, in the past, the Box-Cox transformation has been used to compute the elasticities for food items onlyIn this study, we have applied the Box-Cox transformation to estimate the total expenditure elasticities for food and non-food items.

[25] In the past a number of authors used different functional forms for Engel curve analysis. Allen and Bowley (1935) used the linear Engel function for the analysis of the British family budget data. The topic has further gained importance following the contributions of Working (1943), Prais and Houthakker (1955), Summers (1959), Goreux (1960), Leser (1963), Sinha (1966), Kakwani (1977b), Bewley (1982), Haque (1984), Giles and Hampton (1985) and Hoa.(1986) The Box-Cox Engel function has been used by Zarembka (1972), Chang (1977), and Bensu, Kmenta and Shapiro (1976) for food demand analysis. This function was also used by Zarembka (1968), White (1972), and Spitzer (1976, 1977) for the analysis of the demand for money.

This BC function is a very general form of Engel function, since it is based on non-linear transformations with λ, μ and ν parameters. It is noted here that the functional forms (i) to (v) of Section 2.1 of Chapter 3 are all special cases of this BC Engel function (5.1). More specifically:

if $\lambda = 1$, $\mu = 1$ and $\nu = 1$ then (5.1) = (i);
if $\lambda = 1$, $\mu = 0$ and $\nu = 0$ then (5.1) = (ii);
if $\lambda = 1$, $\mu = -1$ and $\nu = -1$ then (5.1) = (iii);
if $\lambda = 0$, $\mu = 0$ and $\nu = 0$ then (5.1) = (iv); and
if $\lambda = 0$, $\mu = -1$ and $\nu = -1$ then (5.1) = (v).

Many other functional forms can also be obtained by varying the values of λ, μ and ν.[26] However, allowing for more flexibility in the Box-Cox Engel function should not be seen as a substitute for an appropriate theoretical basis.

These commonly used Engel functions can be estimated by using the GLS method on each of the first five functions of Section 2.1 of Chapter 3, and the Maximum Likelihood method is used to estimate the Box-Cox Engel function for various items. More importantly, Powell (1969) has shown that the GLS method yields estimates that automatically satisfy the adding-up criterion for those functions such as linear (L) function (i), which have an independent linear total expenditure (income) variable. However, for other functions including the Box-Cox Engel function, the adding-up criterion can be verified empirically by Cramer's formula (1973a, p. 147), which states that the adding-up criterion is satisfied at a particular point, if the Engel elasticity estimates weighted by the budget shares sum to unity.

3. THE BOX-COX ENGEL FUNCTION

The transformation of variable techniques is a powerful procedure in econometrics to handle the general problem in choosing a functional form, particularly when a functional form is not suggested by theory [see Zarembka 1974,

---

[26] It is noted that for $\lambda=0, \mu=0$, $\nu=0$, the expressions $(Y^\lambda-1)/\lambda$, $(X^\mu-1)/\mu$ and $(S^\nu-1)/\nu$ appear to be indeterminate. However, for any finite number K, we can write $K = e^{(\log K)}$, where e is the base of the natural logarithm and

$e^{(\log K)} = 1 + \log K + 1/2!(\log K)^2 + 1/3!(\log K)^3 + \ldots$. Thus, it follows that

$$\frac{Y^\lambda - 1}{\lambda} \equiv \log Y + \frac{\lambda}{2!}(\log Y)^2 + \frac{\lambda^2}{3!}(\log Y)^3 + \cdots$$

Therefore when $\lambda \to 0$: $\dfrac{Y^\lambda - 1}{\lambda} \to \log Y$.

Similarly

$\dfrac{X^\lambda - 1}{\lambda} \to \log X$ as $\mu \to 0$, and $\dfrac{S^\lambda - 1}{\lambda} \to \log S$ as $\nu \to 0$.

p. 83).[27] This is precisely the case with Engel curve analysis. Also, the inspection of the scatter diagram of family budget data does not give a clear idea of the appropriate functional form. Econometricians often attempt to determine the appropriate functional form of the relationship on an *ad hoc* basis out of a number of simple functions that satisfy some economic and statistical criteria.

This implies that one is often content to fit a local approximation to an unknown function in order to estimate its direction in the observed region. The commonly used functional forms have certain deficiencies with respect to some *a priori* beliefs. For example, Chang (1977) indicated that a linear function implied that the income elasticity for meat was rising and tended toward unity, if it was less than unity. This was inconsistent with the theoretical effect of an increase in income on the demand for food. The share semi-log function is not valid for extreme values of total expenditure (income). On the other hand, the widely used double-logarithmic (DL) functional form gives constant total expenditure (income) elasticity at all levels of total expenditure (income). Although this DL function is quite successfully selected in a number of studies based on the grounds of goodness of fit.

Because of such difficulties in the commonly used functional forms, the Box-Cox Engel function is developed and used in this study, which will represent both the statistical and economic properties of demand analysis. The Box-Cox Engel function given in Equation (5.1) of Section 2.1 in this chapter is considered for our investigation. Note that λ, μ and ν are the transformation parameters, which determine the degree and type of non-linearity, and α, β, and γ are coefficient parameters in the Box-Cox Engel function given in Equation (5.1). A different Box-Cox transformation is applied to the dependent as well as the independent variables (viz., per capita total expenditure and family size).

4. ESTIMATION OF ELASTICITY FROM THE BOX-COX ENGEL FUNCTION

4.1 Elasticity of the Box-Cox Functional Form

In order to derive the total expenditure elasticity (income) of the Box-Cox Engel function, we differentiate the BC Engel function (5.1) and obtain the following.

$$Y^{\lambda-1}dY = \beta X^{\mu-1}dX + \gamma S^{\nu-1}dS$$

or

$$Y^{\lambda}d\log Y = \beta X^{\mu}\log X + \gamma S^{\nu}\log S$$

[27] An excellent review of the literature on transformation of variables can be obtained from the author on request.

Hence,
$$\frac{d \log Y}{d \log X} = \frac{\beta \, X^{\mu}}{Y^{\lambda}}$$

and
$$\frac{d \log Y}{d \log S} = \frac{\gamma \, S^{\nu}}{Y^{\lambda}}$$

Therefore, the total expenditure elasticity at any points (Y, X) satisfying (5.1) is given by

$$\eta_{(X,Y)} = \beta \frac{X^{\mu}}{Y^{\lambda}}$$

The estimated elasticity of total expenditure (income) would be calculated by substituting the estimated value of β, μ and λ in the above formula. The variance of the estimated elasticity cannot be obtained analytically, because it involves products and ratios of random variables. Cramer's (1946) approximation formula can be used for this purpose, which is already presented in Appendix 3A of Chapter 3.

4.2 Estimation of the Box-Cox Engel Function

We estimate the Box-Cox Engel function (5.1) of Section 2.1 by the Maximum Likelihood (ML) method. In order to apply the ML method to Equation (5.1), we assume that the errors are additive and normally distributed with zero mean, constant variance and Cov ($\varepsilon_i, \varepsilon_j$) = 0 if i $\neq$ j. We have used the grouped data.

Therefore, in order to restore constant variance for grouped mean observations, we need to multiply each observation of all the variables by the square root of the number of sample households in respective classes.

The likelihood function for the original variable Y_i is given by

$$L(Y_1, Y_2, \cdots, Y_n | \theta) = (2\pi\sigma^2)^{-n/2}$$

$$\cdot \exp\left\{ -\frac{1}{2\sigma^2} \sum_{i=1}^{n} n_i \left(\frac{Y_i^{\lambda} - 1}{\lambda} - \alpha - \beta \frac{X_i^{\mu} - 1}{\mu} - \gamma \frac{S_i^{\nu} - 1}{\nu} \right)^2 \right\} |J| \qquad (5.2)$$

where the suffix i stands for the ith cell observations for various variables, θ is the vector of parameters (α, β, γ, λ, μ, ν, σ^2), n_i is the weight variable (number of household in the i-th cell) and J is the Jacobian of the transformation on the dependent variable, i.e.

$$|J| = \prod_{i=1}^{n} \left| \frac{\delta(\sqrt{n_i} \cdot ((Y_i^\lambda - 1)/\lambda)))}{\delta Y_i} \right| = \prod_{i=1}^{n} n_i^{1/2} Y_i^{(\lambda-1)}$$

Maximisation of the likelihood function can be accomplished by maximizing its logarithm. The log-likelihood of Equation (5.2) can be written as

$$LL(Y_1, Y_2, \cdots, Y_n | \theta) = -\frac{n}{2}\log(2\pi\sigma^2) - \frac{1}{2\sigma^2}\sum_{i=1}^{n} n_i \left(\frac{Y_i^\lambda - 1}{\lambda} - \alpha - \beta\frac{X_i^\mu - 1}{\mu} - \gamma\frac{S_i^\nu - 1}{\nu} \right)^2$$

$$+ \sum_{i=1}^{n} \left(\frac{1}{2}\log n_i + (\lambda-1)\sum_{i=1}^{n} \log Y_i \right)$$

$$= LL(Y_1, Y_2, \cdots, Y_n | \theta) = -\frac{n}{2}\log(\sigma^2) - \frac{1}{2\sigma^2}\sum_{i=1}^{n} n_i \left(\frac{Y_i^\lambda - 1}{\lambda} - \alpha - \beta\frac{X_i^\mu - 1}{\mu} - \gamma\frac{S_i^\nu - 1}{\nu} \right)^2$$

$$+ (\lambda-1)\sum_{i=1}^{n} \log Y_i + C$$

Excepting a constant term, the above log-likelihood function can be written as

$$LL(Y_1, Y_2, \cdots, Y_n | \theta) = -\frac{n}{2}\log(\sigma^2) - \frac{1}{2\sigma^2}\sum_{i=1}^{n} n_i \left(\frac{Y_i^\lambda - 1}{\lambda} - \alpha - \beta\frac{X_i^\mu - 1}{\mu} - \gamma\frac{S_i^\nu - 1}{\nu} \right)^2$$

$$+ (\lambda-1)\sum_{i=1}^{n} \log Y_i \tag{5.3}$$

The maximization of Equation (5.3) can be done with any non-linear optimisation algorithm. The covariance matrix of all seven parameters is approximated by computing the inverse of Fisher's information matrix for Equation (5.3) and is given by

$$I^{-1}(\theta) = -E\left(\frac{\partial^2 LL}{\partial\theta\partial\theta'} \right)^{-1} \tag{5.4}$$

where θ is the true vector of parameters, and E stands for mathematical expectation. In order to maximise Equation (5.3), we minimise the negative of the right hand side of the equation by the so-called *Quasi-Newton Algorithm*. The required initial values were obtained by some trial and error method: spanning the space (α, β, γ, λ, μ, ν, σ^2) repeatedly and evaluating Equation (5.3) for different sets of parameter values. Thus, our parameter estimates do not depend on any particular set of initial points. In order to find the approximate variances and covariances of the parameters, we took the negative of inverse of the matrix of second and cross derivatives of the parameters, which are derived analytically and evaluated at the optimum parameter values.[28]

5. EMPIRICAL ILLUSTRATIONS

The Australian 1975-76 HES cross-classified data for 10 broad consumption items described in Section 3 of Chapter 3 are considered for our investigation. Engel curves for ten different broad expenditure items were estimated using the Box-Cox functional form (5.1) of Section 2. Different sets of initial values of parameters are used to maximise the log likelihood function. It is observed that the log likelihood values are very close to each other for all sets of initial values of parameters. We took that set of parameter values, which gave the highest log likelihood value. The maximum likelihood estimates of the parameters and the values of the log likelihood are given in Table 5.1. The estimated values of λ, μ and ν clearly show that no widely used well known Engel function is appropriate for Australian 1975-1976 HES data. However, the standard errors of the estimated coefficient parameters, i.e., α, β and γ are found to be very high for most of the cases, although many authors such as Hinkley and Runger (1984) suggest that a smaller variance is highly desirable. This is probably because the data are not sufficiently informative to allow joint estimation of all the free parameters of the Box-Cox Engel function. Moreover, Ramsey (1978) has shown that for Box-Cox type transformations on dependent variables, the usual first order approximation of the log likelihood function is inappropriate in many real situations, so that the actual variance of the ML estimator may be very large, or even infinite. They argued that in most real situations the usual formula does not give correct results.

It is seen that the estimated parameter values of λ, μ and ν of the Box-Cox Engel function are different from those of restricted values -1, 0 and 1; which are used to obtain a number of simple well known Engel functions.

Moreover, in many cases t-ratios of estimates of λ, μ and ν for the Box-Cox Engel function are significantly different from -1, 0 and 1. Therefore, the restrictions we put on λ, μ and ν in the Box-Cox Engel function to obtain a number of simple well known Engel functions may be incorrect for our present study. Thus, any

---

[28] See Kendall and Stuart (1967, vol. 2) and Goldfeld and Quandt (1972). Here we assume that the ML estimates are sufficient in large samples. It is also noted here that this estimation technique has never been used to estimate such a general Engel function.

CHAPTER 5

estimates based on simple well known Engel functions may be inappropriate for our present data set.

Therefore, we come to the conclusion that the Box-Cox Engel function is the most appropriate Engel function for Australian HES data. This function has also flexibility in shape. We have used the Box-Cox Engel function to estimate total expenditure (income) elasticities for various expenditure items.

Table 5.1. Estimated parameters and their standard errors of the general Engel function

Commodities	α	β	γ	λ	μ	v	σ^2	LL (*)
(1) All food	-0.1768 (0.9668)	0.8617 (0.8713)	-0.0347 (0.0299)	-0.64441 (0.0383)	-0.5303 (0.3282)	-0.3600 (0.5638)	0.0099 (0.0013)	261.4345
(2) Current housing costs	1.0567 (0.2055)	0.0421 (0.0315)	-0.0287 (0.0001)	-0.1695 (0.0558)	0.6227 (0.1694)	1.8447 (0.0024)	1.0423 (0.2580)	28.3070
(3) Fuel & power	-12.303 (1.9944)	14.6185 (2.4786)	-0.2869 (0.0225)	-0.4325 (0.1081)	-1.1113 (0.0648)	0.4000 (0.0648)	0.4000 (0.0582)	56.4240
(4) All alcohol & Tobacco	-3.5907 (1.4237)	1.2034 (0.7673)	1.7998 (5.4484)	-0.1522 (0.1056)	-0.0483 (0.1665)	-6.7843 (0.2066	1.3843 (0.3515)	222.6826
(5) Clothing & footwear	-16.730 (5.1892)	10.8985 (4.6862)	0.0095 (0.0001)	0.0866 (0.0594)	-0.5235 (0.1113)	2.5128 (0.0001)	2.2405 (0.5011)	276.9670
(6) Housing equipment & operation	-6.7201 (3.0051)	4.4474 (2.5612)	-0.0020 (0.0001)	-0.2165 (0.3278)	-0.4604 (7.8400)	3.0881 (0.0006)	2.5242 (2.2500)	315.7566
(7) Medical care & health expenses	-7.5351 (4.2290)	3.8948 (3.2629)	-0.0009 (0.0001)	0.2068 (0.1205)	-0.3671 (0.2110)	3.4459 (0.0001)	2.4363 (0.4310)	161.2159
(8) Transport & communication	-8.2227 (2.4098)	2.5597 (1.1050)	0.8062 (0.2394)	0.3408 (0.0863)	0.0406 (0.1242)	-0.3699 (0.3542)	6.0573 (2.5990)	355.7530
(9) Recreation & education	-5.1774 (2.1529)	2.0866 (1.3022)	0.0977 (0.0015)	-0.0731 (0.0086)	-0.1414 (0.1628)	1.0128 (0.0111)	1.5365 (0.4346)	305.2497
(10) Miscellaneous goods & services	-7.8018 (3.6503)	4.2650 (2.8030)	-0.5160 (0.3906)	-0.0518 (0.0884)	-0.3343 (0.1790)	-2.4072 (1.9770)	1.6709 (0.5308)	297.9559

* Except for an additive constant. Standard errors of the estimated parameters are presented in parentheses ( ).

Source: The 1975-1976 Australian Household Expenditure Survey data obtained from a special tape supplied by the Australian Bureau of Statistics.

5.1 Elasticity Estimates

Estimated total expenditure elasticities for various commodity groups for the Box-Cox Engel function are presented in Table 5.2. It is observed from this table that the elasticity estimates obtained from the Box-Cox function are reasonably good for Australian HES data. These elasticity estimates are very close to the estimates of the commonly used Engel functions (i) to (v), which are presented in Section 2.1 of Chapter 3. The standard errors of the estimated elasticities for most expenditure items based on the Box-Cox Engel function are higher than those of simple well-known Engel functions. This is possibly due to the need to estimate the power parameters for the Box-Cox Engel function, which we discussed earlier. However, the conditional standard errors of the elasticities are very close to those of some simple well-known Engel functions.

The weighted elasticity of all the items for the Box-Cox Engel function is 0.97, which is very close to one. This shows that the adding-up criterion is approximately satisfied by the Box-Cox Engel function.

The total expenditure elasticity (η) of the Box-Cox Engel function is given by

$$\eta = \beta \frac{X^{\mu}}{Y^{\lambda}}$$

which implies that the elasticity approaches to β as $X^{\mu}\!/\!Y^{\lambda}$ approaches to unity.

The rate at which the elasticity changes with total expenditure (X) is given by

$$\frac{d\eta}{dX} = \frac{\beta\mu(1+\alpha\lambda-\beta\lambda/\mu-\gamma\lambda/\nu+(\gamma\lambda/\nu)S^{\nu})X^{-\mu-1}}{(\lambda\beta/\mu+(1+\alpha\lambda-\beta\lambda/\mu-\gamma\lambda/\nu+(\gamma\lambda/\nu)S^{\nu})X^{-\mu})^{2}}$$

Table 5.2. Estimated total expenditure elasticities computed at the mean value for the Box-Cox Engel function *.

Commodity groups	Elasticity		
(1) All food	0.47	(0.25)	{0.02}
(2) Current housing costs	0.78	(0.18)	{0.06}
(3) Fuel and power	0.17	(2.48)	{0.26}
(4) All alcohol and tobacco	1.20	(1.79)	{0.31}
(5) Clothing and footwear	1.10	(0.68)	{0.39}
(6) Household equipment and operation	1.00	(1.53)	{0.38}
(7) Medical care and health expenses	0.76	(0.78)	{0.14}
(8) Transport and communication	1.30	(1.01)	{0.28}
(9) Recreation and education	1.32	(1.09)	{0.21}
(10) Miscellaneous goods	1.18	(0.61)	{0.23}

* Figures in parentheses ( ) and brackets { } respectively denote the unconditional and conditional (upon λ, μ and v) approximate standard errors of the estimated total expenditure (income) elasticities.

Source: The 1975-1976 Australian Household Expenditure Survey data obtained from a special tape supplied by the Australian Bureau of Statistics.

Therefore, η increases or decreases with X accordingly as

$$\mu(v + v\alpha\lambda + \lambda\gamma\delta^v) > \lambda(\beta v + \gamma\mu)$$

or

$$\mu(v + v\alpha\lambda + \lambda\gamma\delta^v) < \lambda(\beta v + \gamma\mu)$$

Thus, from the shape of the Box-Cox Engel function, it is seen that its elasticity fluctuates with X subject to certain constraints.

At this point, it should be mentioned that the Box-Cox transformation has been used in the past by several authors to find the total expenditure (income) elasticity for food items only. In this context our ML estimates of λ, μ and v for total food are - 0.6441, -0.5303 and -0.3600 respectively. Since λ, μ and v are less than zero, the total expenditure of food demand declines with rising total expenditure (income), which is consistent with the finding of Chang (1977) who indicated that income elasticity of demand for some specific foods like meat generally should be falling rather than rising. The rate of this decline for the present study is reported below.

Table 5.3. *Food share and its income elasticity estimates at various household income levels*

Food share and elasticity at various household income levels	Weekly household income levels			
	$115.00	*$180.00*	*$320.00*	*$530.00*
$\overline{Y}_f / \overline{X}_{te}$ (Food share)	0.26	0.21	0.16	0.12
$\eta\left(\overline{Y}_f / \overline{X}_{te}\right)$ [Elasticity]	0.53	0.49	0.44	0.40

Source: The 1975-1976 Australian Household Expenditure Survey data obtained from a special tape supplied by the Australian Bureau of Statistics.

Table 5.3 shows that the share of food expenditure, and total expenditure elasticity of food are decreasing as household income increases, which cannot be achieved by the widely used linear or double log Engel functions. This is because as indicated by Chang (1977), income elasticity of demand for some food items is increasing and converses to unity, if it is less than one. This finding is inconsistent with the theoretical effect of an increase in income on the demand for food, which was also observed by Benus, Kmenta and Shapiro (1976). However, this change is not rapid as observed by Paris (1970, p. 50) for the semi-log or log-inverse functional form. There is enough evidence, which shows that income elasticity of food should be falling rather than rising [see Goreux (1960)]. On the other hand, elasticity estimated from the double log Engel function remains constant irrespective of income levels. Therefore the future demand for food could be overestimated if the estimates are based on either linear or double log Engel functions for forecasting purposes, since the expected real per capita income in Australia will be expected to rise in the future as in the past. Elasticity estimates based on our Box-Cox Engel function should be taken as more reliable elasticity estimates for food in Australia.

6. STATISTICAL TESTS FOR SPECIAL ENGEL FUNCTIONS

Now, we would like to show to what extent the Box-Cox Engel function makes an improvement over the usual curves that are cheaply and easily estimated. At this stage, it is helpful to remember that those usual functional forms would be represented by the Box-Cox function only when λ, μ and v take the specified values of 0, 1 and -1. In order to discriminate among the special Engel functions, a joint statistical hypothesis test for λ, μ and v can be performed by a likelihood ratio test.[29] Under general conditions for a large number of observations,

[29] The Wald test can also be used for this purpose on joint parameters of each of these models against the Box-Cox model. See Kendall and Stuart (1967) for more about this test.

$$-2\{LL_{\max}(\hat{\lambda}, \hat{\mu}, \hat{v}) - LL_{\max}(\lambda,,\mu,v)\}$$

approximately follows the χ^2-distribution, with degrees of freedom, equal to the number of parametric restrictions in the null hypothesis, where $LL_{\max}(\lambda,,\mu,v)$ is the log-likelihood value corresponding to the unconditional maximum, and $LL_{\max}(\hat{\lambda}, \hat{\mu}, \hat{v})$ is the log-likelihood value under power parameter restrictions. In our case, each of the functional forms, which can be listed as linear, hyperbola, semi-log, double log, and log-inverse have three restrictions. The Box-Cox Engel function corresponds to the unconstrained maximum. Since all of these models come from the same parametric family of functions, it is possible to use the likelihood ratio test to see whether each of the models is significantly different from that of the Box-Cox Engel function. However, no combination of the models (i)-(v) described in Section 2.1 earlier in Chapter 3 can be compared pair-wise, since these functions are not nested within each other.

The likelihood ratio tests for five different special functions against the Box-Cox Engel function are carried out separately for each expenditure item. The resulting χ^2 values from Table 5.4 show that the linear, hyperbolic and semi-log Engel functions are significantly different from that of the Box-Cox Engel function. The double log Engel function is also significantly different from that of the Box-Cox Engel function excepting a few expenditure items. This function is not significantly different from that of the Box-Cox functional form for all food, fuel and power, all alcohol and tobacco at 1% level of significance and recreation and education at 5% level of significance, and miscellaneous goods and services at 10% level of significance. While the log-inverse functional form is significantly different from that of the Box-Cox functional form for all items except for medical care and health expenses at 1 % level of significance.

Thus, Table 5.4 clearly indicates that none of the commonly used Engel functions are appropriate to estimate the total expenditure elasticities for the Australian HES data, although the double-log Engel function is not significantly different from that of the Box-Cox Engel function for five out of ten expenditure items. Thus, we come to a crucial conclusion that instead of using the commonly used Engel functions, the more flexible Engel function, which is based on the Box-Cox transformation, should be used for any further investigation to estimate total expenditure (income) elasticities for Australian HES data.[30]

---

[30] It should be noted here that in the past Podder (1971) and McRae (1980) used the double log Engel function to estimate the elasticities for various Australian household expenditure items.

*Table 5.4: Likelihood Ratio test**

Consumption items	Linear $\lambda=1,\mu=1,$ $\nu=1$	Hyperbolic $\lambda=1,\mu=-1,$ $\nu=-1$	Semi-log $\lambda=1,\mu=0,$ $\nu=0$	Double-log $\lambda=0,\mu=0,\ \nu=0$	Log-inverse $\lambda=0,\mu=-1,$ $\nu=-1$
(1)All food	80.7 (0.0001)	164.9 (0.00005)	108.82 (0.0001)	11.84 (0.01)	51.1 (0.00005)
(2) Current housing costs	189.24 (0.00005)	294.76 (0.00005)	252.74 (0.00005)	25.99 (0.001)	68.9 (0.0005)
(3) Fuel & power	101.99 (0.0001)	93.62 (0.0001)	73.30 (0.0001)	10.57 (0.014)	51.57 (0.0005)
(4) All alcohol & tobacco	118.20 (0.0001)	205.66 (0.00005)	144.62 (0.00005)	11.09 (0.011)	46.48 (0.0005)
(5) Clothing & footwear	130.77 (0.0001)	141.32 (0.00005)	112.29 (0.0001)	21.05 (0.001)	30.97 (0.0008)
(6) Household equipment & operation	234.92 (0.00005)	274.42 (0.00005)	251.93 (0.00005)	13.86 (0.006)	18.32 (0.001)
(7) Medical care & health expenses	58.08 (0.001)	59.32 (0.001)	39.94 (0.001)	15.4 (0.008)	8.14 (0.035)
(8) Transport & communication	67.26 (0.001)	183.09 (0.00005)	102.21 (0.0001)	24.31 (0.001)	59.27 (0.0005)
(9) Recreation & education	159.57 (0.00005)	227.74 (0.00005)	188.99 (0.00005)	7.07 (0.057)	60.56 (0.0005)
(10)Miscellaneous goods & services	155.48 (0.00005)	213.68 (0.00005)	180.52 (0.00005)	6.18 (0.012)	23.42 (0.0001)

* All these χ^2 ratios have 3 degrees of freedom since we put 3 restictions for all the functional forms considered here.

The parenthetic value is the probability of χ^2 greater or equal to a specified number, for example $P[\chi^2(3) \geq 6.18] = 0.12$.

Source: The 1975-1976 Australian Household Expenditure Survey data obtained from a special tape supplied by the Australian Bureau of Statistics.

7. CONCLUSIONS

The Box-Cox transformation has been used to describe the relationship between dependent and independent variables. Using this transformation, the Box-Cox functional form has been constructed, which turns out to be a natural extension of the class of mathematical functions previously used. The non-linearity of the relationship has been considered in the Box-Cox Engel function and the ML estimation procedure has been applied to estimate the parameters. Initial values of $(\alpha, \beta, \gamma, \lambda, \mu$ and $\nu, \sigma^2)$ have been found by some trial and error methods. It is noted here that different sets of initial values are used to estimate parameters. In almost all cases the log likelihood values are close to each other with slight changes in parameter estimates. We took the set of parameter values, which gave the highest log likelihood value.

We have used the Box-Cox functional form to estimate the total expenditure elasticities for food and nine different non-food items with Australian HES data for the first time. It is seen that none of the commonly used Engel functions are appropriate for Australian 1975-1976 HES data, although the double log Engel function is not significantly different from that of the Box-Cox Engel functions for five expenditure items. We thus come to a crucial conclusion that the more flexible Box-Cox Engel function should be used to estimate total expenditure elasticities for Australian HES data for future studies, although the estimation procedure is complicated and costly compared to ordinary regression analysis. It also yields high standard errors for the estimated elasticities in comparison to the widely used simple Engel functions. A large number of observations are essential to obtain accurate estimates of the parameters for the Box-Cox Engel function. Despite many problems in the Box-Cox Engel function, one should use this function to estimate total expenditure elasticities for various expenditure items, since it is more flexible in nature and a better Engel function than many widely used simple Engel functions. Thus, the Box-Cox Engel function should be used to estimate total expenditure elasticities for various expenditure items, particularly for those items where there is any doubt about the commonly used Engel functions.

A number of problems still remain unsolvable for grouped data. First, to get unbiased estimates of the parameters for grouped data we need an unbiased within group estimate of E $(Y^{(\lambda)})$ to replace $(\overline{Y}^{(\lambda)})$, which is not done for the present study. Second, all the applications of transformation of variables have been performed in a single equation context.

Simultaneous equation systems arising from Engel curve analysis described in Summers (1959) have not been considered for such non-linear transformations. It should be pointed out here that if different λ transformations, are performed within such a system, the identification problem within the non-linear system would be serious, although some progress has been made on the simultaneous system by Tintner and Kadekodi (1971). Lastly, our entire estimation procedure is based on the assumption that the residuals are normally distributed, which might not be appropriate. Normality is not a constraint, rather an assumption. Therefore, it is suggested here that some other distribution function could be tried to estimate the parameters for the Box-Cox Engel function for further study.

CHAPTER 6

A REVIEW OF PERSONAL INCOME DISTRIBUTION

In this chapter, readers will find a brief survey of literature on personal income distribution. It starts to show how the income distribution function evolves, and how theoretical income density functions were developed by a number of authors in various parts of the world. The uses of income distribution in measuring income inequality and poverty for proper public policy formulations are also discussed.

1. INTRODUCTION

From basic economic lessons, we know that income is generated by land, labour, capital and entrepreneurship in various private and public sectors. It is created and distributed among the individuals of a country. Following this process, a number of authors have tried to establish a stable income distribution over time and space. There are three main topics in the theory of income distribution viz., (i) the functional distribution of income; (ii) distribution of national income among various production sectors; and (iii) the personal income distribution. The present chapter is concerned with the last type of income distribution.[31]

The purpose of this chapter is to provide a brief survey of literature on personal income distributions, which were developed by a number of authors. It is mainly concerned with the development of the income distribution function and its application to major public policies. But, it principally deals with the underlying ideas, and hence readers are requested to read the original publications.[32]

Many scholars have tried to establish the shape of income distribution over the last century, but none is entirely satisfactory in measuring income inequality or poverty. This attracts a number of authors to develop probability laws to provide observed distributions over the whole range of income. The Lorenz curve is usually used to measure income and wealth inequality. The original concept of the Lorenz curve is extended and developed to cover distributional considerations into various fields of social sciences. The techniques of the Lorenz curve can be used to analyse relationships among the distributions of various economic variables, which have applications in public taxation, public finance and spending, inflation, estimating Engel elasticities, growth, and in many other areas.

---

[31] Most of the literature is mainly concerned with the first two topics of income distribution. A comprehensive discussion on these two topics can be found in Bronfenbrenner (1971).

[32] See Milanovic (1999) and Schultz (1998) for an extensive review on income distribution.

The outline of this chapter is given as follows. A brief survey of literature is given in Section 2. This section also provides how income is generated and distributed among individuals of a country along with some main income distribution functions developed by various authors. Further development on income distribution is provided in Section 3. This section also provides an interesting discussion of the effect of taxation on income distribution and the measurement of poverty, which has immense application in formulating public policies. Some concluding remarks are made in the final section.

2. SURVEY OF LITERATURE ON PERSONAL INCOME DISTRIBUTION

There are two main schools of thought to explain the distribution of income among individuals. The first is known as the school of 'statistical theory', which was developed by Gibrat (1931), Roy (1950), Champernowne (1953), Aitchison and Brown (1954), Rutherford (1955), Davidson and Duclos (1998), Schultz (2000), and Flemming and Micklewright (1999). These authors developed the personal income distribution with stochastic theory.[33] The second school of thought is generally known as the socioeconomic school. Three groups of authors belong to this school. The first group follows the human capital approach, based on the hypothesis of lifetime income maximization. Mincer (1958), Backer (1962, 1967), Chiswick (1968, 1971, 1974), Husen (1968), De Wolff and van Slijpe (1972), and Atkinson, Rainwater and Smeeding (1995), belong to this group. The major exponents of the second group of authors are Bowles (1969), Dougherty (1971, 1972), Psacharopoulos and Hinchiffe (1972) and Bojer (1998). They only deal with the demand side of the market. The third group of authors developed the supply and demand school. The major contribution of this approach is due to Tinbergen (1975), Wilson (1995), and Attanasio and Szekely (1999). Their approach considers both labour income and incomes from other factors of production.

The authors belonging to the first type of school are criticised due to a partial explanation of the income generation process. The first and second group of authors of the second school of thought are criticised because of their partial dealings with the supply and demand side of the market respectively.

2.1 Income Distribution Function

Let us suppose that there are N individuals and the income of an individual is denoted by x. Now classify the individuals into (N+1) income groups, viz., (0 to x_1), (x_1 to x_2) ... (x_N to x_{N+1}). Income distribution theory can be derived from probability theory. Let us assume that an individual will lie in the $(n + 1)^{th}$ income group if it shows n heads in the tossing of N coins. Hence the probability of an individual belonging to the (X_n to X_{n+1}) group selected at random is ($^{N}C_n$) / 2^N,

---

[33] Bjerke (1961) and Bourguignon and Morrisson (1999) presented reviews of stochastic models on personal income distribution.

where ^NC_n is the number of combinations of N things taken n at a time. This probability is calculated on the assumption that probability (Head) = probability (Tail) = ½. A coin shows either head or tail in a single toss. Therefore there will be 2^N possible outcomes if a single coin is tossed N times. The probability of finding people in different income groups on random sampling can be equated with the relative frequency of people in this group as given in the income distribution. The specification and estimation of the income density function are the major problems in statistics.

Let us take X as an income of an individual whose range varies from 0 to ∞ then the probability distribution function F(x), meaning that the probability of an individual selected at random will have income $\leq$ x is defined by

$$F(x) = \text{Prob. } [X \leq x]$$

The properties of this function are given by

$$\text{Limit}_{x \to \infty} F(x) = F(\infty) = 1$$

$$\text{Limit}_{x \to 0} F(x) = F(0) = 0$$

F(x) is a monotonic, increasing function of x.

This implies that F(x) has the domain (0, ∞), and range (0, 1). Further, if F(x) is continuous and has continuous derivatives at all points of x, then it follows that

$$\frac{d}{dX} F(X) = f(X) \qquad \text{where } f(X) \geq 0.$$

This implies
$$F(x) = \int_0^x f(X) \, dX$$

The probability density function is given by $f(X)$. Specification of the density function $f(X)$ is a major problem in describing an income distribution. A number of theoretical income density functions have been developed by various authors to approximate observed income distributions, some of which are given below.

2.1.1 The Normal Distribution

The normal distribution is widely used to specify the probability density function of a number of random phenomena. Due to the Central Limit Theorem, all the distributions observed in the practical field follow approximately normal distribution.

It is discovered that the shape of the observed income distributions remain unaltered irrespective of time and place. Hence many scholars have tried to explain the generation of income distribution by some probabilistic law. Their arguments rest on the assumption that if income is generated as a result of the sum of a large number of random variables then the Central Limit Theorem asserts that the income variable should approximately follow a normal distribution. But this does not hold good in practice because the theoretical normal distribution is symmetric and has a finite mean and variance. However the observed income distributions are positively skewed with a single mode and a long right tail. Therefore the normal distribution is not sufficiently accurate to describe the observed income distribution.

2.1.2 Pareto's Law

In 1897, Pareto established his famous income distribution law, which is suitable to higher incomes, and can be described as follows.

Let y number of persons having income x or more, then the relation between x and y is given by the following equation, which is known as the Pareto Law of income distribution.[34]

$$y \;=\; A\,X^{-\alpha} \tag{6.1}$$

Taking the log of both sides of the above equation, we get

$$\log y \;=\; \log A - \alpha \log X$$

This demonstrates that the graph of $\log y$ against $\log X$ will lie on a straight line with the slope $-\alpha$. The elasticity of the income distribution function is given by

$$d\left(\log y\right)/\,d\left(\log X\right) \;=\; -\alpha$$

This is also explained as the elasticity of the number of persons y with respect to the lower limit of the income X.

From the equation $y \;=\; A\,X^{-\alpha}$ (Pareto's law), it follows that

$$\frac{d\,y}{d\,X} \;=\; -\alpha\,A\,X^{-(\alpha+1)}$$

Again let y be the number of persons having income x or more then

---

[34] The original formula of Pareto's income distribution is $y = A/(x - a)^{\alpha}$; where a is the lowest income at which the curve begins, considering a = 0, we get Equation (6.1).

$$y \;=\; \int_{x}^{\infty} f(X)\,dX$$

$$\frac{dy}{dX} \;=\; [f(X)]_{x}^{\infty} = f(\infty) - f(x) = -f(x), \text{ since} \qquad f(\infty) = 0$$

$f(X) \;=\; A\,\alpha\,X^{-(\alpha+1)}$, the Pareto density function of X; $\quad 0 \le X \le \alpha$

Now if X_0 is taken as the lower limit of income then

$$\int_{X_0}^{\infty} f(X)\,dx \;=\; 1$$

$$\int_{X_0}^{\infty} A\,\alpha\,X^{-(\alpha+1)}\,dX \;=\; 1$$

or

$$A\,\alpha \int_{X_0}^{\infty} X^{-(\alpha+1)}\,dX \;=\; 1$$

or

$$A\,\alpha \left[\frac{X^{-\alpha}}{(-\alpha)} \right]_{X_0}^{\infty} \;=\; 1$$

$$A\,(X_0)^{-\alpha} \;=\; 1$$

$\therefore$

$$A \;=\; \frac{1}{(X_0)^{-\alpha}}$$

$\therefore$

$$f(x) = \left[\frac{\alpha}{(X_0)^{-\alpha}} \right] X^{-(\alpha+1)}$$

$$=\; \alpha\,(X_0)^{\alpha} \cdot (X_0)^{-(\alpha+1)}, \quad X_0 \le X \le \infty$$

The mean of the Pareto distribution is given by

$$E(X) = \int_{X_0}^{\infty} X \, f(X) \, dX$$

$$= \int_{X_0}^{\infty} X \, \alpha \, (X_0)^{\alpha} . (X_0)^{-(\alpha+1)} \, dX$$

$$= \left[\frac{\alpha}{(\alpha-1)} \right] X_0 = \frac{[\alpha . X_0]}{(\alpha-1)}$$

This shows that the mean of the Pareto distribution is proportional to the lower income X_0 beyond which the Pareto law works. But, it still holds even if we increase X_0.

The variance of the Pareto distribution can be calculated as

$$V(X) = \int_{X_0}^{\infty} X^2 f(X) \, dX - \left[\int_{X_0}^{\infty} X \, f(X) \, dX \right]^2$$

$$= \frac{(\alpha X_0^2)}{[(\alpha-2)(\alpha-1)^2]}$$

which exists only if $\alpha > 2$. In general the value of α varies from 1.2 to 1.9 and on the average $\alpha = 1.5$.[35]

The value of the parameter α may be taken as a measure of inequality of the distribution of income. The greater the value of α, the more concave the hyperbola and the greater the difference between the various income classes of the population.

[35] See Lange (1962, p. 185).

2.1.3 Mandelbrot's Model

Mandelbrot modified a highly abstract model of Pareto's law. He observed that all the income distributions of the upper tails tend to follow Pareto's law. Further he found that the total earning of an individual is the sum of income from various sources. Thus he considered the income variable as the sum of independent random variables with different domains of summation. Since all these sums have the same type of distribution approaching Pareto's law, he turned to the class of stable distributions. Suppose that there are 'n' independent random variables then their sum

$$U_n = u_1 + u_2 + u_n \qquad\qquad (6.2)$$

where U_n have the same distribution up to a linear transformation of their scales for the coefficients $A_i > 0$ and b_i such that $A_1 U_1 + b_1$, $A_2 U_2 + b_2$, ... , $A_n U_n + b_n$ have the same probability distribution $F(x)$, which is stable. More generally if the sum U_n has the same distribution up to a linear transformation so that for some $A_n > 0$, B_n such that $A_n U_n + B_n$ has the probability distribution $F(x)$ and is stable. Levy (1925, 1937) and Feller (1966, ch. 6) have studied these stable distributions. Mandelbrot considered a distribution, which has: (i) a finite mean; (ii) infinite variance; and (iii) skewness towards the right. The single stable distribution that meets these conditions is called the Pareto-Levy distribution. However the density function of the Pareto-Levy law cannot be written in a closed analytic form but is represented indirectly with a Laplace transformation. For large x the probability distribution function is given by

$$F(x) \sim 1 - X^{-\alpha} \{ U^* \, \Gamma \, (1 - \alpha) \}^{\alpha}$$

where $\Gamma \, (1 - \alpha)$ is the gamma distribution,[36] α is the parameter of Pareto's law which lies $1 < \alpha < 2$ and U^* is a positive scalar parameter. This distribution has never been applied to empirical data.

2.1.4 Champernowne's Model

The shape of the income distribution is invariant over time and space. This fact attracted many scholars to work on income distribution by a stochastic process.[37] Gibrat (1931) started to work first on this line. He generated a positively skewed distribution with the 'law of proportionate effect'. A simple stochastic process proposed by Champernowne (1953) is a very familiar work in this line and is briefly described as follows.

---

[36] $\Gamma \, (a) \; = \; \int_0^\infty e^{-x} \, x^{a-1} \, dx$, where e is the base of the Naperian logarithms (log e = 1).

[37] Other stochastic processes have been developed by Simon (1955), Steindl (1965) and Wold and Whittle (1957) that lead to Pareto's law.

Champernowne determined a minimum income x* and then divided the income scale above it into a countably infinite number of income classes. The jth income class is leveled as ($X_{j-1} - X_j$) that satisfies $X_j = C\,X_{j-1}$ for j = 1, 2, ..., ∞ where C is constant. This condition asserts that the boundary points of income classes are equidistant on a logarithmic scale. Hence the class interval with the transformed scale is log C. The income earning elements pass these income intervals from one discrete time point to another. An income recipient who at time t belongs to income class r_1 may move to income class $r_1 + \varepsilon$ at time (t+1), and hence

$$\sum_{\varepsilon=-(r_1-1)}^{\infty} p_t\left(r_1,\varepsilon\right) = 1$$

This means that a recipient in class r_1 at time t will be in any of the income intervals 1,2, 3, ... ∞ with probability 1. If $p_t(r_1)$ is denoted as the probability that a unit is in income class r_1 at time t then the income distribution $p_{t+1}(r_2)$ at time (t+1) will be generated according to

$$p_{t+1}\left(r_2\right) = \sum_{\varepsilon=-\infty}^{r_2-1} p_t\left(r_2-\varepsilon\right) p_t\left(r_2-\varepsilon,\varepsilon\right) \qquad (6.3)$$

This equation is known as the transition equation model and is based on the following assumptions.

(a)   For every dying income receiver there is an heir to his income in the following year.
(b)   For every value of t and r_1 and for some fixed integer N,

$$p_t\left(r_1,\varepsilon\right)=0, \quad \text{if } \varepsilon>1 \text{ or } \varepsilon< \text{-N}, \qquad (b.1)$$

and
$$p_t\left(r_1,\varepsilon\right)= p_\varepsilon >0 \text{, if } -N \le \varepsilon \le 1 \text{ and } \varepsilon > \text{-r}_1, \qquad (b.2)$$

(c)
$$\sum_{\varepsilon=-N}^{1} \varepsilon\, p_\varepsilon < 0$$

Assumption (a) asserts that the number of income recipients remains unaltered over time. First part of assumption (b.1) implies that none of the income units move up by more than one or down by more than N income classes in a year. The second part of assumption (b.2) has two meanings viz., (i) the transition probabilities $p_t(r_1, \varepsilon)$ are constant with respect to time and (ii) they are independent of income level r_1 and determined by ε alone. While assumption (c) shows that initially all the recipients belong to any one of N+1, N+2, ... income classes. The expected number of income classes shifted to the negative number in the following period.

Under certain conditions, a homogeneous Markov chain with a finite number of states leads to an equilibrium distribution. However, Champernowne states that the process defined for an infinite number of states also has the same property. If the equilibrium distribution is denoted by $p*(r_2)$ then the transition Equation (6.3) becomes

$$p^*(r_2) = \sum_{\varepsilon=-N}^{1} p^*(r_2 - \varepsilon) p_\varepsilon \qquad \text{for all } r_1 > 1. \qquad (6.4)$$

To find a unique solution of $p*(r_2)$ from Equation (6.4), we substitute $c_1 z^{c_1}$ for $p*(r_2)$ in Equation (6.4) and the resulting equation in terms of Z is given by

$$g(Z) = \sum_{\varepsilon=-N}^{1} p_\varepsilon Z^{1-\varepsilon} - Z = 0 \qquad (6.5)$$

where $g(Z)$ is a polynomial of degree (N+1). By the first assumption of (b.1), all coefficients are positive and certainly $g(0) = p_1 > 0$; by (b.2) we get $g(1) = 0$ and from (b.2) and (c) we get $g'(1) = 0$. All these conditions imply that (6.5) has a unique real root other than unity lying between zero and one, d (say); and hence the equilibrium distribution is given by

$$p^*(r_2) = C_2 d^{r_2}, \qquad 0 < d < 1 \qquad (6.6)$$

The constant C_2 is adjusted so as to equal the sum of probabilities over all admissible values of r_2 units.

Lastly to establish the link between (6.6) and Pareto's law, the probability that an income taken at random y exceeds y_{r_2} is calculated by

$$P(y > y_{r_2}) = \sum_{j=r_2}^{\infty} p^*(r_1) = \sum_{j=r_2}^{\infty} C_2 d^{r_2} = \frac{C_2}{1-d} \cdot d^{r_2} \qquad (6.7)$$

Further we have mentioned that the condition $X_j = C X_{j-1}$ is satisfied by the income classes and hence it follows that

$$X_{r_2} = C_2^{r_2} X_0 \qquad (6.8)$$

where X_0 is the minimum income. Taking logarithms for both the equations (6.7) and (6.8) and eliminating r_2 we have

$$\log P\left(y > y_{r2}\right) \;=\; \gamma - \alpha \log X_{r2} \tag{6.9}$$

where $\qquad \alpha \;=\; -\dfrac{\log d}{\log c_2}, \text{ and } \gamma \;=\; \log \dfrac{c_2\, x_0^{\alpha}}{(1-d)}$

Since $0 < d < 1$; α is always positive and hence it is interpreted as the Pareto constant.

2.1.5 The Lognormal Distribution

The distribution function of the lognormal distribution of the random variable X is given by

$$F(x) \;=\; \Lambda\left(x/\,\mu,\sigma^2\right) \;=\; \int_0^x \frac{1}{x\sigma\sqrt{2\pi}}e\left\{- \frac{(\log x - \mu)^2}{2\sigma^2}\right\} dx, \quad x > 0$$

$$= \; 0; \qquad\qquad\qquad\qquad\qquad\qquad\qquad\qquad x \le 0$$

The lognormal distribution is widely used for income and for many other size variables. An efficient estimation procedure and statistical inference are readily available for this distribution, because of its close relationship to the normal distribution. It gives reasonable fit in the middle classes of income, covering about two-thirds of the total population. A positively skewed distribution is observed if real income data is fitted.[38]

There are certain disadvantages to this distribution. Firstly, it does not fit well to the end points. Secondly, it over-corrects for the positive skewness of the income distribution. It needs the positive value of income.

Gibrat (1931) frequently used the lognormal distribution to income and many other size variables. He assumed that many independent random factors affect these variables in a multiplicative fashion rather than additive. This is known as Gibrat's law of proportionate effect. This idea is further extended by Rutherford (1955), who developed a new model for income distribution by assuming that new people enter into the society at a constant rate with lognormal income distribution. As time passes its variance increases and the number of survivors declines exponentially with age. With these assumptions he derived the standard symmetrical Gram-Charlier type A distribution.[39] He also gave an experimental method of fitting this distribution.

---

[38] Other interesting properties are discussed by Aitchinson and Brown (1954), Bourguignon and Morrisson (1999), Firebaugh (1999) and Yao and Zhu (1998).

[39] See Cramer (1946, p. 222) for such Gram-Charlier of type A distribution.

2.1.6 Gamma Density Function

The Gamma density function is given by

$$f(x) = \frac{\lambda^{\alpha}}{\Gamma(\alpha)} x^{\alpha-1} e^{-\lambda x}; \qquad 0 < x < \infty; \; and \; \alpha, \lambda > 0$$

where $\Gamma(\alpha)$ is the Gamma function, and α is related to the income inequality measure and λ is a scale parameter. Amoroso (1925) first fitted this density function to income data, and latter Salem and Mount (1974) fitted it to US income data. They showed that the Gamma distribution fitted better than the lognormal distribution. But this is not quite satisfactory since it exaggerates the skewness.

3. FURTHER DISCUSSION ON THE MEASUREMENT OF INCOME INEQUALITIES

In 1905, Lorenz first established the relationship between the cumulative proportion of income and the cumulative proportion of income receiving units when they are arranged in ascending order of their income. This was later popularly known as the Lorenz curve, which was widely used to measure inequalities of income and wealth in many countries in the world.[40]

More formally, if P(x) is the proportion of units having income less than or equal to x, and Q(X) is the proportion of income received by those units whose income is less or equal to x. Then the relationship between P(x) and Q(x) is known as the Lorenz curve. The Lorenz curve derived from the most established income distribution usually does not fit the actual data well. However, the Lorenz curve has a number of properties mentioned in Kakwani and Podder (1973), which can be used to specify the equation of the Lorenz curve that fits the data well. In general it is an increasing function, passing through the points (0, 0) and (1, 1).

When P(x) = Q(x) all income receiving units get equal income, which is popularly known as the egalitarian line. It can be shown that the distance between the Lorenz curve and the egalitarian line is maximum at income level x = E(x). It can also be shown that the Lorenz curve for the Pareto distribution is skewed towards (0, 0); and it is symmetrical for the lognormal distribution.[41]

Mahalanobis (1960) first extended the concept of the Lorenz curve to the concentration curve, which is defined as the expenditure of the ith item made by those units having income less than or equal to x as $Q_i [W_i (x)]$. The relationship between P(x) and $Q_i [W_i (x)]$ is called the concentration curve. Details about the concentration curve are provided in Chapter 7 of this book.

The Lorenz curve is widely used to measure inequality, since it shows the deviation of each unit from exact equality. Atkinson (1970) showed that the Lorenz curve ranking in terms of social welfare and the ranking of the income distribution

---

[40] Piketty (1999), Rongve (1998), Milanovic (1999), Schultz (1998), Garner and Terrell (1998) and Veeernik (1998) have used Lorenz curve to measure inequalities of income.
[41] See Kakwani (1980b) for more properties of the Lorenz curve.

of the Lorenz curve is identical to the ranking of social welfare, irrespective of the form of the utility function of the individual unit, provided they do not intersect. The inequality measure lies between 0 and 1. The following are used to measure income inequality.

(1) The Gini index is widely used to measure inequalities. It is equal to one minus twice the area under the Lorenz curve, which is equivalent to twice the area between the Lorenz curve and the egalitarian line.[42]

$$G = 1 - 2 \int_0^\infty Q(x) f(X) dX$$

(2) Relative Mean Deviation was introduced by Von Bortkiewicz (1930), and Bresciani-Turroni (1910) and investigated by Pietra (1948), which is defined by

$$R = \left(\frac{1}{\mu}\right)\left(\frac{1}{n}\right) \sum_{i=1}^{n} |x_i - \mu|$$

where x_i is the income of the ith unit and i varies from 1 to n. Note that R = 0, when every unit receives equal amount of income, R approaches to 1 as n approaches to ∞, when one unit receives all the income. It can be shown that the relative mean deviation provides the maximum gap between the egalitarian line and the Lorenz curve.

(3)   Elteto and Frigyes (1968) introduced three set of inequality measures:

$$P = \mu / \mu_1; \qquad Q = \mu_2 / \mu_1; \qquad R = \mu_2 / \mu,$$

where $\mu = E(x);$ $\mu_1 = E\left(\frac{x}{x} < \mu\right),$ and $\mu_2 = E\left(\frac{x}{x} \geq \mu\right)$

Note that μ_2 is the mean income of those with an income greater than μ, and μ_1 is the income of those with an income less than μ. These measures can be expressed in terms of the Lorenz curve.[43]

The Lorenz curve can also be used to estimate income elasticity, which is very helpful particularly for grouped data. Mahalanobis (1960) first introduced the concept of the concentration curve to describe the consumption pattern of different commodities. It was also shown that the concentration index of a commodity is closely related to its elasticity. Kakwani (1977b) and Haque (1984) estimated

---

[42] See Garner and Terrell (1998), Van de Ven (2001) and Creedy (1997) for more details about the computation of Gini index from the Lorenz curve.

[43] See Kakwani (1980b) for more measures of inequalities of income.

income elasticities from nonlinear Engel functions, which are based on the concentration curves. They showed that the proposed equation of the Engel curve derived from the concentration curve performed better than other usual well-known Engel functions. Further, it can be shown that for inferior goods the concentration curve of a commodity lies above the egalitarian line, for necessary items the concentration curve lies between the egalitarian line and the Lorenz curve, and the concentration curve lies below the Lorenz curve for luxury goods. Therefore the position of the concentration curve is very important to identify whether the item is a luxury, necessary or inferior. These issues will be discussed further in detail in chapters 7 and 8.

Lorenz curves can also be used effectively for public policy formulation. For example, it can be shown from the analysis of the Lorenz curve that post-tax income is more equally distributed than pre-tax income if the average tax rate increases with income. Further, if the tax-income ratio remains same, inflation does not change the post-tax income distribution even if the tax function is shifted every year. More importantly, it can be shown that the increase in the pre-tax Gini index is a reflection of the fact that the negative income-tax plans cause lower income classes to reduce the supply of their labour proportionally more than higher income classes. The Lorenz curve can also be used extensively to measure poverty.[44]

4. CONCLUSIONS

A brief review of the literature on income distribution is provided in this chapter. This is because the next few chapters are based on the concept and measurement of income distribution. This chapter briefly discusses the issues of the income distribution function, income inequality measured from the Lorenz curve, and its applications in formulating public policies, and its uses in measuring poverty. It is hoped that this background knowledge will help readers to understand the subsequent chapters of the book more clearly.

---

[44] Hilderbrand and Kneip (1990), Wilson (1995) and Sutherland (1996) have studied the effect of income distribution on household expenditures.

CHAPTER 7

ELASTICITY FROM CONCENTRATION CURVES

The readers will learn about the concept of concentration curves, which can be applied to a wide range of social and public policy areas. It is demonstrated here how a new method of estimating the income elasticity of various expenditure items can be calculated from the implicit Engel function based on non-linear concentration curves for grouped data. Our method of estimating income elasticity turns out to be superior to the usual method of least squares in estimating income elasticity from grouped data without any added problems. The reader will also see how the average income elasticity of demand of different expenditure items for the whole population can be obtained when income and expenditure on various expenditure items are provided for several homogeneous groups of the total population.

1. INTRODUCTION

Specification of the functional form is an important issue in computing Engel elasticity from household expenditure data. The importance lies in the fact that the magnitude of elasticity depends largely on the functional form used. A huge body of literature has been devoted to the consideration of the appropriate specification of the functional form. In this regard, we have reviewed the relevant literature and discussed the various issues on specification and discrimination of different functional forms earlier in chapters 3 and 5 of this book.

Engel elasticity can also be estimated indirectly via concentration curves. Iyengar (1960a) proposed an alternative method of computing the elasticity parameter of the double log Engel function, using concentration curves arising from the log normal income density function. Later, Kakwani (1977b) generalized this method and allowed for a variety of specific Engel functions with arbitrary concentration curves. Further, Kakwani (1978) computed the Engel elasticity for an implicit Engel function based on a special type of concentration curve introduced by Kakwani and Podder (1976). Hansen, Formby and Smith (1996) have also estimated income elasticity of demand for housing from concentration curves.[45]

---

[45] See Costa and Michelini (1999), Hansen, Formby and Smith (1996), and Cowell (1995) for more specifications on concentration curves.

In this chapter, we have developed a model in computing Engel elasticity from an unknown Engel function using concentration curves. Our method of estimating Engel elasticity is based on general types of concentration curves rather than the new coordinate system of concentration curves as was used by Kakwani (1978). A nonlinear functional form of the concentration curves for total expenditure and expenditure on each commodity is used to derive the expenditure elasticity for different household commodities. The concentration curves have been fitted to the Australian 1975-76 HES data and then expenditure elasticities were estimated in terms of the estimated parameters of the concentration curves for total expenditure and expenditure on each item. The empirical results show that the proposed Engel function fits better than other commonly used Engel functions in terms of goodness of fit. Moreover, the adding-up criterion is approximately satisfied by this proposed Engel function at all levels of per capita total expenditure.

The outline of this chapter is as follows. The definitions of the Lorenz curve and the concentration curve along with its specification and derivation are discussed in Section 2. A new formulation of the Engel elasticity based on implicit specification of the concentration curve is given in Section 3. Specification of the non-linear concentration curve used to derive the Engel elasticity for this study is described in Section 4. Empirical illustrations are presented in Section 5, while Section 6 gives some indication for further research. Finally, the last section makes a few concluding remarks and limitations of the present study.

2. DEFINITIONS AND SPECIFICATION OF THE CONCENTRATION CURVES

The concentration curve for income is known as the Lorenz curve. For our present purpose, we shall derive both of these curves separately. The Lorenz curve is discussed first.

2.1 Lorenz Curve

The Lorenz curve is defined as the relationship between the cumulative proportion of income and the cumulative proportion of income receiving units when the units are arranged in ascending order of income. This curve is widely used to analyse the size distribution of income and wealth.

2.1.1 Mathematical Definition of the Lorenz Curve

Let X be the per capita total expenditure (income) of a family and if X is assumed to be a random variable with a probability density function $f(X)$, then the proportion of families having per capita total expenditure (income) less than or equal to x is given by

$$P(x) = \int_0^x f(X)dX \tag{7.1}$$

Further, if it is assumed that the mean μ of the distribution exists then the first moment distribution function is defined by

$$Q(x) = \frac{1}{\mu}\int_0^x Xf(X)dX \tag{7.2}$$

This $Q(x)$ is interpreted as the proportion of per capita total expenditure (income) made (received) by those families whose per capita total expenditure (income) is less than or equal to x.

The relationship between $P(x)$ and $Q(x)$ is known as the Lorenz curve. Inverting (7.1) and eliminating x from (7.2), one could obtain the Lorenz curve provided the function (7.1) is invertible, which is true for most commonly used income density functions $f(X)$. On the other hand, the same curve is obtained by plotting $Q(x)$ as the ordinate and $P(x)$ as the abscissa for different arbitrary values of x. This curve is commonly represented in a unit square.

The first and second derivatives of Q with respect to P are respectively given by

$$\frac{dQ}{dP} = g'(p) = \frac{dQ/dx}{dP/dx} = \frac{x}{\mu} > 0 \tag{7.3}$$

$$\frac{d^2Q}{dP^2} = g''(p) = \frac{1}{\mu f(x)} > 0 \tag{7.4}$$

These two positive derivatives show that the Lorenz curve is an increasing convex function of P. This convexity along with the fact that $Q(0, 0) = 0$ and $Q(1, 1) = 1$ implies that $Q \leq P$. When $Q = P$ for all $0 < P < 1$ then the Lorenz curve coincides with the egalitarian line which means that all the families make (earn) an equal amount of total per capita expenditure (income) in the society.

It should be noted here that the Lorenz curve is generally derived from some known income distribution such as the Pareto, or lognormal.[46] But these curves do not give a reasonably good fit to empirical data. In fact, most of the available income density functions with a few exceptions such as the generalized beta of the second kind due to McDonald (1984) are unsatisfactory for practical purposes. As a result, the equation of the Lorenz curve derived from the available income density function is likely to be unsatisfactory. On the other hand, the Lorenz curve has a

---

[46] An excellent review of the literature on income distribution can be found in Cramer (1973a), Kakwani (1980b) and Ebert (1995).

number of properties mentioned by Kakwani and Podder (1973), which can be utilized to specify an equation of the curve directly. Therefore, an alternative approach is to find an equation, which would satisfy the properties of the Lorenz curve and fit the data reasonably well. In general the Lorenz curve must be an increasing function, passing through the origin (0,0) and the point (1, 1).

2.2 Concentration Curves

Mahalanobis (1960) first extended the idea of Lorenz curve to the concentration curve. Later Roy, Chakravarti and Laha (1960) studied some properties of these concentration curves. Iyengar (1960a) used these curves to compute Engel elasticity from the grouped data with two restrictive assumptions. But, the most important study of the concentration curves was made by Kakwani (1980b). Later, many authors such as Haque (1989a), Benabou (1996), Davidson and Duclose (2000), Duclose and Makdissi (2000), Maltagliati and Michelini (1999), and Pradhan, Sudarno and Lant (2000), used concentration curves to analyse poverty and inequality.

2.2.1 Properties of the Concentration Curve

Let $h(X) \geq 0$ for all $X \geq 0$ be a continuous function of X whose mean $E[h(X)]$ and first derivative exist. Then it follows that

$$Q[h(x)] = \frac{1}{E(h(x))} \int_0^x h(X) f(X) dX \qquad (7.5)$$

The parametric relationship between $Q[h(x)]$ and $P(x)$ is known as the concentration curve of $h(X)$. The curve is obtained by inverting $P(x)$ and eliminating x from $Q[h(x)]$. Alternatively, the concentration curve is obtained by plotting $P(x)$ as the abscissa and $Q[h(x)]$ as the ordinate for different arbitrary values of x. This curve must pass through (0, 0) and (1, 1).

The first and the second derivatives of $Q[h(x)]$ with respect to $P(x)$ are given by

$$\frac{dQ(h(x))}{dP(x)} = \frac{h(x)}{E(h(X))} > 0 \qquad (7.6)$$

$$\frac{d^2 Q(h(x))}{dP^2(x)} = \frac{h'(x)}{E(h(X))} \cdot \frac{1}{f(x)} \qquad (7.7)$$

The sign of the second derivative depends on $h'(x)$ as both $E[h(X)]$ and $f(x)$ are positive.

Therefore, if $h'(x) > 0$ for all $x \geq 0$ then $Q[h(x)] < (P(x)$ and hence the concentration curve falls below the egalitarian line (i.e., the line passes through the points $(0, 0)$ and $(1, 1)$ in a unit square). On the other hand, if $h'(x) < 0$ for all x, the curve is concave and will lie above the egalitarian line. If $h'(x) = 0$ then the concentration curve and the egalitarian line coincide. When $h(x) = x$ we obtain the Lorenz curve.

3. ESTIMATION OF ENGEL ELASTICITY FROM CONCENTRATION CURVES: A NEW FORMULATION

Let $W_i(x)$ be the Engel function of the ith commodity. Now if we substitute $W_i(x)$ for $h(X)$ and Q_i for Q in (7.5), we have

$$Q_i[W_i(x)] = \frac{1}{E[W_i(X)]} \int_0^x W_i(X)f(X)dX .$$

Then $Q_i[W_i(x)]$ could be explained as the proportion of the per capita expenditure on the ith commodity made by those families having per capita total expenditure (income) less than or equal to x. Hence, the relationship between $P(x)$ and $Q_i [W_i(x)]$ is known as the concentration curve of the ith commodity.

Now substituting $W_i(x)$ for $h(x)$ in (7.6) and (7.7) we have

$$\frac{dQ_i}{dP} = g'_i(P) = \frac{W_i(x)}{E[W_i(x)]} \qquad (7.8)$$

$$\frac{d^2Q_i}{dP^2} = g''_i(P) = \frac{W'_i(x)}{E[W_i(x)]} \cdot \frac{1}{f(x)} \qquad (7.9)$$

where $E[W_i(x)]$ is the mean expenditure of the ith commodity.

Equations (7.3), (7.4), (7.8) and (7.9) can be used to derive the Engel elasticity of the ith commodity as follows

$$\eta_i(x) = \frac{W_i'(x)x}{W_i(x)} = \frac{g_i''(P)}{g_i'(P)} \cdot \frac{g'(P)}{g''(P)} = \frac{g_i''(P)}{g''(P)} \cdot \frac{g'(P)}{g_i'(P)} \qquad (7.10)$$

The Engel elasticity formula derived in (7.10) is very useful for practical purposes. This formula can be used to estimate the Engel elasticity at any particular total expenditure (income) level x. From the relation (7.3) we have

$$g'(P) = x/\mu , \text{ where } E(x) = \mu.$$

This last relation gives the value of P for any particular value of x, which on substituting in Equation (7.10) gives the expenditure elasticity at any given level of per capita total expenditure (income). For example, the elasticity at mean value is calculated for that particular value of P, which satisfies the relation $g'(P) = 1$.

The above Equation (7.10) could readily be used to estimate the Engel elasticity at the percentile, decile, quartile and median values where the fractile grouping data [vide Mahalanobis (1960)] are available.[47] For example, if we wish to compute the elasticity at the median value $x = M$, we can use the following value for $P(x)$,

$$P(M) = \int_0^M f(x)dx = 0.50 \qquad (7.11)$$

where M stands for the median. This is possible since $f(x)$, the probability density function of x is known.[48]

4. SPECIFICATION OF THE CONCENTRATION CURVE

We have seen that the concentration curve for the ith consumption item is the parametric relationship between Q_i and P, i.e. $Q_i = g_i (P)$.

In Section 2 we have already indicated the drawbacks in constructing the concentration curve from the available income density function. Kakwani and Podder (1973) constructed the concentration curve from its properties. In this study we have constructed the concentration curve directly from its properties so that it fits the data reasonably well. The purpose of this section is to choose a functional form of the concentration curve. Choice of the concentration curve is very important, since this will be used to compute the Engel elasticity using Equation (7.10).

We have fitted a number of concentration curves and the following functional form of the concentration curve is chosen for our present analysis, since it fitted better than other concentration curves

$$Q = [1 - (1-P)^\alpha]^{1/\beta}; \quad 0 < \alpha, \beta < 1 \qquad (7.12)$$

Rasche, Gaffney, Koo and Obst (1980) suggested the above form (7.12) of the concentration curve. This is popularly known as the generalized Pareto concentration curve. This is because, if we put $\beta = 1$, the above curve becomes the

---

[47] The sample households were ranked in ascending order of x, and grouping the households having contiguous ranks formed the fractile groups. The group denoted by 0-5 per cent comprised the bottom 5 per cent of the estimated number of households, the group represented by 5-10 per cent comprised the next 5 per cent of the estimated number of households and so on.
   A new data set measuring income inequality can also be found in Deininger and Squire (1996).
[48] Iyengar (1964a), Prais and Houthakker (1955), and Sinha (1966) computed Engel elasticities at the median values.

equation of the concentration curve when the distribution of income follows Pareto's Law.[49]

Now differentiating (7.12) with respect to P twice we have

$$\frac{dQ}{dP} = (\alpha / \beta)(1 - P)^{\alpha-1}[1 - (1 - P)^{\alpha}]^{(\frac{1-\beta}{\beta})} \qquad (7.13)$$

$$\frac{d^2Q}{dP^2} = (\alpha / \beta)(1-P)^{\alpha-2}[1-(1-P)^{\alpha}]^{(\frac{1-\beta}{\beta})}\left[\alpha(\frac{1-\beta}{\beta})(1-P)^{\alpha}\{1-(1-P)^{\alpha}\}^{-1}-(\alpha-1)\right] \qquad (7.14)$$

For all $\alpha < 1$, the value of the first derivative would be zero and infinite if it is evaluated at zero and one respectively. On the whole, the function (7.12) satisfies all the general properties of a concentration curve. Hence, this curve is taken as the general concentration curve to compute Engel elasticity for various consumption items. Florio (2001) used other types of concentration curves to evaluate the welfare impact of British privatizations in various sectors during 1979-1997.[50]

5.   EMPIRICAL ILLUSTRATIONS

The Australian 1975-76 HES data described earlier in footnote 22 of Chapter 4 are used to illustrate the above method. We have fitted the above equation (7.12) by adding an error term ε and select that set of values of α and β, which minimizes the residual sum of squares. We explore the function step by step at each iteration in the (at most) 2n directions that are parallel to the co-ordinate axis. Any exploratory step that results in an improvement is accepted and the process is repeated. The same method is repeated for total expenditure and expenditure on each item.

---

[49] $a = 1-1/\delta$ where $\delta > 0$, the scalar parameter in the Pareto distribution. The Lorenz curve for the Pareto distribution is defined if $\delta > 1$, which implies that $0 < \alpha < 1$.

[50] Forbes (1999, 2000) and Benabou (1996) also used concentration curves to measure the relationship between inequality and growth.

*Table 7.1.   Estimates of the concentration curve for different commodities for the Australian
1975 to 1976 HES data (per capita).*

Commodities	α	β	Residual sum of squares
Total of all food	0.859593	.889692	.0001037679
All alcohol and tobacco	0.823657	.706045	.0011985776
Current housing costs	0.683137	.838022	.0025185425
Fuel & power	0.853856	.938820	.0001147191
Clothing and footwear	0.889030	.689508	.0008679586
Household equipment and operation	0.671439	.835844	.0010648194
Medical care and health expenses	0.875897	.797294	.0002097013
Transport and communications	0.863714	.675712	.0004542450
All recreation and education	0.819191	.686457	.0010663131
Miscellaneous goods & services	0.794940	.681733	.0011901483
Total expenditure	0.794000	.775957	.0003762444

Source: The 1975-1976 Australian HES data based on the 12 weekly per capita income
groups supplied by the ABS.

The estimated parameters are presented in Table 7.1, together with the residual sums of squares. It is noted that the residual sums of squares are generally low for all commodity items.

Engel elasticity at various per capita income levels is presented in Table 7.2. It is noted that the elasticity for almost all the commodities including total foods are reasonable. It should be mentioned that the elasticity for all food items were estimated and remained more or less constant for almost all the food items for those families whose per capita weekly incomes were $250 or more.[51] This is quite an encouraging result since each food item must reach saturation level.

Further, from Table 7.2 it is also noted that the expenditure elasticity for meals in restaurants and hotels decreases as income increases, although from a common sense

[51] These results are presented later in Chapter 9 where a separate study for various food items are undertaken.

Table 7.2. Total expenditure elasticities at various per capita income levels

Commodity Groups	Weekly per capita income levels in Australian dollars												Mean	Median
	30	50	70	100	130	160	190	220	250	280	310	750		
Total of all food	0.6816	0.6723	0.6706	0.6652	0.6579	0.6478	0.6326	0.6062	0.5741	0.5312	0.4911	0.4440	0.5410	0.5233
All alcohol & tobacco	1.4035	1.2810	1.1795	1.0751	1.0006	0.9431	0.9121	0.8928	0.8797	0.8708	0.8681	0.8560	1.1552	1.1994
Current housing costs	0.7269	0.9100	1.0616	1.2174	1.3282	1.4135	1.4593	1.4875	1.5066	1.5193	1.5230	1.5382	1.0978	1.0318
Fuel & power	0.2554	0.3506	0.4307	0.5147	0.5762	0.6254	0.6529	0.6707	0.6833	0.6923	0.6950	0.7094	0.4501	0.4149
Clothing & footwear	1.4895	1.2672	1.0850	0.9000	0.7708	0.6733	0.6225	0.5917	0.5714	0.5581	0.5543	0.5387	1.0417	1.1206
Household equipment & operation	0.7410	0.9344	1.0944	1.2588	1.3756	1.4654	1.5133	1.5429	1.5628	1.5759	1.5798	1.5950	1.1327	1.0630
Medical care & health expenses	0.8601	0.7957	0.7437	0.6919	0.6568	0.6313	0.6187	0.6116	0.6072	0.6046	0.6039	0.6024	0.7315	0.7538
Transport & communication	1.5947	1.3803	1.2039	1.0237	0.8968	0.8002	0.7491	0.7178	0.6969	0.6830	0.6789	0.6616	1.1618	1.2384
All recreation & education	1.5362	1.3903	1.2693	1.1442	1.0548	0.9852	0.9475	0.9239	.9077	0.8966	0.8933	0.8777	1.2402	1.2930
Miscellaneous goods & services	1.5780	1.4533	1.3490	1.2403	1.1613	1.0988	1.0642	1.0420	1.0265	1.0156	1.0123	0.9954	1.3239	1.3696
Weighted average of elasticities	1.0858	.0484	1.0176	0.9870	0.9656	0.9499	0.9417	0.9369	0.9339	0.9318	0.9311	0.9282	1.0105	1.0235

Source: The 1975-1976 Australian HES data based on the 12 weekly per capita income groups supplied by the ABS

Table 7.3. Total expenditure elasticities for various functional forms at mean total expenditure

Commodity groups	Different functional forms									
	Working curve	Leser curve	Linear	Semi-log	Hyper-bolic	Double-log	Log-inverse	Log log-inverse	Double semi-log	Proposed curve
Total of all food	0.5632	0.5658	0.5365	0.5627	0.4743	0.5574	0.5038	0.5601	0.5512	0.5410
All alcohol & tobacco	1.1078	1.1030	1.0600	1.0638	0.8629	1.1055	1.0079	1.1011	1.0757	1.1552
Current housing costs	1.1025	1.1524	1.2582	1.1679	0.8972	1.0782	0.9455	1.1161	1.2338	1.0978
Fuel & power	0.4737	0.4749	0.4615	0.4807	0.4051	0.4701	0.4244	0.4729	0.4638	0.4501
Clothing & footwear	1.0215	0.9905	0.8641	0.9272	0.7851	1.0003	0.9426	0.9619	0.9263	1.0417
Household equipment & operation	1.1831	1.2234	1.4111	1.2505	0.9483	1.1260	1.0108	1.1392	1.3913	1.1327
Medical care & health expenses	0.7675	0.7571	0.6946	0.7286	0.6183	0.7511	0.7012	0.7296	0.7241	0.7314
Transport & communication	1.1309	1.0942	1.0204	1.0434	0.8621	1.1362	1.0609	1.1036	1.0493	1.1618
All recreation & education	1.1856	1.1743	1.1430	1.1305	0.9106	1.1810	1.0817	1.1707	1.1517	1.2402
Miscellaneous goods & services	1.2626	1.2519	1.2288	1.2030	0.9605	1.2614	1.1562	1.2495	1.2343	1.3239
Weighted average	1.0068	1.0060	0.9935	0.9783	0.7887	0.9892	0.9029	0.9839	1.0054	1.0105

Source: The 1975-1976 Australian HES data based on the 12 weekly per capita income groups supplied by the ABS.

Table 7.4. Weighted residual sum of squares for different functional forms

Commodity groups	Different Functional Forms									
	Working curve	Leser curve	Linear	Semi-log	Hyper-bolic	Double-log	Log-inverse	Log log-inverse	Double semi-log	Proposed curve
Total of all food	0.3600	0.1400	0.1594	0.3613	1.2191	0.1384	0.7937	0.1262	0.1197	0.1336
All alcohol & tobacco	0.1600	0.1400	0.1306	0.1880	0.5634	0.1622	0.2365	0.1390	0.1075	0.0966
Current housing costs	2.9000	2.0600	2.6939	6.1737	10.7208	3.1698	8.3138	2.2777	1.9083	2.1405
Fuel & power	0.0200	0.0100	0.0089	0.0133	0.0221	0.0137	0.0194	0.0099	0.0089	0.0089
Clothing & footwear	0.9900	0.4700	0.8265	0.4605	0.6770	0.9239	0.4274	0.4481	0.4481	0.4551
Household equipment & operation	6.1700	4.8500	6.1597	9.5139	12.5351	6.6270	11.0394	5.7411	4.4760	4.3042
Medical care & health expenses	0.0300	0.0300	0.0304	0.0267	0.0542	0.0274	0.0366	0.0272	0.0240	0.0240
Transport & communication	2.0300	0.4300	1.1496	0.6873	3.3952	2.1740	0.7577	0.4107	0.4129	0.3524
All recreation & education	0.7000	0.6300	0.6056	0.9015	1.9818	0.7092	1.0226	0.6046	0.5803	0.5585
Miscellaneous goods & services	0.8200	0.7500	0.7190	1.0639	2.2072	0.8753	1.1512	0.7323	0.7038	0.6906

Source: The 1975-1976 Australian HES data based on the 12 weekly per capita income groups supplied by the ABS.

point of view, expenditure elasticity for this item should increase with the rise of income. This might happen due to the fact that the item may become stable after income and the consumption of the commodity reach a certain level. The rate of increase in its consumption should diminish progressively as income rises and hence the elasticity of demand falls. It is widely known that the expenditure elasticity of demand for some staple foods will eventually become negative. Therefore, the expenditure elasticity of demand for a specific kind of food like meals in restaurants and hotels generally should fall rather than rise.

The weighted average of the elasticity of all the commodities is given in the last row of Table 7.2, the weights being the budget shares to the expenditures on the items. The adding up criterion asserts that the total expenditure elasticities weighted by the budget shares for all the commodities should be equal to 1 at all income levels [see Cramer (1973a, p. 147), and Nicholson (1949)]. From the last row of Table 7.2, it is seen that the adding up criterion is approximately satisfied at all per capita income levels. The maximum error is about 8% at the extreme minimum and maximum per capita income levels of $30 and $750. The systematic decrease of the weighted average total expenditure elasticity is due to grouping according to per capita income rather than per capita total expenditure. Low-income earners sometimes spend more than their income (by borrowing or some other means) and higher income people spend less than their income. Hence, the weighted average elasticity can be over and underestimated for the lower and higher income groups respectively. Weighted average of the elasticities at the mean value is 1.0105, which is very close to 1.

Elasticity estimates for different commodities at mean total expenditure based on the proposed curve are compared with many commonly used Engel functions and are presented in Table 7.3. In their pioneering work, Prais and Houthakker (1955) investigated the linear, hyperbolic, semi-log, double-log and log-inverse functional forms. These functions were also used by Podder (1971) to describe household consumption expenditure patterns in Australia. The share semi-log Engel function was used by Working (1943) for the United States budget data. Later, Leser (1963) generalized this function. In recent times, the Leser, Working functions became more popular. In fact, Bewley (1982) used the Working function to analyse the same survey data, using 180 observations cross-classified by 12 average weekly household incomes and 15 family compositions. Giles and Hampton (1985) also used the same Working function for New Zealand Household Expenditure Survey data. Goreux (1960) selected the log log-inverse functional form for this larger FAO study, while Sinha (1966) used this form to estimate income elasticities for food items in India. The double semi-log Engel function is used by Haque (1984, 1996) to analyse the Australian Household Expenditure Survey data.[52]

The last row of Table 7.3 gives the weighted avenge of elasticities for all the functions. This shows that the adding up criterion is not satisfied for the hyperbolic, semi-log and log-inverse functional forms. However, this property is approximately

---

[52] We have also tried the quadratic Engel function due to Banks, Blundell and Lewbel (1994, 1997), but this function did not perform well compared to other familiar Engel functions such as the double semi-log or the log log-inverse Engel functions.

satisfied by all other functional forms. In general, the proposed curve performs better than the other Engel functions except the linear, double semi-log, Working and Leser functional forms, where the adding up criterion is supposed to be exactly satisfied.

The weighted residual sum of squares is used to compare the goodness of fit among the alternative functional forms, taking the proportion of the estimated population in each per capita income class as weights. It is clear from Table 7.4 that the proposed curve is superior to all other curves as judged by the minimum weighted residual sum of squares criterion. This curve is selected for seven out of ten items.

However, for clothing and footwear the log-inverse functional form gives a lower value of the weighted residual sum of squares than the proposed curve. It is interesting to note that the double semi-log functional form performs well and occupies the position next to the proposed curve. Earlier Haque (1984, 1996) showed that this function performed better than the other usual functional forms on the basis of the minimum weighted residual sum of squares.

The choice of an appropriate functional form for an Engel curve on theoretical grounds depends on the relative weights attached to the various properties by the investigator. In this analysis, we base our choice of an appropriate functional form on the minimum weighted residual sum of squares. On this basis, our proposed implicit Engel function is better than the commonly used Engel function.

6. INDICATION FOR FURTHER RESEARCH

Sampling properties of the estimated elasticities presented above have not been established. One can estimate the large sample standard error of the elasticity by standard techniques from the estimated dispersion matrix of the coefficients. This is possible since the estimated elasticities are functions of the estimated coefficients $\hat{\alpha}$ and $\hat{\beta}$ of the equation of the concentration curves. In cross-section data particularly from household expenditure surveys, econometricians often make the unrealistic assumption of constancy of the parameters for different households or different regions. For example, Houthakker (1961, p. 723) noted that maximising a quadratic utility function with non-negative variables, yields Engel functions which are 'continuous broken curves with linear segments' rather than straight lines. Spline functions may be used to compute Engel elasticities with our formula.   Spline functions are not widely used, but Spahn (1974) has used cubic splines to approximate the income distribution of West Germany.[53] For the 'structural change' in the income distribution Spahn splices on an exponential segment to the cubic spline. A spline function is a piecewise function in which the pieces are joined together in a suitably smooth fashion. Generally, polynomials are chosen for pieces,

---

[53] Bourguignon and Morrison (1990), De Gregorio and Lee (1998), Coulter, Cowell and Jenkins (1992a, 1992b), and Shorrocks (1995) have also used various techniques in estimating income distributions for various data sets.

and the smoothness requirement is interpreted in terms of continuity of the spline and its derivative. Interested readers are referred to Poirier (1976).

7. CONCLUSIONS AND LIMITATIONS

This study is based on data from a general survey, but the data are not suitably presented for the specific needs of this study to be fulfilled. For example, data on consumption items have been grouped according to per capita income rather than per capita total expenditure. Hence the total expenditure elasticity obtained from this data may not be very accurate because of the fact that the ordering of the per capita income is not the same as the ordering of per capita total expenditure.

However, close examination of the total expenditure and (gross) income figures shows that the distributions of these two variables are very similar within the range of per capita income classes. Thus, it is hoped that the orderings of the per capita income classes would be the same as the orderings of the per capita total expenditure classes of the families. Moreover, the elasticity of total expenditure with respect to income in our case is 1.02, which is not significantly different from unity. Hence, any bias in the estimated total expenditure elasticity based on the per capita income classes may be considered as negligible.

The proposed method of estimation of Engel elasticity has not yet been developed to take into account the effects of other variables. However, it is important to note that if the data are classified according to total expenditure (income) for different family compositions then the effect of family composition and economies of scale could be considered by computing the total expenditure (income) elasticities for different family compositions and then these elasticities could be combined to find the average total expenditure elasticity of demand for the whole population.[54] Some data of this nature are in fact available for the Australian 1974-75 HES and the relevant results have been presented in Table 7.A1 of Appendix 7A.

It should be pointed out that the regression estimates for grouped data are biased for the non-linear Engel functions because of the use of arithmetic means as proxies for geometric and harmonic means for logarithmic or reciprocal relationships. As a result, Engel elasticities computed from non-linear Engel functions are biased, when the least squares method of estimation is used for grouped data. The present method could be used to compute Engel elasticity from grouped data without such an added problem.

In this chapter, we have developed a method of estimating Engel elasticity from the implicit Engel function based on non-linear concentration curves, using grouped data. The empirical results show that the proposed Engel curve fits better than the other commonly used Engel functions on the grounds of goodness of fit. The adding-up criterion is also approximately satisfied by this proposed Engel function at all levels of per capita total expenditure. Hence, our method of estimating Engel elasticities based on concentration curves may be considered as superior over the

[54] See Appendix 7A for more details about this technique.

usual method of least squares in computing Engel elasticities from grouped data. Additionally we have developed a method of estimating income elasticity for the whole population when the population is divided into several homogeneous groups.

APPENDIX 7A: THE METHOD OF OBTAINING WEIGHTED ELASTICITY

In many household expenditure surveys the data are classified according to household income rather than per capita income. In such cases, our method fails to reflect the family size effect on consumer patterns. However, family size or family composition effects can be taken into account in the estimation of Engel elasticity from concentration curves, when the data are classified according to family income and size/composition. The method is given below.

Suppose that the total population is divided into several homogeneous groups. Let us see how total expenditure (income) elasticity for the entire population would be obtained from the total expenditure (income) elasticity for various groups. The problem is relatively simple since it amounts to finding the weighted elasticity. The procedure is discussed below.

Let us assume that we have N Engel functions with respect to all family total expenditure (income) i.e. $Y_1 = f_1(X)$, $Y_2 = f_2(X)$, ...,$Y_N = f_N(X)$ with total expenditure (income) elasticity η_1, η_2, ..., η_N respectively, and if Y_i's are the expenditures for different family compositions on a particular item. Then the elasticity of the sum of the functions, $f_1(X) + f_2(X) + ... + f_N(X)$ is given by

$$\eta = \frac{\eta_1 Y_1 + \eta_2 Y_2 + \cdots + \eta_n Y_N}{Y_1 + Y_2 + \cdots + Y_N}$$

This is true by definition since we know that

$$\eta_1 = f_1'(X)\frac{X}{Y_1}$$

$$\eta_2 = f_2'(X)\frac{X}{Y_2}$$

$$\vdots$$

$$\eta_N = f_N'(X)\frac{X}{Y_N}$$

and hence the elasticity of the sum of the functions $f_1(X)$, $f_2(X)$, ... $f_N(X)$ is

$$\eta = [f_1(X) + \cdots + f_N(X)]'\frac{X}{Y_1 + Y_2 + \cdots + Y_N}$$

$$= [f_1'(X) + \cdots + f_N'(X)]\frac{X}{Y_1 + Y_2 + \cdots + Y_N} \qquad (7.A1)$$

$$= \frac{\eta_1 Y_1 + \eta_2 Y_2 + \cdots + \eta_N Y_N}{Y_1 + Y_2 + \cdots + Y_N}$$

In the 1974-75 Australian HES, eight types of family composition data are available for 12 income groups (1974-75 HES data are not classified according to per capita income).[55] Effects of family composition and economies of scale may be taken into consideration if total expenditure elasticities are computed for each separate family composition. The expenditure elasticities are computed by using the above expression (7.A1) for the whole population. The results of our new formulation for computing Engel elasticities for 10 broad commodity groups for various family compositions as well as for the whole population in Australia are presented in Table 7.A1.

To compute the Engel elasticities for various family compositions, we estimated the same concentration equation (7.12) by the direct search method. Total expenditure (income) elasticities are computed at different levels of income as well as at mean and median values. Because of the shortage of space we only present the total expenditure elasticities at mean and median values. The elasticities presented in Table 7.A1 are reasonable for almost all goods for the Australian household expenditure pattern. Superiority of the proposed Engel curve used in this study is also verified in two respects viz. the adding up criterion and goodness of fit according to the minimum weighted residual sum of squares.

---

[55] Alternative measures of welfare in the absence of expenditure data are discussed in Sahn and Stifel (2000).

Table 7.A1. Total expenditure elasticities for various household composition
at mean for the 1974 to 1975 HES Data*

Commodity groups	Head only	2 adults no child	3 or more adults no child	Head with children	2 adults 1 child	2 adults 2 children	2 adults and 3 or more children	3 or more adults with children	Total of all households
				Household composition					
Total of all food	0.4655 (0.4359)	0.4462 (0.4446)	0.6177 (0.5818)	0.7174 (0.7819)	0.6182 (0.6042)	0.6163 (0.5705)	0.4270 (0.3963)	0.6944 (0.6604)	0.5892 (0.5686)
All alcohol & tobacco	1.6015 (1.6645)	1.0224 (1.0508)	1.1121 (1.0984)	1.0170 (1.1603)	0.7074 (1.0820)	1.4470 (1.2773)	0.5345 (0.4462)	0.9673 (1.0825)	1.0203 (1.0708)
Current housing cost	1.1067 (1.1235)	1.2948 (1.3010)	1.0567 (1.0236)	0.5588 (0.5157)	0.6366 (0.7485)	0.7921 (0.8924)	0.8918 (0.8042)	0.5602 (0.4919)	0.8405 (0.8433)
Fuel & power	0.1237 (0.1020)	0.1444 (0.1428)	0.2631 (0.2378)	0.5375 (0.6306)	0.5929 (0.4668)	0.8803 (0.7897)	0.5354 (0.4998)	0.6192 (0.6441)	0.4996 (0.4770)
Clothing & footwear	.8148 (0.8384)	1.2309 (1.2007)	1.0984 (1.0499)	1.4133 (1.9656)	1.5409 (1.5984)	1.3491 (1.6771)	1.1928 (1.3530)	1.1675 (1.1645)	1.2314 (1.3399)
Household equipment & operation	0.8802 (0.8739)	1.0437 (1.0068)	1.3572 (1.5102)	-0.2691 (-0.4890)	1.1808 (1.1223)	0.9379 (0.8613)	1.6066 (1.6390)	1.2862 (1.2525)	1.0747 (1.0501)
Medical care & health expenses	0.7582 (0.7636)	0.7376 (0.7760)	0.8014 (0.8852)	1.1038 (1.1990)	0.4165 (0.3307)	0.6029 (0.6774)	0.5511 (0.6048)	0.7980 (0.7732)	0.7034 (0.7315)
Transport & communication	1.5550 (1.5933)	1.1076 (1.1568)	0.9882 (1.0484)	2.0373 (2.2764)	0.9553 (1.0902)	0.5003 (0.5658)	0.8648 (1.0254)	1.0362 (1.2414)	1.0381 (1.1654)
All recreation & education	1.6375 (1.6357)	1.4930 (1.4750)	1.1764 (1.1114)	1.3784 (1.5446)	1.2001 (0.9797)	1.5753 (1.5173)	1.8997 (1.8017)	1.3917 (1.1718)	1.4447 (1.3498)
Miscellaneous goods & services	1.3157 (1.3210)	1.1838 (1.1973)	1.3608 (1.4141)	1.8699 (1.6662)	2.2515 (2.1699)	2.1130 (2.1541)	1.6452 (1.8867)	1.3776 (1.4314)	1.5951 (1.6239)
Weighted average of elasticities	1.0651 (1.0725)	1.0139 (1.0193)	1.0067 (1.0160)	1.0388 (1.1176)	0.9683 (0.9988)	0.9757 (0.9933)	0.9910 (1.0205)	0.9891 (1.0012)	0.9986 (1.0216)

* Figures in parentheses indicate the total expenditure elasticities at median.

Source: The 1974-1975 Australian HES data based on 12 weekly household income groups for various household compositions supplied by the ABS.

CHAPTER 8

ESTIMATING INCREASE IN CONSUMER DEMAND

In this chapter readers will find an alternative method of estimating increased consumer demand for various expenditure items due to increase in income and decrease in income inequality. The present method of estimating increased consumer demand differs from those of previous studies in two respects, viz., an arbitrary Engel function rather than the double log, and an equation of the Lorenz curve instead of a density function for income distribution. The present method of estimating the increase in consumer demand with respect to changes in total expenditure and total expenditure inequality makes an empirical contribution in the field. Empirical illustrations are made with reference to the Australian 1975-76 HES data, and many interesting observations are made, which contradict with the previous findings.[56]

1. INTRODUCTION

Any planned public investment should lead to an increase in real income and expenditure of households. As a consequence, the demands for different consumption items would increase. Unless necessary steps are taken in advance to meet the increased demand for consumption, inflationary pressure is likely to build up in particular sections of the economy. Therefore, it is of considerable importance to forecast aggregate demand for different items for proper production planning.

In the past, several attempts have been made to estimate the increased consumer demand. A huge body of literature has been published by many authors on the problem of estimating the increase in consumer demand with respect to changes in both income and income inequality. A review of these studies may be found in Deininger and Olinto (2000), Forbes (2000), Jain (1976), and Iyengar and Jain (1973). It should be noted that most of these studies on demand forecasting are based on the assumption of an unaltered theoretical total expenditure distribution (for example pareto or log-normal) and an invariant Engel function (say, double log). These assumptions are, however, subject to criticism. The double log Engel function may not be considered as the best functional form for all the commodities.

---

[56] Materials presented here were published earlier in *Sankhya* [see Haque (1991b)].

On the other hand, the equation of the Lorenz curve derived from the available income density function is likely to be unsatisfactory.[57]

In this chapter we estimate the increase in consumer demand by using a new coordinate system of the Lorenz curve, introduced by Kakwani and Podder (1976). Thus, our method of estimating the increase in consumer demand differs from those of previous authors in two respects. First, we can estimate the increase in consumer demand for any arbitrary Engel function instead of the double log Engel function. Second, an equation of the Lorenz curve is used to estimate the increase of consumer demand instead of using an income distribution function. Our method of estimating the increase in consumer demand with respect to total expenditure and total expenditure inequalities makes an empirical contribution in the field.

We have estimated the increase in consumer demand with respect to various percentage increases in per capita total expenditure by changing one parameter, and various percentage changes (decrease or increase) in the Lorenz ratio by changing only one other parameter in the Lorenz equation, while the rest of the parameters remain unaltered over the projected period. A number of interesting results are observed from our study and in some cases our empirical results contradict previous studies.

An increase in the demand for any commodity depends on many factors: (i) growth of income; (ii) changes in relative prices; (iii) net increase in population growth; (iv) changes in consumption patterns (due to changes in tastes and preferences); (v) changes in family composition; and (vi) shifts of income distribution, etc.

In this chapter, we will restrict ourselves to the study of the effects of the rise in income and changes in income inequality in estimating the increase in consumer demand for various consumption items in Australia. This is important, because Williams (1978a, 1978b) has indicated that over the years 1966-67 to 1974-75 real personal disposable income per head increased by nearly 40 per cent while studies on inequality measures for the Australian family total expenditure have decreased over the same period of time.

This chapter is organised as follows. A method of estimation of increasing in consumer demand from the equation of the Lorenz curve is given in Section 2. Numerical estimates of the increase in consumer demand for various consumption items are presented in Section 3. Finally, some conclusions and limitations of the study are given in Section 4.

2. METHOD OF ESTIMATION OF INCREASE IN CONSUMER DEMAND FROM THE EQUATION OF THE LORENZ CURVE

Unlike many previous studies such as Roy, Chakravarty and Laha (1960), Iyengar (1960b), and Pendakur (1998, 2001), etc., we start with an equation of the Lorenz curve introduced by Kakwani and Podder (1976). Using the equation of this

---

[57] See Atkinson et al. (1995), Atkinson (1996), and Gottschalk and Smeeding (2000) for further discussion on income distribution functions.

Lorenz curve, we have estimated the increase in consumer demand for various household consumption items. The procedure is given below.

The equation of the Kakwani-Podder (1976) Lorenz curve is given by

$$V = \alpha U^{\beta} (\sqrt{2} - U)^{\gamma} \quad \alpha, \beta, \gamma > 0, \quad 0 \leq U \leq \sqrt{2} \tag{8.1}$$

with
$$U = \frac{P+Q}{\sqrt{2}}, \quad V = \frac{P-Q}{\sqrt{2}}$$

where $P = P(x)$ is the proportion of families having total per capita expenditures less than or equal to x and $Q = Q(x)$ is the proportion of total expenditure made by these families.

It is noted here that Jain (1975) fitted this function to about 500 observed income distributions for 70 different countries. It is clear from her study that the density function underlying this Lorenz equation provides a good fit to a wide range of observed income distributions for different countries.[58]

Inequality of total expenditure is measured by the Gini index. Under the new coordinate system, the Gini concentration ratio is equal to twice the area between the egalitarian line and the Lorenz curve. Thus, the concentration ratio of the above curve (8.1) is given by

$$CR = 2 \int_0^{\sqrt{2}} \alpha U^{\beta} (\sqrt{2} - U)^{\gamma} dU$$

$$\tag{8.2}$$

$$= 2\alpha(\sqrt{2})^{1+\beta+\gamma} B(1 + \beta, 1 + \gamma)$$

where $B(1+\beta, 1+\gamma)$ is the widely used Beta function.

Now if $f(X)$ is continuous and the derivatives of $P(x)$ and $Q(x)$ with respect to x i.e. $dP/dx = f(x)$ and $dQ/dx = xf(x)/\mu$ exist; where μ is the overall mean of total expenditure, then using these values in (8.1) we can get the derivative of V with respect to U as

$$\frac{dU}{dV} = \frac{\mu - x}{\mu + x} \tag{8.3}$$

which gives

---

[58] Bell and Richard (1998), Goodman and Web (1995) and Machin (1996) fitted other types of income distributions to measure income inequalities for Germany and the UK respectively.

$$x = \frac{\mu\{1 - dV/dU\}}{\{1 + dV/dU\}} \tag{8.4}$$

While again from Equation (8.1) it can be shown that the density function of X is given by

$$f(x) = \frac{1}{\sqrt{2}}(1 + \frac{dV}{dU})\frac{dU}{dx} \tag{8.5}$$

Now let Y = φ (X) be any known time invariant Engel function and if V = g(U) is any known Lorenz equation (a new co-ordinate system) and remains unaltered (although undergoing some changes in its parameters), then the expected expenditure is given by

$$E = \int_0^{\sqrt{2}} \phi\left\{\frac{\mu(1 - g'(U))}{(1 + g'(U))}\right\}\frac{1}{\sqrt{2}}(1 + g'(U)dU) \tag{8.6}$$

If μ and G are the mean and the Gini index respectively of per capita total expenditure for the current period and if μ and G change to μ* = (1+δ)μ and G* = (1-λ)G in the future, where δ and λ are certain fractions of μ and G, then the future expected expenditure on any particular item could be estimated by possible changes of mean per capita total expenditure and the Gini index. Thus, due to change of both per capita mean total expenditure and the Gini index, the future expected expenditure on any particular item is given by

$$E^* = \int_0^{\sqrt{2}} \phi\left\{\frac{\mu^*(1 - g^{*'}(U))}{(1 + g^{*'}(U))}\right\}\frac{1}{\sqrt{2}}(1 + g^{*'}(U)dU) \tag{8.7}$$

where for a given δ

$$\mu^* = (1 + \delta)\mu \tag{8.8}$$

and from Equation (8.1) we can find dV/dU, i.e.

$$g'(U) = \alpha\beta U^{\beta-1}(\sqrt{2} - U)^\gamma - \gamma\alpha U^\beta(\sqrt{2} - U)^{\gamma-1} \tag{8.9}$$

which shows that g'(U) is a multiple of α. Further, from Equation (8.2) we can say that the Gini concentration ratio is also a multiple of α. Therefore, a one per cent change of α means a one per cent change of the Gini index, assuming β and γ will remain unchanged over the projected period.[59] Thus for a given λ, if we put

$$\alpha^* = (1-\lambda)\alpha \qquad (8.10)$$

in Equation (8.9) we get,

$$g^{*\prime}(U) = \alpha^* \beta U^{\beta-1}(\sqrt{2}-U)^{\gamma} - \gamma\alpha^* U^{\beta}(\sqrt{2}-U)^{\gamma-1}$$

It is noted that $g^{*\prime}(U)$ is obtained from $g'(U)$ just by putting α^* in (8.9) instead of α.

Therefore, the two directional changes of μ and α could estimate the expected expenditure on a particular item.

Thus, the percentage change in consumer demand for a commodity is given by

$$I_{(\delta,\lambda)} = 100(\frac{E^*}{E}-1) \qquad (8.11)$$

As a special case, if $\lambda=0$, i.e., if the per capita total expenditure distribution remains unaltered, then for a proportionate change in per capita mean total expenditure E^* becomes

$$E_1^* = \int_0^{\sqrt{2}} \phi\left\{\frac{\mu^*(1-g'(U))}{(1+g'(U))}\right\}\frac{1}{\sqrt{2}}(1+g'(U)dU) \qquad (8.12)$$

and hence the increased consumer demand is given by

$$I_{(\delta,0)} = 100(\frac{E_1^*}{E}-1) \qquad (8.13)$$

On the other hand if per capita mean total expenditure is stable over time, i.e. if $\delta=0$ and the per capita total expenditure distribution is at all close to the line of equal distribution then E^* becomes

---

[59] We have empirically verified the effects of β and γ on the Lorenz ratio and found that the effects are negligible for various changes of these parameters. Therefore, it is assumed that any change in the Gini index is due to change in α.

$$E_2^* = \int_0^{\sqrt{2}} \phi \left\{ \frac{\mu (1 - g^{*\prime}(U))}{(1 + g^{*\prime}(U))} \right\} \frac{1}{\sqrt{2}} (1 + g^{*\prime}(U)) dU \tag{8.14}$$

for a given λ, $\alpha^* = (1-\lambda)\alpha$, where $g^{*\prime}(U)$ is obtained as previously. Thus, the increased consumer demand can be calculated by the following formula

$$I_{(0,\lambda)} = 100(\frac{E_2^*}{E} - 1) \tag{8.15}$$

3. NUMERICAL ILLUSTRATIONS ON DEMAND PROJECTIONS

Australian Household Expenditure Survey (HES) 1975-76 data are used to illustrate the above method in this section. Data used here are obtained from a special table prepared by the Australian Bureau of Statistics (ABS). Commodity-wise, weekly arithmetic mean household expenditure, average number of persons per household and estimated number of households were available for twelve per capita (gross) income groups for the Australian population, the ranking being in ascending order of the average weekly per capita income of the households. Per capita income data are used here, because per capita income data, which include the basic economies of scale, welfare changes of the households, etc., are necessary for precise short-term demand projections.[60]

To compute the increased consumer demand for various consumption items, we assume that the above Lorenz equation (8.1) remains unaltered (even though the parameters might have changed) over time and can be estimated by the ordinary least squares method after applying the logarithmic transformation. The estimated parameters of the above equation (fitted to the per capita income data) are given by $\hat{\alpha} = 0.2369$, $\hat{\beta} = 0.9561$, and $\hat{\gamma} = 0.8827$. Putting these values in Equation (8.9) and replacing $g'(U)$ in (8.6) we can estimate E. E* can be obtained from Equation (8.7) for different values of δ and λ. Simpson's numerical integration rule is used to evaluate the integral.

All the functional forms (i) to (vii) given in Section 2.1 of Chapter 3 are estimated by the weighted least squares method, taking the estimated sample proportion of the population in each per capita income class as the weights.[61]

---

[60] See Footnote 22 for more about these data.

[61] In addition to these seven functional forms, we have also used two other functional forms: the share semi-log (SSL) Y/X = α + β log X + γ log S; and share semi-log inverse (SSLI) Y/X = α + β log X + γ /X + δ log S to estimate the increased demand for various expenditure items. It should be noted that Working (1943) first used the SSL Engel function for the USA budget data. Later Bewley (1982) and Giles and Hampton (1985) used this function respectively for the Australian and New Zealand budget data analysis. Leser (1963) generalized the SSL Engel function by adding an inverse term and called this generalized version of the form as share semi-log inverse (SSLI) function. This SSLI allows the

Parameters estimated by the weighted least squares method for different functional forms are used to estimate the percentage change in demand with respect to change in income and income inequality for 16 commodity groups. We have computed the percentage change in demand with respect to change in income and income inequality, for all the items by each functional form separately. Results of change in demand are only presented for the best functional form of the item as judged by the distance function, D^2-criterion, which is given in Equation (3.4) earlier in Chapter 3. Table 8.1 presents the percentage increase/decrease in demand for different items due to two dimensional changes, viz., (i) percentage increase in per capita total expenditure, and (ii) percentage change in Lorenz ratio (a decreased Lorenz ratio implies increased income equality).

Table 8.1 shows that the percentage demand for a necessary item (as judged by the criterion that the elasticity lies between 0 and 1) increases as the percentage of the Lorenz ratio decreases. But, fuel and power, and education do not follow this trend. The percentage demand for these two items decreases as the Lorenz ratio decreases, although the elasticities of these two items show that these are necessary items.[62] The reason for this might be that in Australia, if some money is transferred from the richer group to the poorer group, the latter group of the population probably spends this money on items other than fuel and power, and education.

On the other hand, the percentage change in demand for luxury goods (as judged by the criterion that the elasticity is greater than 1) decreases as the Lorenz ratio falls. However, wine, alcohol and tobacco, and transport and communication are exceptions. The elasticities of these items show that they are luxury items, however their percentage change in demand increases as the Lorenz ratio decreases. These findings directly contradict Iyengar's results. Iyengar (1960b) used Indian data and showed that the percentage demand would rise or fall with the percentage decrease of the Lorenz ratio for necessary and luxury goods respectively. But our results do not show these trends. This difference might be observed due to the differences of the consumption patterns between the developing and developed countries.

The percentage increase/decrease in demand for necessary/luxury goods simply implies that if the distribution of per capita total expenditure is equalised among the individuals then people will demand more necessary goods and less luxury goods. This really means that if the purchasing power of the poor people increases by transferring some money from the higher income class to the lower income class via some government instrument, like progressive taxation and transfer payments, then the poor people spend their money on necessary items. On the other hand, because of the government mechanism the purchasing power of the rich people will decrease and ultimately they would spend their money on necessary commodities first and then luxury goods. As a result the demand for necessary/luxury commodities will increase/decrease due to the reduction of the

---

simultaneous testing of the constancy of the elasticity demand and marginal outlay for any commodity.

[62] Hansen, Formby and Smith (1996) estimated income elasticity for housing from the concentration curve.

Table 8.1.   Percentage increase/decrease in demand (per capita)

Commodity groups	Percentage increase in per capita expenditure (100α)	Percentage change in Lorenz ratio (100β)						Best functional form* chosen by the D^2 criterion	Corresponding elasticity of the best function
		10	5	0	-5	-10	-20		
(1) Bread cakes & cereals	0	-0.653	-0.3176	0	0.3003	0.5836	1.1004		
	5	-0.0277	0.3077	0.6253	0.9256	1.2089	1.7257		
	10	0.5226	0.858	1.1756	1.4759	1.7592	2.276	DSL	0.11
	20	1.4238	1.7592	2.0768	2.3771	2.6604	3.1773		
	50	3.0639	3.21	3.5279	3.8282	4.1115	4.6284		
(2) Meals in restaurants & hotels	0	5.675	2.7604	0	-2.6097	-5.0718	-9.5639		
	5	15.2118	12.2971	9.5367	6.9269	4.4647	-0.0274		
	10	25.4007	22.486	19.7254	17.1156	14.6533	10.1611	DSL	2.47
	20	47.51	44.5952	41.8345	39.2245	36.7622	32.2696		
	50	124.7212	121.806	119.045	116.435	113.972	109.478		
(3) All foods	0	-0.3619	-0.176	0	0.1664	0.3234	0.6097		
	5	2.3862	2.5721	2.7481	2.9145	3.0714	3.3578		
	10	5.0927	5.2785	5.4545	5.6209	5.7779	6.0642	DSL	0.55
	20	10.3951	10.5809	10.7569	10.9233	11.0802	11.3665		
	50	25.6077	25.7935	25.9695	26.1358	26.2927	26.5790		
(4) Wine	0	-2.9888	-1.4686	0	1.4146	2.7730	5.3114		
	5	6.0799	7.7768	9.4164	10.9951	12.5114	15.3449		
	10	15.6065	17.4901	19.3097	21.0625	22.7456	25.8911	LLI	1.92
	20	36.0469	38.3342	40.5438	42.6724	44.7164	48.5369		
	50	108.695	112.442	116.063	119.551	122.202	129.166		
(5) All alcohol & tobacco	0	-0.9124	-0.4438	0	0.4195	0.8153	1.5373		
	5	4.877	5.3455	5.7893	6.2088	6.6046	7.3266		
	10	10.5614	11.0299	11.4737	11.8932	12.289	13.0109	DSL	1.08
	20	21.6516	22.1201	22.5638	22.9833	23.379	24.101		
	50	53.1709	53.6394	54.083	54.5025	54.8981	55.62		
(6) Current housing costs	0	2.2394	1.0893	0	-1.0298	-2.0014	-3.774		
	5	7.5312	6.381	5.2917	4.2619	3.2903	1.5176		
	10	13.0802	11.93	10.8407	9.8108	8.8392	7.0665	DSL	1.23
	20	24.8616	23.7113	22.6219	21.592	20.6203	18.8475		
	50	64.4998	63.3494	62.2598	61.2297	60.2578	58.4846		

(Table 8.1. Continued)

(7) Fuel & power	0	0.0054	0.0027	0	-0.0027	-0.0053	-0.0107		
	5	2.207	2.2041	2.2013	2.1985	2.1957	2.1901		
	10	4.4086	4.4056	4.4027	4.3997	4.3968	4.3909	L	0.46
	20	8.8118	8.8086	8.8053	8.8021	8.7989	8.7925		
	50	22.0214	22.0174	22.0134	22.0093	22.0053	21.9973		
(8) Medical care & health expenses	0	-0.9053	-0.4403	0	0.4163	0.8090	1.5255		
	5	2.91550	3.3804	3.8208	4.2370	4.6298	5.3462		
	10	6.63220	7.0971	7.5374	7.9537	8.3464	9.0629	DSL	0.72
	20	13.7891	14.2541	14.6944	15.1107	15.5034	16.220		
	50	33.5228	33.9877	34.4280	34.8442	35.2369	35.953		
(9) Transport & Communica- tion	0	-3.8269	-1.8721	0	1.7887	3.493	6.6454		
	5	2.4759	4.482	6.4022	8.2358	9.9819	13.209		
	10	9.6727	10.7263	12.6908	14.566	16.35	19.647	LLI	1.10
	20	20.7463	22.8846	24.9281	26.877	28.73	32.195		
	50	54.5024	56.8352	59.0603	61.178	63.189	66.89		
(10) Recreation	0	0.0143	0.0071	0	-0.007	-0.014	-0.024		
	5	5.8832	5.8757	5.8682	5.8607	5.8532	5.8383		
	10	11.7521	11.7442	11.7364	11.729	11.721	11.705	L	1.16
	20	23.4899	23.4814	23.4728	23.464	23.456	23.439		
	50	58.7034	58.6927	58.682	58.671	58.661	58.639		
(11) Books, newspapers & magazines	0	2.1526	1.047	0	-0.99	-1.924	-3.628		
	5	6.9491	5.8435	4.7965	3.8065	2.8726	1.1686		
	10	11.9929	10.8873	9.8402	8.8503	7.9163	6.2123	DSL	1.13
	20	22.7373	21.6317	20.5845	19.595	18.661	16.956		
	50	59.0984	57.9926	56.9453	55.955	55.021	53.316		
(12) Education	0	0.0119	0.006	0	0.006	-0.012	-0.024		
	5	4.9272	4.9209	4.9146	4.9084	4.9021	4.8896		
	10	9.8424	9.8359	9.8293	9.8227	9.8161	9.803	L	0.98
	20	19.6729	19.6657	19.6586	19.651	19.644	19.63		
	50	49.1643	49.1554	49.1464	49.138	49.129	49.111		

(Table 8.1. Continued)

Commodity groups	Percentage increase in per capita expenditure 100α)	Percentage change in Lorenz ratio (100β)						Best functional form chosen by the D^2 criterion	Corresponding elasticity of the best function
		10	5	0	-5	-10	-20		
(13) All recreation & education	0	0.0141	0.0070	0	-0.0070	-0.141	-0.028		
	5	5.8039	5.7965	5.7891	5.7817	5.7743	5.7596		
	10	11.5937	11.586	11.578	11.571	11.563	11.547	L	1.14
	20	23.1733	23.1649	23.156	23.148	23.14	23.123		
	50	57.9122	57.9017	57.891	57.881	57.87	57.849		
(14) Clothing & footwear	0	-4.3212	-2.1141	0	2.0199	3.9446	7.5044		
	5	1.6192	3.8505	5.9855	8.0234	9.9635	13.547		
	10	7.339	9.5877	11.737	13.787	15.737	19.335	LI	0.94
	20	18.1343	20.401	22.564	24.624	26.58	30.182		
	50	45.8601	48.0948	50.219	52.236	54.144	57.644		
(15) Household equipment & operation	0	4.4701	2.1743	0	-2.056	-3.995	-7.533		
	5	9.4692	7.1734	4.999	2.9434	1.004	-2.534		
	10	14.982	12.6861	10.512	8.456	6.5166	2.9782	DSL	1.39
	20	23.3715	25.0756	22.901	20.845	18.906	15.367		
	50	73.1132	70.8169	68.642	66.586	64.646	61.107		
(16) Miscellaneous goods & services	0	0.0152	0.0076	0	-0.008	-0.015	-0.031		
	5	6.2884	6.2804	6.2724	6.2644	6.2564	6.2404		
	10	12.5615	12.5532	12.554	12.536	12.528	12.511	L	1.23
	20	25.1078	25.0987	25.089	25.068	25.071	25.053		
	50	62.7467	62.7353	62.724	62.711	62.709	62.678		

* Symbols of the functional forms are defined in Section 2.1 of Chapter 3.

Source: The 1975-1976 Australian HES data based on the 12 weekly per capita income groups supplied by the ABS.

income inequality. Recently Barrett, Crossley and Worswick (1999a, 1999b) studied the effect of income inequality in Australia and observed similar phenomenon.[63]

In another direction the percentage increase in demand is effectively increased due to increase in per capita total expenditure. One interesting point is that the percentage increase in demand for a commodity due to a change in per capita total expenditure is directly linked with its elasticity. For example, the elasticity of bread, cakes and cereals is 0.11 and its demand rises only 3.53% for a 50% rise of per capita total expenditure. But for high elasticity commodities like meals in restaurants and hotels whose elasticity is 2.47, the demand rises as much as 119.04% for only 50% rise in per capita total expenditure. This shows that higher elasticity indicates higher demand and lower elasticity indicates lower demand due to the change of per capita total expenditure.

Another point to observe is that the percentage demand of bread, cakes and cereals does not equi-proportionally decrease with the percentage increase of income, but it decreases at a lesser rate, which is desirable from an Engel curve analysis for a necessary food item. Unlike this, the percentage demand of meals in restaurants and hotels increases more rapidly than the percentage increase in income. Results of all other items can be interpreted in a similar manner.

Thus, Table 8.1 shows that for one per cent increase in total expenditure, the demand for luxury and necessary goods will increase more or less than one per cent respectively. These findings corroborate with the general demand theory.

Further interpretation of Table 8.1 is quite straightforward. For example, if the per capita total expenditure increases by 20 per cent and the Lorenz ratio decreases by 10 per cent, then the per capita increases in demand for meals in restaurants and hotels, all food, wine, current housing costs, household equipment and operation, medical care and health expenses, transport and communication, and books, newspapers and magazines, are 36.76, 11.08, 44.72, 20.62, 18.91, 15.50, 28.73 and 18.66 per cent respectively.

However, if one does not consider the effect of change in the Lorenz ratio then the percentage increase in demand is fully accounted for by the percentage change in total expenditure. In that case the per capita increase in demand for the above items would be 41.83, 10.76, 40.54, 22.62, 22.90, 14.69, 24.93 and 20.58 per cent respectively. In general this investigation shows that the per capita increase in demand for necessary and luxury goods would be underestimated and overestimated respectively, if the change of income distribution is not considered.

For a fixed rise in per capita total expenditure, the demand for necessary goods does not vary substantially in comparison to the variation in demand for luxury goods due to a change in the Lorenz ratio. For example, suppose there is a 10% increase in per capita total expenditure then the percentage increase in demand for all foods would be 6.06 for a 20 per cent decrease in the Lorenz ratio as opposed to 5.45 per cent demand without any reduction of the Lorenz ratio. On the other hand,

---

[63] The effects of income inequality on consumption were also studied by Blundell and Preston (1998) and Pendakur (2001) for other developed countries.

the corresponding figures for meals in restaurants and hotels are 10.16 and 19.73 respectively.

On the whole, the increase in demand for future consumption of the various Australian household expenditure items depends mainly on the rise of the per capita total expenditure rather than a reduction in the Lorenz ratio. This suggests that income is fairly equally distributed among the individuals in Australia.

3. CONCLUSIONS AND LIMITATIONS

The invariance assumption on the Lorenz equation is used to estimate the increase in consumer demand. Our result satisfies the theoretical aspects as well as *a priori* beliefs that demand will increase (decrease) for necessary (luxury) goods due to a decrease in the Lorenz ratio. The method proposed here for estimating the increase in consumer demand gives a better understanding for future consumption patterns in Australia.[64]

Due to the unavailability of data, we are not able to predict the aggregate increase in consumer demand for the nation as a whole. The idea could easily be extended to estimate the aggregate increase in consumer demand. If we multiply the right hand side of Equation (8.11) by the factor $D^* = D \ (1+r)$ then the aggregate increase in consumer demand would be estimated for the whole nation; where D and D^* are the demand in the base year and target year respectively, r is the rate of growth of population after adjusting the specific and overall consumer scales. Note that, in that case r should also be changed along with the mean per capita total expenditure and the parameter α. It is interesting to mention here that because of the structure of the population, the rate of growth of the young adults group is about 0.3 per cent per annum. However, the net reproduction rate is less than unity in cross sectional analysis. Hence, our estimates might be taken as the aggregate percentage increase in consumer demand with respect to change in income and income inequality for the Australian economy if we multiply the obtained results by the base year aggregate demand.

These results are especially helpful for production policy decisions. This is the first study of its nature in Australia. Finally, it should be pointed out that the Engel functions we have used to compute increased demand were based on a simple relationship between the per capita expenditure on a particular commodity and the per capita total expenditure. Family size and other sociological, demographic and cultural factors have been omitted from the specification of the Engel functions. At this stage it is not possible to cover all those factors, which together may have substantial influence on consumption spending. Generalisation of our method to

---

[64] Clark and Oswald (1996), Blundell and Preston (1995), Clark and Taylor (1999), DSS [Department of Social Security] (2000), Goodman, Johnson and Webb (1997) and Johnson (1996) have also provided a better understanding about income, consumption and patterns of living standards for other countries.

include all these variables in the specification of the functional form is possible and is left for further investigation. A more comprehensive study may be carried out using expenditure data on individual commodities.

CHAPTER 9

FOOD DEMAND ANALYSIS IN AUSTRALIA

In this chapter, readers will get a clear picture of the expenditure patterns of seven widely used broad types of food items, using the 1975-76 Australian HES data. Percentage expenditures of these food items with respect to total expenditure are provided for various household compositions, income levels and ethnicity. It is seen that sole parent households consistently spend less on food compared to married couple households. More importantly, it is seen that the smaller the household size, the better the living standard in Australia. Higher quintile households spend more than one third of their total food expenditure on 'meals in restaurants and hotels', while expenditures on 'fruits and vegetables' have been reduced drastically in recent years, which has tremendous impact on health for Australian people. Total expenditure elasticities are calculated for various food items based on several Engel functions and it turns out that 'meals in restaurants and hotels' is a luxury item in Australia. Estimation of elasticity indices of various food items are also presented, and it is shown how each food items is contributing to make the elasticity index for 'all food' item. Additionally, the percentage change in demand due to changes in total expenditure and total expenditure inequalities for various food items are provided, which are useful for future production planning.

1. INTRODUCTION

Overall expenditure patterns of some broad expenditure items are provided in previous chapters. The present chapter is entirely devoted to analyse food expenditure patterns of the households in Australia. Food is very important, not only because a minimum quantity is absolutely needed for everyone's survival, but also because it is the largest single expenditure item in the Australian family budgets. The percentage expenditure of food can also be regarded as a measure of the standard of living for various families. The lower the percentage of expenditure on food, the better the living standard, since food is regarded as a necessary household expenditure item. Hence, there is demand for a comprehensive study into the variation of expenditure on various types of food in different income groups for different household compositions. However the scope for an intensive investigation into any single category of expenditure item, for different surveys, is severely limited. This is because the components of the broad category of food items vary vastly from survey to survey. The income groupings used to report the expenditure

125

data for classifying households, also differ in various surveys. That is why various data sets from different surveys are used for the analysis in this chapter.

Here, we have extended our food demand analyses in two main directions. First, total food expenditure is disaggregated into several food items, which is also limited by the availability of detailed information. Second, the present chapter examines the possible differences of food consumption patterns among various socio-economic and demographic characteristics.

The present chapter is organized as follows. A brief description of expenditures for various food items of different socio-economic and demographic characteristics is given in Section 2. The patterns of food expenditure for various household compositions, income levels and ethnicity are provided in Section 3. Section 4 is mainly concerned with the estimation of income elasticities for various food items of different socio-economic and demographic characteristics, while estimation of elasticity indices for various food items are presented in Section 5. The effects of demand of various food items due to an increase in total expenditure and reduction of total expenditure inequality are presented in Section 6. Finally, limitations and some concluding remarks about the Australian food demand analyses are provided in the final section.

2. FOOD EXPENDITURES BY VARIOUS SOCIO-ECONOMIC AND DEMOGRAPHIC CHARACTERISTICS

An important feature of food consumption is the limitations of people's capacity to consume it, and hence a little variation is expected to be observed in terms of volume of food consumption. Yet, real expenditure of per head food expenditure increases with the growing economic prosperity in Australia. In this study, we explore how the nature and composition of foods are affected due to improved economic prosperity. We have seen from our past experience that when people get more money to spend, they usually buy more food on a per capita basis, even though they don't consume it all, probably because of psychological satisfaction. But, the most important variation is possibly coming from the use of quality and composition of foods as well as getting better food services. The composition of food can be changed due to substitution of one item by another better quality item when people get more money. The Australian HESs do not provide information on food quality and services, and hence our analyses are mainly based on money expenditures made by various households for different food items, which encompasses quantity, quality and services.

Inter-household expenditure on food varies due to a number of factors, such as household composition, income and many others. In measuring the differences of expenditures on foods among households, investigators generally estimate income elasticity from the Engel function, where household expenditure of food is mainly determined by household total expenditure and family size. But, there are other important socio-economic and demographic characteristics, which also can explain substantial differences in food expenditures among household. A detailed study of the effect of household composition on the expenditures of food items is provided in this chapter. Also, expenditure patterns of food for sole parent and married couple households differ significantly, because of economic vulnerability [see Cass (1986), Raymond (1987), Haque (1996), and Birrell and Rapson (1997)] of the sole parent households. Therefore, it is of great interest to see the food expenditure habits of sole parent households, who are economically most vulnerable as well as homogeneous. Their food expenditure is then compared with married couple households. Estimated total expenditure elasticities of various food items for different sole parent and married couple households will be compared to see whether there is any significant difference among them.

It is a common practice to classify households on the basis of the level of household income. This makes us to examine whether lower income households have a different dietary habit than higher income households. Also, we want to investigate whether the estimated income elasticity for lower income households differs from that of higher income households. More importantly, Australia is a multicultural society and its population is composed of migrants from different countries around the world. Australian migrants are mostly European, yet they differ sociologically and culturally. There are also migrants from Asia and Africa, who also differ socially, religiously and culturally. It is thus anticipated that migrants' food expenditure habits and patterns differ among themselves as well as from Australian-born population. For example, Muslims are not allowed to drink any alcohol and/or eat pork. It is thus interesting to see how expenditures on various food items differ among migrant groups. A comprehensive study of differences in food expenditures among various ethnic groups is also provided in this study.

3. PATTERNS OF FOOD EXPENDITURES CLASSIFIED BY VARIOUS HOUSEHOLD COMPOSITIONS, INCOME LEVELS AND ETHNICITY

Table 9.1 presents the percentage expenditure of each household commodity with respect to total expenditure for different years at different major cities in Australia. This table clearly shows that Australian households spend the highest amount of money on food at different cities in various years. It is also interesting to note that as time passes, the percentage of expenditure on food has dropped since 1974-75, while luxury items such as current housing costs, transport and communication, and recreation have increased significantly over time. This is consistent with a rising standard of living over the study period 1974-75 to 1998-99.

Table 9.1. Expenditures on commodity groups as percentages of total expenditure in various capital cities in Australia: 1967-1968 to 1998-1999*

Commodity groups	Years	Sydney	Melbourne	Brisbane	Adelaide	Perth	Hobart	Canberra	All capital cities
Current housing costs	1967-68	10.37	9.35	9.56	8.87	10.43	8.84	-	9.78
	1974-75	15.34	14.2	14.9	12.62	13.7	13.39	14.55	14.47
	1975-76	16.00	13.92	13.92	13.02	15.18	11.85	15	14.62
	1984	15.34	13.17	14	12.15	12.93	12.34	12.82	13.91
	1988-89	16.12	14.35	16.7	14.96	13.34	14.88	17.07	15.29
	1993-94	16.25	14.36	14.24	12.63	13.62	12.64	14.49	14.76
	1998-99	16.18	12.93	15.12	13.3	12.75	12.55	13.07	14.37
Fuel & power	1967-68	3.13	4.32	3.36	3.61	2.96	4.41	-	3.55
	1974-75	2.08	2.7	1.81	2.01	1.9	2.71	2.63	2.26
	1975-76	2.06	2.58	1.92	1.95	2.14	2.67	2.47	2.22
	1984	2.43	3.25	2.61	3.12	2.92	3.31	2.86	2.83
	1988-89	2.07	2.69	2.25	2.86	2.56	3.25	2.6	2.43
	1993-94	2.34	3.46	2.02	2.88	2.79	4.1	2.77	2.75
	1998-99	2.1	2.92	1.82	3.22	2.61	3.57	2.6	2.49
Food**	1967-68	29.12	29.03	32.18	28.64	32.97	30.91	-	30.89
	1974-75	21.01	20.51	21.14	20.06	20.12	20.32	17.91	20.63
	1975-76	19.11	19.31	19.32	18.68	19.34	17.49	16.78	19.1
	1984	19.39	19.73	19.61	19.44	18.99	18.97	18.2	19.44
	1988-89	18.48	18.71	18.59	18.76	18.78	19.98	18.14	18.64
	1993-94	19.38	18.34	18.14	17.8	18.21	18.94	17.09	18.58
	1998-99	17.85	18.62	17.65	17.97	17.91	18.02	16.37	18.01
Alcohol & tobacco	1967-68	5.3	4.93	4.25	4.79	4.33	4.53	-	4.96
	1974-75	6.24	5.59	6.04	5.29	6.18	5.8	5.55	5.89
	1975-76	6.08	6.18	4.69	5.54	5.92	5.62	5.07	5.88
	1984	5	4.72	4.71	5.39	5.03	5.16	4.1	4.92
	1988-89	4.19	4.22	4.88	4.91	4.68	4.85	4.33	4.42
	1993-94	4.14	3.91	4.56	4.44	4.81	4.79	3.66	4.25
	1998/99	3.96	3.97	3.98	3.96	4.81	4.83	4.55	4.10

* Canberra was excluded from the 1967-68 Survey. It is noted from the 1975-76 HES data that the % expenditure on Transport and Communication exceeds the % expenditure on food in Australia.

** Including non-alcohol beverages.

*** Personal care is included in recreation and education.

Sources: Australian Household Expenditure Surveys: 1974-1975 to 1998-1999.

(Table 9.1. Continued)

Commodity Groups	Years	Sydney	Melbourne	Brisbane	Adelaide	Perth	Hobart	Canberra	All capital cities
Clothing & footwear	1967-68	7.99	8.33	8.84	8.51	6.65	10.02	-	7.97
	1974-75	8.35	9.59	8.34	9.42	8.07	9.18	8.36	8.86
	1975-76	8.95	9.47	7.51	8.66	7.91	10.02	7.83	8.55
	1984	7.29	6.69	5.4	6.53	5.96	7.15	6.28	6.65
	1988-89	6.52	6.34	6.09	6.18	6.08	5.62	5.71	6.29
	1993-94	5.95	6.47	5.5	5.51	5.53	5.8	5.94	5.91
	1998-99	4.82	5.1	4.29	4.8	4.53	4.92	4.38	4.77
Housing equipment & operations	1967-68	10.88	10.29	10.11	11.07	11.65	10.64	-	10.56
	1974-75	9.08	9.18	8.83	10.34	9.5	11.09	10.83	9.33
	1975-76	9.51	9.92	11.19	10.29	11	11.51	11.87	10.11
	1984	11.37	11.42	11.13	13.62	12.19	11.16	11.83	11.66
	1988-89	12.23	12.21	11.87	11.05	13.5	12.18	10.74	12.16
	1993-94	12.02	10.62	11.08	11.58	13.24	12.33	11.6	11.6
	1998-99	11.99	11.14	12.23	11.53	12.09	11.86	12.53	11.77
Medical care & health expenses	1967-68	4.11	3.99	3.3	4.34	3.78	4.28	-	4.04
	1974-75	3.74	3.83	3.29	4.05	3.6	2.98	3.17	3.72
	1975-76	2.94	2.95	3.01	3.11	2.71	2.68	2.37	2.92
	1984	3.66	4.15	3.52	3.95	3.51	3.7	3.36	3.79
	1988-89	4.41	4.31	3.95	4.42	3.87	4.16	3.72	4.25
	1993-94	4.67	4.43	4.34	5.3	4.24	5.08	3.83	4.54
	1998-99	4.64	4.75	4.5	5.4	4.5	5.44	4.19	4.69
Transport & communication	1967-68	9.62	9.95	9.86	10.02	9.18	8.8	-	9.58
	1974-75	16.35	15.99	17.74	18.15	17.63	16.37	19.41	16.73
	1975-76	18.93	18.64	18.91	19.17	19.12	19.03	19.27	18.89
	1984	14.38	15.76	17.17	15.99	17.12	15.84	17.05	15.61
	1988-89	14.5	14.65	14.63	15.44	14.8	13.29	15.24	14.66
	1993-94	13.14	15.21	16.77	14.9	15.71	13.81	17.22	14.74
	1998-99	15.96	17.8	16.56	13.77	17.06	15.05	16.81	16.51

(Table 9.1. Continued)

Commodity groups	Years	Sydney	Melbourne	Brisbane	Adelaide	Perth	Hobart	Canberra	All capital cities
Recreation & education***	1967-68	6.14	6.06	5.89	6.6	5.06	4.39	-	5.87
	1974-75	8.15	9.07	8.65	8.9	10.73	7.26	9.05	8.79
	1975-76	8.44	9.02	8.98	11.12	9.59	9.98	11.09	9.16
	1984	13.42	14.5	13.73	13.49	14.41	16.12	14.34	13.95
	1988-89	14.34	14.13	13.25	13.87	12.92	14.42	14.38	13.99
	1993-94	15.1	15.62	15.16	16.65	14.73	15.91	15.7	15.4
	1998-99	14.52	14.82	14.61	16.09	15.02	14.92	16.21	14.86
Miscellaneous goods & services	1967-68	-	-	-	-	-	-	-	-
	1974-75	9.64	9.33	9.25	9.16	8.97	10.89	8.54	9.31
	1975-76	8.76	7.97	10.52	8.46	7.07	9.14	8.23	8.51
	1984	7.72	6.59	8.12	6.31	6.94	6.24	9.06	7.23
	1988-89	7.16	8.39	7.79	7.54	9.47	7.37	8.06	7.89
	1993-94	7.01	7.58	8.2	8.3	7.11	6.6	7.7	7.47
	1998-99	7.98	7.95	9.34	9.96	8.72	8.84	9.29	8.4

Table 9.2. Per capita expenditures on food item for sole parent and married couple households with children based on the 1988 to 1989 HES Data

Number of children	Types of households	
	Sole parent	Married couple
One dependent child	32.2	34.80
Two dependent children	26.14	29.81
Three or more dependent children	20.29	24.87

Source: The 1988-1989 Australian HES Unit Record Tape Supplied by the ABS.

Inter-city differences are again insignificant except for Canberra. Observations on Canberra, when compared with other cities tend to verify Engel's law.

Per capita expenditure on food of sole parent and married couple households with children are presented in Table 9.2. This table shows that on a per capita basis, sole parent households consistently spend less money on food than married couple households. More importantly, this table shows that per capita expenditure on food decreases as the number of people increases in both sole parent and married couple households. This may happen due to economies of scale in food purchasing and/or preparation.

The expenditure patterns of foods of various household compositions in different quintile groups are presented in Table 9.3. It is of considerable interest to know the expenditure patterns of various household compositions, because it is the most important determinant of household expenditure other than income. It also helps to identify a class of households who need financial assistance to maintain a minimum level of living standard.

First, Table 9.3 shows that the percentage of total expenditure on food decreases as the income of the household increases, which is consistent with Engel's law. This is true for all types of household compositions. Observations for six or more person households indicate that these type of households maintain a lower level of living standard compared to smaller family sizes based on the food share criterion, which states that the smaller the food share the better the living standards. On the basis of this food share criterion it can be concluded from this table that the smaller the family size the better the living standard in Australia. However, a different picture emerges when the expenditure for different household compositions within an income quintile group is examined. For example, percentage expenditure on food at the lowest quintile for married couple households was 24.04%, compared to 20.47% for married couple with one dependent child households. Moreover, single parent with 2 or more dependent children, and married couple with 3 or more dependent children households spend a higher percentage of total expenditure on food compared to other family compositions. Additionally, households of the lowest income quintiles of the latter two types spend 27.06% and 26.93% respectively on food, which is significantly higher compared to other household compositions within the same income quintile group, showing that these types of households tend to verify Engel's law when compared with other households.

Table 9.3. Percentage of total expenditure on food by household income
quintile groups and compositions in Australia: 1988-1989[*]

Household compositiopns	Gross income quintiles					
	Lowest quintile	*Second quintile*	*Third quintile*	*Fourth quintile*	*Highest quintile*	*All house-holds*
Single person	23.83	22.10	16.30	15.41	15.40	17.37
Two persons	23.25	23.04	18.76	16.71	15.23	18.30
Three persons	21.71	20.61	19.79	17.87	16.31	18.71
Four persons	23.31	20.12	20.71	18.34	17.18	19.34
Five persons	24.59	22.14	22.77	18.70	18.15	20.40
Six or more persons	29.05	26.42	21.14	21.31	20.76	22.88
Single parent household with one dependent child	17.38	24.02	24.03	19.19	14.90	18.93
Single parent household with 2+ dependent children	27.06	22.27	22.75	20.82	19.01	21.66
Single parent household with dependent child	22.34	22.93	23.60	19.76	17.39	20.50
Married couple household with 1 dependent child	20.47	18.82	19.33	18.07	15.11	17.81
Married couple household with 2 dependent children	23.63	20.34	19.88	20.16	16.52	19.52
Married couple household with 3+ dependent children	26.93	22.35	22.46	19.40	17.69	21.04
Married couple with dependent children	23.51	20.87	20.52	19.14	16.61	19.55
Married couple households : husband and wife only	24.04	22.79	19.69	17.02	14.89	18.55
All households	**22.18** (19.84) [19.59]	**21.47** (20.28) [20.16]	**19.67** (18.93) [18.85]	**18.83** (18.06) [18.06]	**17.05** (17.20) [16.64]	**19.06** (18.44) [18.17]

[*] 1993-1994 results for all households are given in parentheses; 1998-1999 results for all
households are given in brackets [ ].

Source: The 1988-1989 Australian HES Unit Record Tape Supplied by the ABS; and the
Australian 1993-1994 to 1998-1999 HESs.

However, observations for single parent with one-child households contradict
Engel's law, because the percentage expenditures on food do not decrease as income
increases for the next three income quantities. Moreover, it shows from Table 9.3
that this type of households, which belong to the lowest and highest income quintiles
maintain a very high standard of living compared to other household types, which is
not true. This is because we have observed that these types of households spent

more money on housing than food, and, as a result, the percentage of expenditure on food dropped. It is also noted from Table 9.3 that household living standards vary widely from one income class to another income class. In fact, overall, households belonging to the highest income quintiles maintain more than 30% higher level of living standards than the households of the lowest income quintiles. Most importantly, we notice that the maximum disparity (61.45%) in the standard of living occurs between the highest and lowest gross income quintile households for married couple only (i.e., husband and wife only). The corresponding figures for married couple with 3 or more children, and single parent with 2 or more children households were 52.23% and 42.35% respectively. This shows that households of married couple with 3 or more children, single parent with 2 or more children, and married couple only, who belong to the lowest income quintile group, should be given priority for any further financial assistance in terms of improving living standards in Australia.

Table 9.4. Percentage of total expenditure and total food expenditure for some broad food items in various household income quintile groups in Australia: 1988-1989 to 1998-1999*

Broad food items	Survey years	Bakery products & cereals	Meat & seafood	dairy Products	Fruits & vegetables	Miscellaneous foods	Non-alcohol beverages	Meals-out & take-away food	Total food
Lowest quintile	1988-89	2.95 (13.31)	5.12 (23.09)	2.76 (12.46)	3.71 (16.73)	3.24 (14.59)	1.11 (5.02)	3.29 (14.82)	22.18 (100)
	1993-94	2.63 (13.27)	3.74 (18.87)	2.36 (11.91)	3.02 (15.24)	3.38 (17.05)	1.09 (5.500)	3.60 (18.16)	19.82 (100)
	1998-99	3.01 (15.37)	3.63 (18.55)	2.18 (11.14)	3.12 (15.94)	2.42 (12.38)	1.88 (9.58)	3.34 (17.04)	19.58 (100)
Second quintiles	1988-89	2.70 (12.60)	4.78 (22.27)	2.56 (11.94)	3.35 (15.59)	3.01 (14.04)	1.36 (6.32)	3.70 (17.25)	21.46 (100)
	1993-94	2.63 (13.27)	3.74 (18.87)	2.36 (11.91)	3.02 (15.24)	3.38 (17.05)	1.09 (5.50)	3.60 (18.16)	19.82 (100)
	1998-99	3.13 (15.54)	3.63 (18.02)	2.17 (10.74)	3.03 (15.02)	2.49 (12.37)	1.90 (9.45)	3.80 (18.86)	20.16 (100)
Third quintiles	1988-89	2.27 (11.54)	3.80 (19.30)	2.16 (11.00)	2.61 (13.25)	2.76 (14.02)	1.51 (7.66)	4.57 (23.22)	19.68 (100)
	1993-94	2.26 (11.93)	3.18 (16.79)	2.10 (11.09)	2.31 (12.20)	3.36 (17.74)	1.43 (7.55)	4.30 (22.70)	18.94 (100)
	1998-99	2.62 (13.87)	2.94 (15.59)	1.86 (9.88)	2.40 (12.74)	2.39 (12.69)	1.98 (10.49)	4.66 (24.74)	18.85 (100)
Fourth quintiles	1988-89	2.13 (11.32)	3.59 (19.05)	1.87 (9.94)	2.44 (12.94)	2.53 (13.45)	1.48 (7.84)	4.79 (25.46)	18.83 (100)
	1993-94	2.04 (11.29)	2.72 (15.05)	1.76 (9.74)	2.14 (11.84)	2.98 (16.49)	1.40 (7.75)	5.03 (27.84)	18.07 (100)
	1998-99	2.44 (13.53)	2.65 (14.65)	1.61 (8.92)	2.18 (12.08)	2.15 (11.90)	1.84 (10.20)	5.19 (28.72)	18.06 (100)

* Expenditure with respect to total food expenditure is presented in parentheses ( ).

Sources: The 1988-1989 Australian HES Unit Record Tape supplied by the ABS; and the Australian HESs 1993-1994 to 1998-1999

(Table 9.4 Continued)

Broad food items	Survey years	Bakery products & cereals	Meat & seafood	Dairy products	Fruits & vegetables	Miscellane-ous foods	Non-alcohol beverages	Meals-out & take-away food	Total food
Highest quintiles	1988-89	1.69 (9.91)	2.94 (17.27)	1.44 (8.43)	2.16 (12.68)	2.05 (12.04)	1.35 (7.93)	5.42 (31.75)	17.04 (100)
	1993-94	1.73 (10.06)	2.42 (14.08)	1.37 (7.97)	1.87 (10.88)	2.52 (14.66)	1.30 (7.56)	5.98 (34.79)	17.19 (100)
	1998-99	2.13 (12.80)	2.26 (13.59)	1.31 (7.87)	1.99 (11.94)	1.82 (10.92)	1.63 (9.80)	5.50 (33.08)	16.64 (100)
All households	1988-89	2.16 (11.35)	3.72 (19.49)	1.96 (10.27)	2.62 (13.74)	2.54 (13.35)	1.39 (7.29)	4.67 (24.50)	19.06 (100)
	1993-94	2.12 (11.50)	2.97 (16.11)	1.83 (9.93)	2.28 (12.36)	3.01 (16.32)	1.33 (7.21)	4.90 (26.57)	18.44 (100)
	1998-99	2.52 (13.87)	2.81 (15.44)	1.69 (9.30)	2.36 (13.02)	2.16 (11.87)	1.81 (9.95)	4.82 (26.55)	18.17 (100)

Table 9.5: Average per capita expenditure of the households by food groups, ethnicity and reference person's age over 65 and under 65years*

Food groups	Under 65 years					Over 65 years				
	Australia	ESC	NESC All	NESC Asia & Europe	NESC Africa	Australia	ESC	NESC All	NESC Asia & Europe	NESC Africa
Bakery product & cereals	3.80 (10.52)	3.93 (10.63)	3.83. (10.49)	3.52 (10.27)	4.01 (10.63)	4.59 (11.86)	4.69 (12.15)	4.59 (11.60)	6.80 (14.24)	5.22 (10.96)
Meat & fish	6.38 (17.66)	6.44 (17.42)	7.64 (20.92)	6.44 (18.79)	8.30 (21.99)	8.54 (22.07)	8.22 (21.30)	11.29 (23.69)	10.95 (22.94)	11.37 (23.88)
Dairy product oils & fats	3.47 (9.61)	3.76 (10.17)	3.60 (9.86)	3.01 (8.78)	3.93 (10.41)	3.94 (10.18)	4.70 (12.18)	5.34 (11.23)	4.58 (9.60)	5.54 (11.64)
Fresh fruits & nuts	2.13 (5.90)	2.05 (5.55)	2.53 (6.93)	2.57 (7.50)	2.52 (6.68)	3.15 (8.14)	2.83 (7.33)	3.84 (8.09)	4.51 (9.49)	3.67 (7.71)
Vegetables	2.54 (7.03)	2.87 (7.77)	2.89 (7.91)	2.86 (8.35)	2.91 (7.71)	3.53 (9.12)	3.48 (9.01)	4.30 (9.02)	5.05 (10.58)	4.11 (8.63)
Sweets & confectioneries	2.47 (6.84)	2.48 (6.71)	2.19 (6.00)	1.97 (5.75)	2.30 (6.09)	2.41 (6.23)	2.39 (6.19)	2.23 (4.68)	2.26 (4.73)	2.22 (4.66)
Tea, coffee Food drinks	1.06 (2.93)	1.11 (3.00)	1.14 (3.12)	1.01 (2.95)	1.21 (3.21)	1.59 (4.11)	1.67 (4.33)	2.24 (4.69)	1.50 (3.14)	2.43 (5.10)
Other foods	1.71 (4.73)	1.82 (4.92)	1.68 (4.60)	1.67 (4.87)	1.69 (4.48)	1.79 (4.63)	1.64 (4.25)	2.81 (5.89)	2.24 (4.69)	2.94 (6.18)
Non-alcoholic soft drinks	2.89 (8.00)	2.76 (7.47)	2.71 (7.42)	2.28 (6.65)	2.94 (7.79)	1.92 (4.96)	1.83 (4.74)	2.87 (6.03)	2.33 (4.88)	3.01 (6.32)
Take-away food	9.67 (26.77)	9.74 (26.35)	8.31 (22.75)	8.94 (26.09)	7.93 (21.10)	7.24 (18.70)	7.14 (18.50)	7.20 (15.11)	7.51 (15.73)	7.10 (14.91)
All food	36.12	36.96	36.52	34.27	37.74	38.7	38.59	47.66	47.73	47.61

* Percentage expenditures on various food items with respect to total food expenditure are presented in parentheses ( ).

Source: The 1988-1989 Australian HES Unit Record Tape supplied by the ABS.

Seven types of food expenditures are presented in Table 9.4. These are considered in this analysis in order to explore what percentage of expenditures (total expenditure as well as food expenditure) are spent on different food items by various households in different quintile income groups in different years. It is noted that the expenditures of these seven food components should add up to total food expenditure for all income quintile groups.

It is seen that the largest percentage of food expenditure is made up with 'meals out and take-away food', although it seems a luxury item (percentage expenditure increases with the increase of income) for Australian households. In 1993-94 the households belonging to the highest gross income quintile spent about 35% of their total food expenditure on this item, as against about 18% of the lowest gross income quintile households. Similarly, non-alcohol beverages can also be classified as a luxury good for Australian households. In 1988-89, the highest income quintile households spent about 8% of the total food expenditure on this item, compared to only 5% of their lowest counterparts. The rest of the other food items can be considered as necessary goods, although households with lower incomes spend a higher proportion of expenditure on food compared to the higher income families. 'Meat and seafood' is the second largest expenditure item among the food items, where the lowest income quintile households spend about 23.09% of their total food expenditure, compared to 17.27% by the highest income quintile households. This shows that households belonging to higher income groups enjoy better quality of food, including marketing services, compared to the lower income households. "Miscellaneous food" which comprises with sugar, honey, jam, potato-chips, savory, chocolate, ice and other confectioneries; is considered to be evenly distributed across all Australian households.

It is found from Table 9.4 that most Australian households spend a higher percentage of expenditures on 'meals out and take away food' over time. This implies that there is a growing tendency for Australian households including lower quintile income groups to use more and more 'fast and take away food' over time. The lowest quintile income households spend 17.04% of total food expenditure on 'meals-out and take away' in 1998-99 compared to 14.82% in 1988-89. Similar patterns are observed for all income quintile groups. More importantly, households of the highest quintile income group spend more than one third of their total food expenditure on 'meals-out and take away' food compared to only 17% in the lowest quintile income group in 1998-99.

Another important observation is that expenditure on 'fruits and vegetables' has drastically reduced in 1998-99 compared to 1988-89 across all households. Also, expenditures on 'miscellaneous goods and services' as well as 'fast food' have increased significantly over this period of time for all quintile income groups. This can be interpreted as an indication that Australian households are giving up eating healthy foods such as fresh fruits and vegetables, and tending to consume more and more unhealthy foods such as 'miscellaneous foods, and fast foods', which might have long term bad effects on the health of the Australian people.

Per capita expenditures of various food items for different ethnic and age groups are shown in Tables 9.5. It reveals from this table that migrants from Non English Speaking Countries (NESC) usually spend more money for 'all foods' than the

Australian born or the migrants from English Speaking Countries (ESC) at an old age. The expenditures on cereals, fresh fruits and nuts, and vegetables are generally higher for the NESC of Asian and African migrants compared to other groups. However, NESC of both Asia and Africa and Europe spend more money on meat and fish when they become old compared to their younger age (under 65 years). At an older age (over 65 years) all groups spend approximately 22% of their total food expenditure on meat and fish. This implies that at an older age, migrants from NESC spend more on meat and fish than their traditional expenditure behaviour in their home countries. The expenditures on dairy products and fats, tea, sweets, coffee and food drinks, and other non-alcohol beverages are higher for migrants from NESC of Europe than other groups. Expenditure patterns of various food items are very similar for the Australian born and the ESC migrants, although the ESC migrants spend slightly more on sweets, tea and coffee and dairy products than Australian born people.

It is appropriate to mention here that expenditure is not necessarily a proxy for actual consumption, yet it is noted from Young (1986) that with a few minor exceptions, the mortality levels between Australian born and migrants from ESC are similar, and their consumption patterns are also similar. It is thus expected that some informed suggestions regarding health outcomes are possible from this study if higher expenditure indicates higher consumption, i.e., expenditure is one of a mix of variables that is salient in health status, which are discussed below.

3.1 Protective Effects of Plant Foods

Nutritional epidemiology suggests that populations with lower mortality report higher expenditure on cereals, vegetables and fresh fruits and nuts. This analysis indicates that expenditure is generally higher for migrant households from NESC than Australian born and migrants from ESC, which might be the reason for lower mortality levels for the migrants from Asia and Africa, and NESC of Europe [see Young (1986)].

3.2 Expenditure on Dairy Products and Fats

Expenditure on dairy products and fats is substantially higher in migrant households of European NESCs. This might affect their health with saturated fat related diseases such as heart disease.

3.3 Expenditure on Meat and Fish

Expenditure on meat and fish is generally high for migrants of NESC households. This is contrary to the popular belief that lower mortality is associated with lower expenditure on meat and fish. On the other hand, such expenditure is below average for the ESC group with the exception of females aged more than 65 years, whose mortality levels are similar to those born in Australian. Meat consumption has significantly risen among migrant households of Asian and European NESCs, the majority of who came from low meat consuming cultures. This might ultimately lead them to attain the higher levels of mortality of Australian born people in the long run.

These findings should be treated with caution, as expenditure data cannot be used directly for the measurement of health. Although, expenditure can be taken as a proxy for quantity consumed that might affect health. This is true particularly for some directly health-related consumption items, such as eggs, beer and tobacco, where there is little variation in unit price and waste. Moreover, there is a very high positive correlation between household expenditure and consumption. There are still many drawbacks in expenditure data because of the exclusion of home-made fruits and vegetables, which may underestimate the consumption practice of some migrant groups (particularly among households of European NESCs) compared to others. Besides many problems with the expenditure data, it is expected that the above suggestions regarding health outcomes are useful in explaining different levels of mortality and disease patterns for various ethnic groups living in Australia.

4. ESTIMATION OF TOTAL EXPENDITURE ELASTICITY FOR VARIOUS FOOD ITEMS

The analysis of food expenditure given above is important and useful, but not rigorous. In this section, we will estimate total expenditure elasticities for various food expenditure items based on the 'best' functional form chosen from various alternatives. Like Chapter 3, here we also discriminate among various functional forms on the basis of the distance function D^2-criterion and the non-nested hypothesis testing procedure to choose the best functional form, and then we estimate total expenditure elasticities for different food items based on this 'best' Engel function. Additionally, we also estimate total expenditure elasticities of various food items by the new method described in Chapter 7, which is based on concentration curves for various food items at different income levels.

First, we choose a best functional form among seven different functional forms described in Section 2.1 of Chapter 3, based on the D^2-criterion, which are presented in Table 9.6. This table clearly shows that no single Engel function is appropriate for various food items. It turns out that the double semi-log (DSL) function fits best for four out of eight food items as well as for all foods, The linear (L) and log log-inverse (LLI) each fits for two items. Thus, it can be concluded that the DSL is the best functional form for most of the Australian food expenditure items on the grounds of goodness of fit. This function also has the advantage that it automatically satisfies the adding up criterion. More importantly, it is observed that the double semi-log (DSL), log log-inverse (LLI) and double log (DL) Engel functions are consistently accepted against each other and the rest of the other functions for all food items when the non-nested hypothesis testing procedure based on the Mackinnon, White and Davidson P_E-test was performed (see Chapter 3 for more details about this test).

Table 9.6. D^2 –statistics for different types of Engel curves fitted to various food consumption items: 1974 to 1975

Commodity groups	Functional forms considered							Best function
	L	SL	HYP	DL	LI	LLI	DSL	
(1) Bread	0.0000335	0.0000319	0.0000368	0.0000315	0.0000370	0.0000286	0.0000288	LLI
(2) Flour, cakes, & other cereals	0.0000655	0.0000576	0.0000550	0.0000601	0.0000580	0.0000518	0.0000509	DSL
(3) Meat	0.0012170	0.0011489	0.0012265	0.0013719	0.0013369	0.0011829	0.001089	DSL
(4) Fish	0.0000294	0.0000296	0.0000327	0.0000340	0.0000348	0.0000331	0.0000299	L
(5) Dairy products, oils & fats	0.0000176	0.0001795	0.000199	0.0001833	0.0002063	0.0001693	0.0001720	LLI
(6) Fruit	0.0001113	0.0000897	0.0000910	0.0001108	0.0000989	0.0000950	0.00008734	DSL
(7) Vegetables	0.0001132	0.0001148	0.0001371	0.0001383	0.0001524	0.0001268	0.0001131	DSL
(8) Other food	0.0588000	0.0677000	0.0824000	0.0604000	0.0769000	0.0592000	0.0593000	L
(9) All food	0.0141000	0.0198000	0.0299000	0.0154000	0.0240000	0.0154000	0.0139000	DSL

Source: The Australian 1974 to 1975 HES data based on 120 observations supplied by the ABS

We have estimated the total expenditure elasticities for all seven functions. However, we only present the elasticities for the DSL, LLI and DL functions, since these functions dominated the other functions on the basis of the specification tests and goodness of fit criteria as indicated above. The estimated total expenditure elasticities, together with their standard errors, as well as the percentages of expenditures of various food items with respect to total expenditure, are presented in Table 9.7. This table clearly indicates that Australian households spend the highest percentage of total expenditure on 'other food', which encompasses 'take away foods'. This food item turns out to be a luxury item in Australia on the grounds that its total expenditure elasticity is greater than 1, which is consistently observed by all three Engel functions as well as on the basis of the best Engel function among seven alternatives. While, the elasticity of bread is consistently negative for all three functions and it turns out to be an inferior good in Australia. 'dairy products, oils and fats' becomes an inferior good when elasticity is estimated based on the LLI functional form, but it becomes a necessary item based on the DSL and DL functions. All other food items become necessary items on the grounds that their elasticities lie between 0 and 1.

Table 9.7. Estimated total expenditure elasticities at mean values of X and S for the Australian 1974 to 1975 HES data.

	Elasticity estimated by different functions					Percentage of food share expenditure with respect to total expenditure
	DSL	DL	LLI	Best form by D^2-criterion		
(1) Bread	-0.1100 (0.0410)	-0.1200 (0.0292)	-0.1400 (0.0675)	-0.1400 (0.0675)	(LLI)	1.01
(2) Flour, cakes biscuits & other cereals	0.1400 (0.0992)	0.1300 (0.0330)	0.1000 (0.0745)	0.1400 (0.0992)	(DSL)	1.25
(3) Meat	0.3200 (0.1686)	0.3200 (0.0405)	0.2900 (0.0938)	0.3200 (0.1686)	(DSL)	0.39
(4) Fish	0.5200 (0.3502)	0.5000 (0.0678)	0.4700 (0.1624)	0.4300 (0.0624)	(L)	4.64
(5) Dairy products, oils & fats	0.0100 (0.0246)	0.0100 (0.0238)	-0.0100 (0.0551)	-0.0100 (0.0551)	(LLI)	2.98
(6) Fruit	0.3900 (0.1608)	0.3900 (0.0350)	0.3700 (0.0799)	0.3900 (0.1608)	(DSL)	1.45
(7) Vegetables	0.2900 (0.1456)	0.2800 (0.0364)	0.2600 (0.0863)	0.2900 (0.1456)	(DSL)	1.55
(8) Other Food	1.3400 (1.8700)	1.2000 (0.0563)	1.2300 (0.1352)	1.4100 (0.1569)	(L)	7.38
(9) All Food	0.5500 (0.0947)	0.5400 (0.0216)	0.5400 (0.0527)	0.5500 (0.0947)	(DSL)	20.64

* Figures in parentheses denote the approximate standard errors of the estimated elasticities [See Cramer (1946) for the estimation of standard errors].
Source: The Australian 1974-1975 HES data based on 120 observations supplied by the ABS.

As indicated earlier in Chapter 4, the use of grouped arithmetic means would introduce biases when the Atkin's GLS method is used to estimate Engel elasticities for various non-linear Engel functions such as DL or SL. We have estimated the within group geometric/harmonic means for the logarithmetic/inverse relationships as discussed in Chapter 4 and estimated unbiased Engel elasticities for various non-linear Engel functions. Further, in Chapter 3, we have shown that due to the simultaneity of the model, the traditional GLS method produces inconsistent estimates of the Engel elasticities. We have used the instrumental variable approach as described in Chapter 3 to obtain consistent estimates of Engel elasticities for various food items. These unbiased and consistent elasticities along with the elasticity estimates based on the traditional GLS method are presented in Table 9.8. This table clearly shows that there are discrepancies in elasticity estimates based on the traditional GLS method with those obtained from the unbiased and consistent estimates. The differences of elasticities of various food items vary from commodity to commodity and from function to function. Most notably, it is observed that the hyperbolic function produces the lowest elasticity estimates based on all methods. This analysis again reconfirms that 'Meals in restaurants and hotels' and 'snacks and take-away food' are luxury food items in Australia. All other food items are considered to be necessary items.

Table 9.8. Estimation of Engel elasticities by methods A, B and C

Methods used	Food items	Functional forms						
		L	SL	HYP	DL	LI	LLI	DSL
Method A Elasticity at 'AMs' for various Engel functions	(1) Bread, cakes, dairy products, oils & fats	0.03	0.09	0.10	0.09	0.10	0.06	0.08
	(2) Meat and fish	0.31	0.46	0.36	0.48	0.42	0.40	0.43
	(3) Fruits & vegetables	0.35	0.39	0.26	0.41	0.31	0.40	0.40
	(4) Miscellaneous foods	0.24	0.37	0.27	0.38	0.31	0.34	0.35
	(5) Meals in restaurants & hotels	2.50	1.37	0.35	2.12	1.47	2.13	2.49
	(6) Snacks, take-away food	0.74	0.89	0.61	1.12	0.88	1.00	0.88
	(7) Total food	0.50	0.49	0.29	0.52	0.37	0.53	0.54
Method B Elasticity at 'GMs & HMs' for various Engel functions	(1) Bread, cakes, dairy products, oils & fats	0.03	0.14	0.11	0.15	0.11	0.04	0.02
	(2) Meat and fish	0.31	0.47	0.36	0.58	0.43	0.23	0.31
	(3) Fruits & vegetables	0.35	0.29	0.30	0.42	0.33	0.40	0.34
	(4) Miscellaneous foods	0.24	0.36	0.26	0.43	0.30	0.23	0.16
	(5) Meals in restaurants & hotels	2.50	1.63	0.39	2.64	1.61	3.62	1.75
	(6) Snacks, take-away food	0.74	1.08	0.71	1.47	0.92	1.24	1.53
	(7) Total food	0.50	0.24	0.31	0.47	0.40	0.46	0.45
Method C Elasticity estimates by instrumental variable approach	(1) Bread, cakes, dairy products, oils & fats	0.02	0.12	0.11	0.12	0.12	0.06	0.08
	(2) Meat and fish	0.29	0.49	0.34	0.56	0.44	0.40	0.44
	(3) Fruits & vegetables	0.34	0.36	0.20	0.42	0.27	0.40	0.40
	(4) Miscellaneous foods	0.22	0.39	0.25	0.42	0.29	0.34	0.36
	(5) Meals in restaurants & hotels	2.55	0.87	0.38	2.09	1.20	2.13	2.44
	(6) Snacks, take-away food	0.70	0.86	0.48	1.20	0.81	1.02	0.86
	(7) Total food	0.49	0.44	0.20	0.52	0.31	0.52	0.53

Source: The 1975-76 Australian HES data based on the twelve weekly per capita income groups (these groups are given in Foot note 22) supplied by the ABS.

Table 9.9. Total expenditure elasticities of different food items at various per capita income levels.

Weekly per capita income levels in Australian $	Bread, cakes & cereals	Meat & fish	Dairy products, oils & fats	Fruits & vegetables	Miscellaneous foods	Meals in restaurants & hotels	Snacks & take-away food	Total food
A$ 30	0.1626	0.5600	0.1254	0.3702	0.3737	3.0155	1.4213	0.6816
A$ 50	0.1245	0.4998	0.1183	0.4031	0.3320	2.7267	1.2093	0.6723
A$ 70	0.0936	0.4515	0.1131	0.4315	0.2987	2.4782	1.0356	0.6706
A$ 100	0.0627	0.4040	0.1084	0.4623	0.2663	2.2091	0.8596	0.6652
A$ 130	0.0415	0.3723	0.1059	0.4859	0.2449	2.0038	0.7376	0.6579
A$ 160	0.0260	0.3499	0.1046	0.5057	0.2300	1.8313	0.6445	0.6478
A$ 190	0.0181	0.3391	0.1044	0.5173	0.2231	1.7293	0.5964	0.6326
A$ 220	0.0134	0.3332	0.0146	0.5252	0.2194	1.6596	0.5674	0.6062
A$ 250	0.0104	0.3297	0.1044	0.5311	0.2173	1.6074	0.5484	0.5741
A$ 280	0.0085	0.3277	0.1052	0.5354	0.2162	1.5681	0.5360	0.5312
A4 310	0.0079	0.3272	0.1053	0.5368	0.2159	1.5555	0.5325	0.4911
A$ 750	0.0058	0.3265	0.1064	0.5446	0.2159	1.4766	0.5181	0.4440
Mean	0.0863	0.4402	0.1119	0.4385	0.2910	2.4171	0.9944	0.5410
Median	0.0996	0.4609	0.1140	0.4258	0.3051	2.5278	1.0695	0.5233

Source: The 1974-1975 HES data based on the twelve per capita income groups supplied by the ABS.

We also estimate total expenditure elasticities for various food items by the new method of estimating Engel elasticities based on the concentration curves described in Chapter 7. Elasticity estimates based on this new method for different food items at different income levels are presented in Table 9.9. This table also shows that 'all food' decreases as the level of income increases, which is quite expected for food. 'Meals in restaurants and hotels' turns out to be a luxury item at all income levels in Australia. However, 'snacks and take away foods' is considered to be a luxury item for those households whose per capita income is A\$70 or less per week, but it becomes necessary item for those households whose per capita income exceeds A\$70 per week. All other food items seem necessary on the basis that their elasticities are less than 1 and elasticities for all these food items are decreasing with the increasing level of incomes, which is quite expected for any food items. More importantly, it was found that the elasticities for almost all food items remain the same for those households whose per capita incomes are more than A\$280 per week. This is quite encouraging since the level of saturation must be reached by all of food items.

At this point, we want to estimate total expenditure elasticity for various sole parent and married couple households to examine their living conditions. For that reason, the following seven different functional forms have been tried to find the best functional form among various Engel curves, which are listed below.

(i)   Linear   : $Y_{ij} = \alpha_i + \beta_i X_j + \varepsilon_{ij}$

(ii) Double semi-log   : $Y_{ij} = \alpha_i + \beta_i X_j + \gamma_i \log X_j + \varepsilon_{ij}$

(iii) Share inverse   : $W_{ij} = \alpha_i + \beta_i / X_j + \varepsilon_{ij}$

(iv) Working-Leser   : $W_{ij} = \alpha_i + \beta_i \log X_j + \varepsilon_{ij}$

(v)   Addilog   : $\log[\widetilde{W}_{ij} / W_j] = \alpha_i + \beta + \beta_i \log X_j + \varepsilon_{ij}$

(vi) Log share linear   : $\log[W_{ij} / \widetilde{W}_j] = \alpha_i + \beta_i X_j + \varepsilon_{ij}$

(vii) Log share inverse: $\log[W_{ij} / \widetilde{W}_j] = \alpha_i + \beta_i / X_j + \varepsilon_{ij}$

where $W_{ij} = Y_{ij} / X_j$, $\log \widetilde{W}_j = \sum \log W_{ij} / K$, $K > 0$; Y_{ij} is the expenditure on the ith commodity for the jth household, and X_j is the total expenditure of the jth household. These functional forms can all be derived from more general expenditure systems, which can satisfy the adding-up criterion.

The GLS method is used to estimate each of the above Engel functions to estimate elasticity for various food items of different sole parent and married couple households. All the above functions were fitted to the 1988-89 HES data, and a best functional form among these alternatives was chosen on the basis of the distance function, D^2-criterion and the non-nested hypothesis testing procedures, which are described in Chapter 3. On the basis of these criteria the double semi-log (DSL) Engel function turns out to be the best functional form again for the 1988/89 Australian HES data.

Total expenditure elasticity of 'all foods' for different household composition is estimated based on the seven Engel functions given above. However, we only present expenditure elasticity for the DSL Engel function, since this function dominates the other functions on the basis of specification tests and the goodness of fit criterion as indicated in Chapter 3. The calculated expenditure elasticities, together with the estimates of their standard errors and the number of households on which these estimates are based are presented in Table 9.10. This table clearly shows that total expenditure elasticity increases with the increase of number of children for both sole parent and married couple households. For example, total expenditure elasticity for married couple households with one child is 0.52 compared to 0.58 for those who have three or more children. More importantly, this table shows that total expenditure elasticities are consistently higher for sole parents than for married couple households with children. For example, total expenditure elasticity for sole parent with three or more children is 0.65 compared to 0.58 for married couple households with three or more children. This indicates that sole parent households with three or more children would spend 65 cents more for food if their income increases by one more dollar compared to 58 cents by married couple households with three or more children. Thus, this study shows that sole parent households with 3 or more children spend approximately two thirds of their incomes on food, if additional monies are made available to these households. This implies that both sole parent and married couple households with three or more children need financial assistance to improve their economic conditions.

Elasticities of 'all food' for more detailed household compositions are further estimated at the mean and median values from the new method based on the concentration curve given in Equation (7.12) of Chapter 7, using the 1974-75 HES

Table 9.10. Total expenditure elasticity for all foods for various household compositions at mean values: 1988 to 1989 HES Data[*]

Household compositions					
Married couples with children			Sole parents with children		
With 1 child	0.52	(0.14)	[574]	0.60 (0.15)	[226]
With 2 children	0.53	(0.15)	[998]	0.63 (0.12)	[145]
With 3 or more children	0.58	(0.12)	[609]	0.65 (0.12)	[67]

*   Standard errors of estimated total expenditure elasticities are presented in parenthes, and figures in brackets [ ] represent the number of households on which these calculations are based.

Source: The 1988-1989 Australian Household Expenditure Survey Unit Record Tape supplied by the ABS.

*Table 9.11:   Total expenditure elasticity for all foods for various household
compositions at mean values: 1974 to 1975 HES data*[*]

Household compositions	Total expenditure food elasticity
Head only	0.4655 (0.4359)
Two adults no children	0.4462 (0.4446)
Three or more adults no children	0.6177 (0.5818)
Head with children	0.7174 (0.7819)
Two adults with one child	0.6182 (0.6042)
Two adults two children	0.6163 (0.5705)
Two adults & three or more children	0.4270 (0.3963)
Three or more adults with children	0.6944 (0.6604)
Total of all households	0.5892 (0.5686)

* Elasticities based on median values are presented in parentheses.

Source: The Australian 1974 to 1975 HES data based on 120 observations supplied by the
ABS.

data and are presented in Table 9.11. This table clearly indicates that households
with children maintain very poor living standards in Australia. They seem to spend
about two thirds if additional incomes are made available to these households, which
is quite consistent to our earlier findings stated above. We thus recommend that in
order to improve living standards, the government should provide further financial
assistance to those families who have children. Recognizing this fact very recently
(June 2004) the Australian federal government provides A$600 for each child for
those families who have children, which surely helps them to improve their living
standards.

5. ESTIMATION OF ELASTICITY INDEX FOR FOOD ITEMS

Mahalanobis (1960) first used the concentration curves to describe and compare
the consumption patterns at different levels of total expenditure in different regions
of India. Later, Kakwani (1980b) showed that the concentration curve lies above or
below the Lorenz curve according to whether the elasticity η_i (x) is less or greater
than unity for all x $\geq$ 0, η_i (x) being the elasticity for the ith commodity.[65] Again it
follows from Equation (7.5) of Chapter 7 that the larger the absolute difference
$| \eta_i$ (x) $- 1 |$ for all per capita total expenditure x $\geq$ 0, the greater the area between
the concentration curve of the ith commodity and the Lorenz curve for x. Hence, the
area between the two curves can be taken as a measure of elasticity or inelasticity for
the commodity. Therefore, the elasticity index of the ith commodity is defined by

$$I_{ei} = C_i - G \qquad\qquad (9.1)$$

[65] See Corollary 2 in Kakwani (1977a). The position of the concentration curve of a commodity indicates
whether the commodity is a luxury, necessary or inferior item.

where C_i and G are the concentration index of the ith commodity and the Gini index of the per capita total expenditure (income) respectively. In fact, I_{ei} represents twice the area between the two curves. The ith commodity is elastic or inelastic according to whether it is strictly positive or negative.

The magnitude of I_{ei} indicates how much the elasticity of the ith commodity deviates from unity over the whole income range. Hence, this measure is only used for comparative purposes. The advantage of this index is that it can be computed from grouped data without specifying any particular Engel function.

Further, if expenditure on any broad commodity group, say 'all food', is expressed as the sum of expenditure on different sub-items, then from corollary 3 of Kakwani (1977a) we can write the following expression

$$C_f = \frac{1}{E_f} \sum_{i=1}^{6} E_i C_i \qquad (9.2)$$

where E_f and E_i are the mean per capita expenditure on 'all food', and on the ith sub-item of the group respectively, C_f is the concentration index of the whole group concerned, i.e., 'all food', and C_i is the concentration index for the ith sub-item of the group. Using Equation (9.1), we can re-express the above Equation (9.2) as follows

$$C_f = \frac{1}{E_f} \sum_{i=1}^{6} E_i \{I_{ei} + G\}$$

$$= \frac{1}{E_f} \sum_{i=1}^{6} E_i I_{ei} + \frac{1}{E_f} \sum_{i=1}^{6} E_i G$$

$$C_f - G = \frac{1}{E_f} \sum_{i=1}^{6} E_i I_{ei}; \qquad because \quad E_f = \sum_{i=1}^{6} E_i$$

$$I_{ef} = \frac{1}{E_f} \sum_{i=1}^{6} E_i I_{ei} \qquad (9.3)$$

This shows that the elasticity index of 'all food' is the weighted average of its individual sub-items.

5.1   Computation of Elasticity Index

The elasticity index given above in Equation (9.1) is now estimated for various Australian food items, using the Kakwani and Podder (1976) Lorenz curve (8.1) discussed in Chapter 8. The ordinary least squares (OLS) method is used to estimate Equation (8.1) of Chapter 8, after taking the logarithm on both sides. Table 9.12 presents the estimated parameters of the Lorenz equation (8.1) together with the values of the coefficient of determination (R^2) between the actual and estimated values of V for all the commodities. It is noted that R^2 is generally very high for all the commodities. It is mentioned here that the original and estimated values of V are very close, up to two decimal places for the entire range of the expenditure. This shows that Equation (8.1) fits well for the Australian data.

Concentration indices and elasticity indices are also given in this Table 9.12. Figures of the Gini indices for per capita total expenditure and income show that per capita family total expenditure is more equally distributed than per capita family income. Further, it is seen from this table that most of the food items are evenly distributed among households except 'meals in restaurants and hotels' and 'snacks and take-away food' in Australia. 'Meals in restaurants and hotels' is very unevenly distributed in Australia. This may imply that higher income households take meals in restaurants and hotels more frequently than poorer households, probably because these foods are more expensive than other foods. Elasticity indices for both per capita total expenditure and income are also given in Table 9.12. The estimate of elasticity index for 'meals in restaurants and hotels' indicates that this item is highly elastic, which means that if household total expenditure is increased by 1%, a household is likely to increase expenditure on this item by more than 1%. 'Snacks and take-away food' appears to have very small elasticity. The total of 'all food' items is also inelastic probably because of a large share of expenditure on other food items. It should be noted here that most food items turn out to be inelastic in Australia.

The contribution of each food item to the elasticity index of 'all food' is presented in Table 9.13. If the elasticity index of 'all food' is taken to be – 100.00, then the contributions of bread, cakes, cereals, dairy products, oils and fats; meat and fish; fruits and vegetables; and miscellaneous foods are –53, –529, –517 and –27 respectively. 'Meals in restaurants and hotels' and 'snacks and take away food' are elastic, and their contributions are 21 and 5 respectively. This indicates that 'meals in restaurants and hotels' is a major expenditure item in total household food expenditure. If this item was not included, 'all food' would become highly inelastic. This indicates that it would not be appropriate to estimate elasticity for 'all food' as a single group rather than individual food items, which are much needed for future food projection, production, marketing and distribution purposes.

6. ESTIMATING CHANGE IN CONSUMER DEMAND DUE TO CHANGES IN INCOME AND INCOME INEQUALITY

We now estimate the increase in consumer demand for various food items due to the rise in total expenditure and changes in total expenditure inequalities in Australia. The new co-ordinate system of the Lorenz equation (8.1) introduced by

Table 9.12. Estimates of the Lorenz function and the elasticity index of the various food items in Australia: 1975 to 1976

Food items	α_i	β_i	γ_i	R^2	Concentration index	Elasticity index	
						Total expenditure	Income
(1) Bread, cakes, cereals, oils & dairy products	0.0319	0.9231	1.1318	0.9199	0.0295	-0.213	-0.312
(2) Meat & fish	0.1034	0.8184	0.9128	0.9955	0.1115	-0.1305	-0.230
(3) Fruits & vegetables	0.1187	1.0192	0.9423	0.9789	0.1142	-0.1278	-0.2276
(4) Miscellaneous foods	0.0715	0.8888	0.9261	0.9820	0.0738	-0.1682	-0.2680
(5) Meals in restaurants & hotels	0.5064	0.9983	0.9763	0.9968	0.4835	+0.2460	+0.1417
(6) Snacks & take-away food	0.2384	0.9464	1.0285	0.9926	0.2278	+0.0580	-0.1140
(7) All foods	0.1286	0.9445	0.8387	0.9979	0.13451	-0.107	-0.207
(8) Per capita total expenditure	0.2369	.09561	0.8827	0.9996	0.2420	-	-
(9) Per capita income	0.3199	0.8568	0.8890	0.9997	0.3418	-	-

Source: The 1975 -1976 Australian HES data based on the 12 weekly per capita income groups supplied by the ABS.

*Table 9.13. Decomposition of the elasticity index of all food
with respect to its individual food items*

Food items	Per capita expenditure on each item	Percentage expenditure on each item	Elasticity index	Contribution to the total elasticity index	Percentage contribution
(1) Bread, cakes, cereals, oils & dairy products	2.90	26.62	-0.213	-0.0566	- 53.00
(2) Meat & fish	2.61	23.96	-0.1305	-0.0313	- 29.00
(3) Fruits & vegetables	1.56	14.32	-0.1278	-0.0183	- 17.00
(4) Miscellaneous foods	1.84	16.90	-0.1682	-0.0284	- 27.00
(5) Meals in restaurants & hotels	0.99	9.10	+0.2460	+0.0224	+ 21.00
(6) Snacks & take-away food	0.99	9.09	+0.0580	+0.0053	+ 5.00
(7) All foods	10.89	100	-0.1069	-0.1069	-100.00

Source: The 1975-1976 Australian HES data based on the 12 weekly per capita income groups supplied by the ABS.

Kakwani and Podder (1976) given in Chapter 8 is also used for this purpose. More details about the general formulation and estimation of the increase in consumer demand can also be found from Chapter 8.

We have estimated the increase in consumer demand with respect to various percentage increases in per capita total expenditure and various percentage changes of the Lorenz ratio by changing only two parameters (one for increasing income and another for changing Lorenz ratio) of the Lorenz equation. There was no effect from other parameters on the changes in consumer demand. The percentage changes in demand estimates based on various changes of level of total expenditure and total expenditure inequalities for various food items are presented in Table 9.14.

Table 9.14 shows that the percentage change in demand effectively increases with per capita total expenditure, and with the decrease of the Lorenz ratio for all food items except 'meals in restaurants and hotels'. This shows that for food items, which are considered to be necessary because their elasticities lie between 0.00 and 1.00, the percentage change in demand for those food items would increase as the Lorenz ratio decreases. On the other hand, the percentage change in demand decreases even if total expenditure inequality reduces for 'meals in restaurants and hotels', which is considered to be a luxury item in Australia. These findings are quite consistent with the findings of Iyengar (1960b), who argued that the percentage change would rise/fall for necessary and luxury goods as the Lorenz ratio decreases.

It is also noted that the percentage increases in demand for a commodity due to changes in per capita total expenditure are directly linked with its elasticity. For example, the elasticity of 'meat and fish' is 0.44 and its demand rises only 10.03% for a 20% rise in per capita total expenditure. But the demand rises as much as 41.83% for a similar rise in per capita income for 'meals in restaurant and hotels', whose elasticity is 2.47. It should be noted that these estimates are based on a simple relationship of per capita expenditure on each food item, and per capita total household expenditure for 12 per capita household income groups.

In another direction, if the per capita total expenditure increases by 50% and the Lorenz ratio decreases by 10%, then the per capita increases in demand for 'fruits and vegetables' and 'meals in restaurants and hotels' are 21.4% and 113.97% respectively. However, if one does not consider the effect of change in the Lorenz ratio, then the percentage increase in demand for the above items would be 20.09% and 119.04% respectively. In general, this investigation shows that the estimation of demand for 'fruits and vegetables' and 'meals in restaurants and hotels' would be under/over estimated for necessary/luxury food items if the effects of income distributions are not considered. However, overall income distribution has no significant effect on the estimation of demand for most of the food items except 'meals in restaurants and hotels'. This again reconfirms that in estimating increase in food demand, it would be inappropriate to use the aggregate elasticity for 'all food', and hence dis-aggregation of 'all food' by different types of food is essential for proper food planning, marketing and projection purposes.

7. LIMITATIONS AND CONCLUSIONS

Investigation of household expenditure patterns of various food items based on a general survey is problematic. More importantly, examining only food items does not provide an accurate picture of the living conditions of households because household expenditure depends on many expenditure items, which have a significant impact on living standards. All our estimates are based on grouped data and hence estimated Engel elasticities loose their large sample properties. Expenditure elasticities of various food items also cause problems in estimating logarithmic/inverse Engel functions due to lack of grouped geometric/harmonic means, as well as simultaneous nature of the model, when single equation models are estimated by the Aitken's (1934) GLS method. However, both of these problems are dealt with procedures developed in this book and elasticities are estimated for various food items, using appropriate methods.

Elasticity estimates indicate most food items are necessary in Australia except 'meals in restaurants and hotels'. This latter food item is considered to be a luxury item on the grounds that its elasticity is significantly higher than unity and its demand decreases with the decrease of income inequality, a criterion emphasized by Iyengar (1960b). We have observed that the elasticity estimates for various food items decrease with the rise of income levels, which is expected for food demand analysis. More importantly, we have noted that elasticity estimates remain more or less stable, when the income level reaches A$280 or more for most of the food items except 'meals in restaurants and hotels'. This is quite encouraging, since levels of saturation must be attained for all food items at some income level. The elasticity estimate for 'meals in restaurants and hotels' continues to decrease up to the highest income level, indicating it is highly likely that households are not willing to spend more money on this food item as they get more and more money in their hands. It should be noted that these elasticity estimates are computed from a specified function at some representative values (usually the means), which are arbitrary and hence subject to criticism.

There is no unique measurement of elasticity and for that reason we have estimated the elasticity index for each food item, which is a single measure of elasticity or inelasticity of a commodity. However, it should be used with caution, because the magnitude of the elasticity index indicates how much the elasticity of the ith commodity deviates from unity over the full range of total expenditure (income). Hence, this measure is only used for comparative purposes. The advantage of this index is that it can be computed from grouped data without specifying any particular Engel function. Additionally, we have decomposed the elasticity index of 'all foods' into its individual food items to see the contributions of each food item to the total food elasticity index. More importantly, as in Chapter 8, here we have also provided an estimate of increase in consumer demand of various food items due to an increase in income and a decrease in income inequality. It is thus hoped that these estimates will describe the real picture of the quantitative nature of food expenditure in Australia, because it incorporates the effect of total expenditure (income) distribution along with the rise of total expenditure (income).

CHAPTER 9

Table 9.14. Percentage increase in consumer demand (per capita)

Commodity groups	Percentage increase in per capita expenditure (100α)	Percentage change in Lorenz ratio (100β)						Best functional form* chosen by the D^2 criterion	Corresponding elasticity of the best function
		10	5	0	-5	-10	-20		
(1) Bread, cakes & cereals	0	-0.653	-0.3176	0.00	0.3003	0.5836	1.1004		
	5	-0.0277	0.3077	0.6253	0.9256	1.2089	1.7257		
	10	0.5226	0.858	1.1756	1.4759	1.7592	2.276	DSL	0.11
	20	1.4238	1.7592	2.0768	2.3771	2.6604	3.1773		
	50	3.0639	3.21	3.5279	3.8282	4.1115	4.6284		
(2) Meat & fish	0	-2.0534	-0.9986	0.00	0.9437	1.8337	3.4571		
	5	0.7573	1.7904	2.7680	3.6915	4.5620	6.1489		
	10	3.3824	4.3940	5.3508	6.2543	7.1056	8.6567	LI	0.44
	20	8.1419	9.1116	10.0279	10.8925	11.7067	13.1888		
	50	19.3985	20.2542	21.0615	21.8219	22.5370	23.8358		
(3) Dairy products, oils & fats	0	-0.5298	-0.2566	0.00	0.2408	0.4663	0.8740		
	5	0.1933	0.4554	0.7015	0.9324	1.1487	1.5395		
	10	0.8553	1.1071	1.3435	1.5653	1.7731	2.1484	LI	0.11
	20	2.0243	2.2577	2.4769	2.6825	2.8750	3.2227		
	50	4.6440	4.8355	5.1052	5.1837	5.3414	5.6262		
4) Fruits and vegetables	0	-0.8810	-0.4295	0.00	0.4077	0.7938	1.5019		
	5	1.3269	1.7884	2.2275	2.6442	3.0390	3.7628		
	10	3.4778	3.9491	4.3975	4.8231	5.2262	5.9654	DL	0.45
	20	7.6242	8.1144	8.5807	9.0234	9.4426	10.211		
	50	19.0331	19.5753	20.0910	20.5806	21.0443	21.894		

* Symbols of the functional forms are defined in Section 3.1.1 of Chapter 3.

Source: The 1975-76 Australian HES data based on the 12 weekly per capita income groups supplied by the ABS.

(Table 9.14. Continued)

(5) Miscellane-ous foods	0	-1.3536	-0.6570	0.00	0.6189	1.2007	2.2575		
	5	0.4968	1.1724	1.8096	2.4096	2.9735	3.9974		
	10	2.2090	2.8648	3.4831	4.0651	4.6121	5.6047	LI	0.29
	20	5.2758	5.8949	6.4782	7.0271	7.5426	8.4776		
	50	12.3507	12.8790	13.3761	13.8434	14.2818	15.076		
(6) Meals in restaurants &hotels	0	5.675	2.7604	0	-2.6097	-5.0718	-9.5639		
	5	15.2118	12.2971	9.5367	6.9269	4.4647	-0.0274		
	10	25.4007	22.486	19.7254	17.1156	14.6533	10.1611	DSL	2.47
	20	47.51	44.5952	41.8345	39.2245	36.7622	32.2696		
	50	124.7212	121.806	119.045	116.435	113.972	109.478		
(7) Snacks, take-away food	0	-4.1884	-2.0484	0	1.9558	3.8184	7.2603		
	5	1.5679	3.7274	5.7922	7.7619	9.6359	13.095		
	10	7.1005	9.2731	11.3485	13.3265	15.207	18.6742	LI	.091
	20	17.5176	19.7009	21.7833	23.765	25.6463	29.1082		
	50	44.1411	46.2795	48.3118	50.2394	52.0635	55.4062		
(8) All foods	0	-0.3619	-0.176	0	0.1664	0.3234	0.6097		
	5	2.3862	2.5721	2.7481	2.9145	3.0714	3.3578		
	10	5.0927	5.2785	5.4545	5.6209	5.7779	6.0642	DSL	0.55
	20	10.3951	10.5809	10.7569	10.9233	11.0802	11.3665		
	50	25.6077	25.7935	25.9695	26.1358	26.2927	26.579		

CHAPTER 10

DEMAND FOR TRANSPORT AND COMMUNICATION

In this chapter, we investigate the expenditure pattern of the transport and communication item, since it is the second highest expenditure item in Australia. The percentage expenditure on transport and communication with respect to total expenditure is examined for various household compositions, income levels and ethnicity. We have also estimated total expenditure elasticity for this item based on several alternative Engel functions. But, we only provide total expenditure elasticity estimated from the double semi-log Engel function, because this function dominates other functions on the basis of the distance function D^2-criterion, and the non-nested hypothesis testing procedure as we have seen in Chapter 3. The percentage changes in consumer demand due to changes in total expenditure and total expenditure inequalities are also discussed. The results of the analyses demonstrate that transport and communication is a necessary item in Australia on the basis of two criteria, viz., its elasticity is not significantly greater than unity, and the demand increases with the decrease of the total expenditure inequalities, a criterion emphasized by Iyengar (1960b). Policy implications of the analyses on 'transport and communication' have also been discussed.[66]

1. INTRODUCTION

Transport and communication is very important, not only because it shows the indication of people to go from one place to another, but also it is the second highest expenditure item in Australian family budgets. The percentage of expenditure on 'transport and communication' indicates the dynamics of an individual for socio-economic linkages in the society. The higher the percentage of expenditure on 'transport and communication', the better the socio-economic links within the society and probably creates better prospects for socio-economic development. Hence, it is better to undertake a thorough investigation into the variation of expenditure on 'transport and communication' for different household characteristics. However, the scope for such an analysis is severely limited due to the variation of definitions of the commodity itself from survey to survey, and even the income classes reported in the surveys for classifying households also differ in various HESs in Australia. In the present analysis, we investigate the possible

---

[66] This is a revised version of a paper earlier published in *Transportatipon* [see Haque 91992)].

variations of 'transport and communication' expenditure among households based on various socio-economic and ethnic characteristics.

The present chapter is organized as follows. The patterns of 'transport and communication' expenditure for various household compositions, income levels and ethnicity are provided in Section 2. Section 3 is mainly concerned with the estimation of income elasticity for the 'transport and communication' item for various socio-economic and demographic characteristics. While, the effects of demand on the 'transport and communication' item due to an increase in total expenditure and a decrease in income inequalities are discussed in Section 4. The implication of this research for transport planning is discussed in Section 5. Section 6 deals with problems and future options, and finally some concluding remarks are made in the final section.

2. EXPENDITURE PATTERN OF 'TRANSPORT AND COMMUNICATION' BY CITY, HOUSEHOLD COMPOSITION, INCOME LEVEL AND ETHNICITY

Australia is a big country and its business centres are scattered far and wide. It also has a very well developed transport network system across all its cities, which encourages people to travel from one end to other. These, together with government taxation policies, increase high transport exposure. In this chapter, we investigate whether low-income households have a different 'transport and communication' expenditure pattern from those of high-income households. Further, expenditure patterns of 'transport and communication' will also be investigated to see whether there are any differences in expenditure patterns among various household compositions and ethnic groups in Australia.

It is clear from Table 9.1 of Chapter 9 that 'transport and communication' is the second highest expenditure item in Australian family budgets. More importantly, percentages of expenditures on the 'transport and communication' item are provided for different cities at different times in Table 9.1. It shows that inter city variation of 'transport and communication' expenditure is more or less similar, even though Melbourne, Perth and Canberra spend a higher percentage of total household expenditure than other cities in Australia. The high quality environment and landscape surrounding these cities may encourage people to travel more, which may be responsible for higher expenditure on 'transport and communication' in these cities than others. It is interesting to note that percentage expenditure on 'transport and communication' remains more or less stable over time.

Table 10.1. *Per capita expenditure on transport and communication for sole parent and married couple households with children*

Per capita expenditure/week in A$					
Sole parent households with dependent children			Married couple households with dependent children		
1	2	3 or more	1	2	3 or more
31.52	20.91	9.49	27.27	22.24	17.71

Source: The Australian 1988-1989 HES Unit Record Tape supplied by the ABS.

Per capita expenditure per week (in Australian dollars) on 'transport and communication' is presented in Table 10.1. It is clear from this table that sole parent with one-child households spend the highest per capita expenditure on 'transport and communication'. This is probably because these households may drive a car with only two people, who pay all the expenses to run a car like other households, but are unable to save from economies of scale that may arise due to larger households. It is also apparent from the above table that per capita expenditure for 'transport and communication' decreases as the number of people in the household increases, probably because larger households may make greater savings due to economies of scale. It should be noted that married couple households with three or more children spend approximately twice as much as sole parent households with three or more children. This probably happens due to the fact that usually at least one member of a married couple household works, which may require long distance travel to go and come from work, while most sole parent households are unemployed [see Haque (1996)] and they only drive short distances to go to schools, shops and visit friends mostly in their neighbourhood.

Percentages of total expenditure on 'transport and communication' for various household compositions are also presented in Table 10.2. This table shows that percentages of total expenditures on 'transport and communication' are more or less stable over time for most of the household types except two adults with three or more children households. In later years, the latter type of households may spend less on 'transport and communication' probably because of government subsidies for those households who have two or more children allow them free travel in public transport.

Table 10.2. Percentage of total expenditure on transport and communication by household composition

| Year | Household compositions | | | | | |
	One adult only	One adult with children	Two adults	Two adults, one child	Two adults, two children	Two adults & three or more children
1974-75	13.46	14.85	16.05	16.26	16.40	15.06
1975-76	16.67	14.26	19.30	19.57	18.34	18.58
1984	13.46	13.78	16.19	15.96	14.13	14.50
1988-89	13.51	14.64	15.37	12.53	13.51	13.59
1993-94	14.57	12.96	15.15	16.46	14.13	13.20
1998-99	14.26	14.16	16.85	16.96	17.25	13.35

Source: The Australian Household Expenditure Surveys: 1974-1975 to 1998-199.

Table 10.3. Percentage of total expenditure of transport and communication by household income quintile groups in Australia: 1993-94 and 19998-99.

| Years | Gross income quintiles | | | | | |
	Lowest quintile	2nd quintile	3rd quintile	4th quintile	Highest quintile	All House-holds
1993/94	13.25	15.26	15.58	16.26	15.83	15.54
1998/99	14.04	14.98	16.24	18.19	17.72	16.85

Source: The 1993-1994 and 1998-1999 Australian HES data conducted by the ABS.

The percentages of total expenditure on 'transport and communication' in various income quintiles are presented in Table 10.3. This shows that households of all income quintiles spent a higher percentage of total expenditure in 1998-99 than in 1993-94. Higher petrol prices and transport costs may be the cause for such a higher percentage of total expenditure in more recent years in Australia than previous years. It is also interesting to note that percentage of total expenditure increases as households move from lower to higher income quintiles except the highest quintile. This implies that to earn more and more money, household members have to travel more from one place to another place and probably they also have larger family size. However, percentage expenditures are lower in the highest quintile group than in the 4th quintile group. This may probably happen due to the fact that the households of the highest income quintile group may have a high proportion of retired and rich households with one or two people, who have less exposure with more expensive cars.

*Table 10.4. Average per capita expenditure of transport and communication
for various ethnic households by reference person's age over
65 and under 65 years: 1988 to 1989**

Age of reference person	Ethnic background (place of birth)				
			NESC		
	Australia	ESC	All	Asia & Africa	Europe
Under 65 years	30.65 (15.11)	31.70 (14.70)	26.96 (14.71)	23.52 (13.42)	28.89 (15.41)
Over 65 years	23.78 (12.67)	27.40 (13.82)	31.96 (15.18)	54.92 (21.72)	26.25 (13.13)

*   Percentage expenditure on transport and communication with respect to total expenditure are
presented in parentheses.

Source: The Australian 1988-1989 HES Unit Record Tape supplied by the ABS.

Table 10.4 shows that when a household reference person's age is less than 65 years, ESB households spend more money on 'transport and communication' on a per capita basis, but their percentage of expenditure on 'transport and communication' is less than any other ethnic groups. This implies that their expenditures on other items are also higher than other ethnic groups. On the contrary, households from Asia and Africa spend significantly less money on transport and communication, and their percentage expenditure on this item with respect to total expenditure is also lower than any other groups when the reference person's age is lower than 65 years. This implies that migrants from Asia and Africa have low exposure in the early phase of their lives in Australia, probably because of their high unemployment situation and unawareness of the locality, which is quite expected from early settlers in a new country. On the other hand, households from Asia and Africa, whose reference person's age is more than 65 years, spend more money on a per capita basis, and their percentage expenditure on 'transport and communication' with respect to total expenditure is also significantly higher than any other groups. This may probably happen due to the isolation of older migrants from Asia and Africa, who do not have many family members and friends at an old age. As a result these people do not get any or very little assistance from other people to travel to any place, and pay a very high travel costs (probably by hiring a taxi). However, per capita and percentage expenditure with respect to total expenditure on 'transport and communication' for older Australian households are significantly less than any other groups, probably because these people may get reasonable travel assistance from family members, friends and neighbours, which is quite expected from their own countrymen.

3. ESTIMATION OF INCOME ELASTICITY FOR TRANSPORT AND
COMMUNICATION ITEM

In the previous section, we analysed the expenditure patterns of the 'transport and communication' item by various socio-economic and ethnic characteristics in Australia, which are both important and interesting, but not sophisticated. In this section we will estimate total expenditure elasticity for the 'transport and communication' item in Australia. Elasticity estimate for this item is important, because it provides the percentage change in expenditure on 'transport and communication' due to a 1% rise in household total expenditure (income), which is very helpful for planning and forecasting purposes.

In the past, a number of authors, viz., Podder (1971), Williams (1976a, 1976b, 1977), McRae (1980), Morris and Wigan (1977, 1978, 1979), Bewley (1982) and Haque (1993) etc., analysed the Australian HES data, using various Engel functions. They attempted to give a picture of the broad spectrum of the Australian household expenditure pattern. More importantly, their findings clearly indicate that the 'transport and communication' is a luxury item in Australia on the basis that its elasticity estimate is greater than unity.[67]

This chapter has two basic aims. First, we will find a best Engel functional form from various alternatives for the 'transport and communication' item. Second, we estimate total expenditure elasticity on the basis of this best functional form in order to examine whether the previous elasticity estimates are affected by using a new Engel function, which may be different from those used in previous studies.

To find a best Engel function among various alternatives, we have used two criteria: (i) the distance function, D^2-criterion; and (ii) the non-nested hypothesis testing procedure; which have already been discussed extensively in Chapter 3. We then estimate total expenditure elasticity on the basis of an Engel function, which will turn out to be the best among various alternative functional forms.

3.1 Data

The 1988-89 Australian HES data obtained from unit tape records were used for this study. This survey was designed to find out how the expenditure pattern of private households varies according to different income levels and characteristics. Most of the information was collected from households on a recall basis with a particular reference period (which varies according to the type of expenditure), using interview techniques. In addition, all members of households aged 15 years and over were requested to record all 'expenditure related to goods acquired during the reference period' over a two-week period in a diary provided to each of them. The stratified multi-stage probability (proportional to the households and collector's districts) sampling procedure was followed for selecting 7500 households, which

[67] Many other authors such as Working (1943), Prais and Houthakker (1955), Summers (1959), Leser (1963), Kakwani (1977b), Bewley (1982), Giles and Hampton (1985), Hoa (1986), Haque (1991a), Alperovich, Deutsch and Machnes (1999), and Shahabi-Azad (2001) have also estimated income elasticity for the transport and communication item for a number of other countries.

were interviewed evenly over the enumeration period (July 1988 – July 1989) to ensure that seasonal expenditure patterns did not affect the final data. Any expenditure made by members of the selected households for business purposes were not considered in the survey. The survey collected 'household expenditure' which included expenditures on those goods (both durable and non-durable) and services by the members of the selected households for private consumption. Other components of household expenditure such as income tax, superannuation contributions, life insurance premiums, purchases of and deposits on dwellings and land are classified as 'other payments'.

In this chapter, the broad 'transport and communication' item includes the purchase of cars and other vehicles (net of sales and insurance claims); petrol, oils and lubricants; vehicle registration and insurance; other running expenses of vehicles (tyres, tubes, spare parts, accessories, crash repairs and services, license fees etc.); rail, bus, tram and other public transport (excluding holiday fares) freight; and air fares, etc. However, postal charges, telephones and telegrams are also included.

3.2 Choice of Functional Form

In order to choose a best Engel function, we have fitted all seven functional forms given in Section 2.1 of Chapter 3, and functional forms (iii) to (vii) [share inverse, Working-Leser, Addilig, log share-linear, and log share-inverse] of Section 4 of Chapter 9. Note that functional forms (i) and (vii) of Section 2.1 of Chapter 3, and (iii) to (vii) of Section 9.2 of Chapter 9, all satisfy the adding-up criterion, which asserts that the sum of expenditures on a set of mutually exclusive and exhaustive expenditure items should add up to total expenditure. The ordinary least squares (OLS) method is used to estimate each of the above 12 equations in order to find a best Engel function from these alternatives based on the distance function D^2-criterion.

The values of the distance function D^2-statistic for different Engel curves for the 'transport and communication' item are presented in Table 10.5. A function would be regarded as the best fit among various alternatives whose D^2-statistic is smaller. The figures from Table 10.5 clearly indicate that the double semi-log (DSL) Engel function performs best when compared with other functions, although there is little difference between the linear, addilog, log share inverse and DSL functions.

We have also used the Mackinnon, White and Davidson (1983) non-nested hypothesis testing procedure to compare the different Engel functions, which has already been discussed in Chapter 3. This test has been applied on a pair-wise basis for all non-nested Engel functions considered for this study and the values of the t-statistic for the 'transport and communication' item have been calculated.[68] Many interesting and important observations are made from these results for the transport and communication item. First, in many two-way comparisons, both functional

---

[68] These t-values are not significantly different from the results obtained from the 1975-76 HES data, which are presented in Table 3.1 of Chapter 3.

forms are rejected. For example the linear form is rejected when tested against the semi-log form, and similarly the semi-log form is also rejected against the linear form. Second, all the LLI, DSL, LSL and LSI forms are accepted against each other and all other forms treating each of the other forms as H_1. The DSL Engel function is also accepted against all functions. The hyperbolic, semi-log and log-inverse functions are rejected against most of the other functions. On the whole, the non-nested hypothesis testing procedure suggests that the DSL is the most suitable functional form for the 'transport and communication' item.

Thus, on the grounds of goodness of fit and the non-nested hypothesis testing procedure, it turns out that the DSL Engel function fits well to the 'transport and communication' item for the 1988-89 Australian HES data. Thus, all our subsequent analyses will be based on the DSL Engel function.

The estimated equation of the DSL function is given by

$$\hat{Y} = -2.3244 + 0.1885\ X + 0.7661\ \text{Log } X + 0.3259\ \text{Log } S; \qquad R^2 = 0.7896$$
$$(0.232)\quad (0.0418)\quad (0.302)\qquad\quad (0.072)$$

The estimated standard errors for different parameters are presented in parentheses.[69] This clearly shows that all the estimated parameters of the DSL function are significantly different from zero. No serious multicollinearity problem is observed between X and Log X.

Table 10.5. D^2-statistics for various functional forms

Functional forms	D^2-statistics
Linear (L)	0.0592
Semi-log (SL)	0.0819
Hyperbolic (Hyp)	0.1268
Double-log (DL)	0.0830
Log-inverse (LI)	0.1587
Log log-inverse (LLI)	0.0645
Double-semi-log (DSL)	0.0503
Share inverse (SI)	0.0672
Working-Leser (WL)	0.0686
Addilog (AL)	0.0567
Log share linear (LSL)	0.0756
Log share inverse (LSI)	0.0588

Source: The Australian 1988-1989 HES Unit Record Tape supplied by the ABS.

[69] The estimated parameters of the DSL function for the 1988-1989 HES data are not significantly different from that of the 1975-1976 HES data.

3.3 Estimation of Engel Elasticity

Total expenditure elasticity is estimated on the basis of the DSL Engel function. The empirical estimation of the total expenditure elasticity is very important, which can be calculated using the following formula

$$\eta = (\beta \, X + \gamma) / (\alpha + \beta \, X + \gamma \log X + \delta \log S) \qquad (10.1)$$

This shows that the elasticity for the DSL Engel function increases with the rise of total expenditure of the household. The rate at which the proportional expenditure on the 'transport and communication' item changes with total expenditure is already given in Equation (3.5) of Chapter 3.

We have estimated the total expenditure elasticity at mean values of total expenditure and family size for the Australian 'transport and communication' item, using the above Equation (10.1). It turns out that the estimated elasticity for the 'transport and communication' item is 1.19 with an estimated standard error of 0.16. The conventional one-tailed t-test at the 5% level of significance shows that the estimated elasticity for the 'transport and communication' item is not significantly greater than unity, when the value of the elasticity estimate 1 is tested in the null hypothesis against greater than 1 in the alternative hypothesis. This shows that 'transport and communication' is a necessary, *not a luxury* item in Australia.

Expenditure shares and estimated elasticities at various per capita income levels are expected to give the real picture of the expenditure behaviour of the 'transport and communication' item in Australia. Hence, these are of great importance to the transport planner for future operational and construction point of view. These values for 'transport and communication' item are presented in Table 10.6

Table 10.6. Expenditure shares, and elasticities at different weekly per capita income levels

Income groups*	$30	$50	$70	$100	$150	$200	$250	$300	$350	$400	$500	$700	ALL
Expenditure share in	18.3	17.5	22.5	23.7	22.9	21.6	19.2	17.6	17.7	17.0	14.5	17.2	19.7
Elasticities	1.69	1.44	1.26	1.12	0.92	0.85	0.75	0.70	0.68	0.69	0.65	0.66	1.19

* These income groups are given in Footnote 22, supplied by the ABS.

Source: The Australian 1988-1989 HES Unit Record Tape supplied by the ABS

It is clear from Table 10.6 that the share of expenditure on the 'transport and communication' item varies from one per capita income level to another per capita income level. The higher share of expenditure on the 'transport and communication' item is observed for the $70 - $250 income groups, meaning those households who work but do not get a higher salary probably due to inexperience at a young age, but want to drive more new and sophisticated cars and want to travel more at a young age. This might cause high expenditure on the 'transport and communication' item, due to the purchase of new cars and their maintenance. However the expenditure share on this item is relatively lower for higher income households, probably because of their low family size and low transport exposure. On the other hand, the elasticity estimate shows that transport is a luxury item to poorer households whose weekly per capita incomes are lower probably because of low income and larger family size. While, elasticity estimates show that the 'transport and communication' item is a necessary item to the majority of Australian households. We have also estimated the total expenditure elasticities at mean values for various sole parent and married couple households with children, which are presented in Table 10.7

Table 10.7 clearly shows that 'transport and communication' is a necessary good for most households except sole parent households with two or more children, when the conventional one-tailed t-test is applied, taking the elasticity value $\eta = 1$ as the null hypothesis (Ho), against the elasticity value $\eta > 1$ as alternative hypothesis H_1.

Further, in order to avoid the problem of simultaneity of the model indicated by Summers (1959), because of using total expenditure as one of the independent variables in a single equation, we have re-estimated the parameters of the DSL Engel function by the Instrumental matrix approach [vide. Liviatan (1961)], using Equation (3.5) of Chapter 3, and obtained the consistent estimates of the parameters of the DSL function.

Using the consistent estimates of the parameters of the DSL Engel function, we have re-estimated the total expenditure elasticity at mean values. The consistent estimate of the total expenditure elasticity for the 'transport and communication' item turns out to be 1.16 with an asymptotic standard error of 0.16. The standard one-tailed t-test again suggests that this elasticity estimate is not significantly greater than 1. This finding further re-confirms our earlier conclusion that 'transport and communication' is a necessary item to most of the Australian households.

Table 10.7. Estimates of total expenditure elasticity of transport and
communication for sole parent and married couple households
*with children**

Per Capita expenditure					
Sole parent households with dependent children			Married couple households with dependent Children		
1	2	3 or more	1	2	3 or more
0.78	2.14	2.74	1.18	1.08	0.87
(0.24)	(0.19)	(0.15)	(0.22)	(0.17)	(0.23)
[215]	[139]	[66]	[537]	[961]	[581]

* Estimates of standard errors are presented in parentheses ( ). Number of households on which these
estimates are based are given in brackets [ ].

Source: The Australian 1988-1989 HES Unit Record Tape supplied by the ABS.

It should be noted that in the present study, a statistical significance test is done on the estimated elasticity of the transport and communication item and it is shown that this is a necessary item on the grounds that its elasticity is less than 1. While previous authors such as Podder (1971), Williams (1976a), Morris and Wigan (1979), McRae (1980), Bewley (1982 and Haque (1984) classified transport and communication as a luxury item on the basis that its elasticity is greater than unity. Thus, it has been proved in this chapter that the elasticity estimate, when interpreted more scientifically, is different from the previous interpretation.

The results of the present analyses contradicted with the previous findings made by many authors who found that transport and communication was a luxury item in Australia. This might have happened due to different interpretations of the estimated elasticity, the uses of different functional forms and data sets together with the variation of the definition of the item. Moreover, it is observed that the previous elasticity estimates are based mainly on the double logarithmic functions with few exceptions (viz., the Klen-Rubin and Addilog functions), which usually produces high elasticity estimates [see Prais and Houthakker (1955) and others]. Thus, the use of the appropriate HES data, functional form and more scientific interpretation of the estimated elasticity demonstrate that transport and communication is not a luxury, but a necessary item in Australia.

This shift could also occur due to the structural change in the economy as shown by Williams (1978a, 1978b, 1978c). This can be supported by the fact that the percentage expenditure on the transport and communication item with respect to total expenditure increased sharply from 9.6% in 1966 to 19.9% in 1975.

It is interesting to note that the 1975-76 HES data show that the percentage expenditure on transport and communication exceeds the percentage expenditure on food in Australia. This is an important observation, which has never been detected in Australia. This observation is very important for future planning in the transport industry including the transport safety area.

This rapid increase of expenditure on transport may be due to government policy on taxes and the availability of well-developed transport systems in Australia, in recent times. Re-distribution of the population in Australian cities is also a factor for such increases in expenditure on transport. Thus, social, demographic, economic and environmental factors are also responsible for such a change of elasticity estimate for the transport and communication item in Australia.

4. FURTHER EVIDENCE FROM INCOME DISTRIBUTION

Iyengar (1960b) demonstrated that the percentage change in demand would rise with the percentage decrease in the Lorenz ratio for necessary items. In order to verify Iyengar's preposition, we have estimated the percentage change in demand for the 'transport and communication' item due to the changes in the total expenditure and total expenditure inequalities at various levels, using the Kakwani-Podder (1976) Lorenz curve [see Chapter 8 for more details about this curve]. The empirical results are presented in Table 8.1 of Chapter 8, which is based on the 1975-76 HES data.[70]

The results of Table 8.1 for the 'transport and communication' item show that the percentage change in demand is effectively increased due to an increase in per capita total expenditure. More importantly, the percentage change in demand increases with the decrease of the Lorenz ratio, an attribute of a necessary item established by Iyengar (1960b). This is also satisfied for the 'transport and communication' item in Australia and is in accord with our earlier conclusion.

Interpretation of Table 8.1 is quite straightforward. For example, if the per capita total expenditure increases by 10% and the total expenditure inequality decreases by 10%, then the per capita increase in demand for the transport and communication item is 16.35%. However, if one does not consider the effect of the income inequality then the percentage increase in demand is fully accounted for by the percentage change in total expenditure. In that case the per capita increase in demand would be only 12.69%. Overall, this analysis shows that the per capita increase in demand for the 'transport and communication' item would be underestimated if the income distribution is not considered. These results are very helpful for transport policy decisions.

5. IMPLICATION OF THE RESEARCH ON TRANSPORT PLANNING

The HES data enable us to quantify the importance of transport vis-à-vis other household expenditure items. This also helps to show the variation of transport expenditure across population groups, time and space. Thus, it provides valuable information in forecasting transport demand. Knowledge of household expenditure by different income groups helps to assess the social impact for transport planning and policies. The relative importance of various expenditure items to different

---

[70] For this part of the analyses, we have used the ascending order of twelve per capita income (gross) grouped data of weekly expenditure on the transport and communication item, total expenditure and estimated number of households.

income groups and their shares in the total expenditure are very critical issues when assessing social impacts.

Income elasticity derived from the HES data is of considerable important to forecast the future transport demand from both operational and construction points of view. The HES data gives long-term elasticity because cross-sectional variations in real income are usually larger than the time series data. Income elasticities measure the responsiveness of expenditure due to change in income. It also helps to measure the relative importance of expenditure items for different income groups. Thus, elasticities indicate which groups are most likely to gain or lose due to changes in policies. Some policies will directly benefit particular groups more than others. For example, a reduction in bus fares will clearly benefit those people who use buses. However, the overall scale of the impacts is a crucial-factor. The car is an overwhelming important mode of transport to all income groups in Australia. Consequently, policies affecting private transport will have the greatest overall impact. For example, removal of car registration and insurance fees would be of great absolute benefit to low income groups rather than a reduction in bus fares, despite the fact that higher income groups would also benefit to a large extent. Newbridge (1999) also studied the benefit of transport networking through the Internet Protocol.

It should be noted that during 1990-1992 the Victorian Government (the motorist state in Australia) removed the car registration fees to increase the standard of living of the people of that state. We have noted that the effect of this measure was positive on the grounds that the demand for transpor increased by about 3%, even though there was no increase in real disposal household income in Australia. This might have happened due to the implementation of the government's social justice policy (equal distribution of wealth and spending is one of the government's policies). In this respect, our estimates of percentage increase in consumer demand due to an increase in total expenditure and a decrease in total expenditure inequality is useful to the planners for future transport planning.

Income elasticities provide some indication of the probable *ceteris-paribus*, long-term effects of any increase in income on consumption expenditures. The income elasticity when weighted by the budget share gives the proportion of income, which is expected to be spent on any particular item if income changes. In this regard, our analysis shows that the larger proportion of any increase in income will be spent on transport in Australia. This finding would really enhance the ability to estimate the transport demand, because we have seen from the 1988-1989 HES data that the highest proportion of household total expenditure has been spent on transport alone in Australia if 'meals in restaurants and hotels' was excluded from the 'all food items'.

6. PROBLEMS AND FUTURE OPTIONS

There are several limitations in using the HES data for transport planning, because demand numbers include the purchase of cars and other rolling stocks, which has nothing to do with a single year's income. However, economists generally work arguably with non-durable items and stock-flow demand problems. They cannot also tell us anything about the price responsiveness of demand, which is very important in times of high inflation and changing government policies with respect to taxes and tariffs. The Senate Regional Affairs and Transport Reference Committee of the Australian Parliament (1999) has studied deregulation of the Australian dairy industry and seriously investigated the effect of government policies of taxes and tariffs for the Australian dairy industry, which also significantly affects the transport industry.

The present study is based on individual data and therefore the estimated coefficients satisfy their large sample properties and the estimated elasticities are efficient. More importantly, our estimates are free from the problems raised due to using arithmetic means as a proxies for geometric and harmonic means to estimate logarithmic (such as log X and log S) or inverse (such as 1/X) functions when estimates are made from grouped data. More importantly, the survey did not collect data on the quantity of the commodity purchased by the households. As a result, it was not possible to estimate quality elasticity. Finally, we did not consider other economic, demographic, geographical and environmental factors, which might affect our calculated elasticities.

The present analysis did not consider anything about the demand for any specific form of transport like Morris and Wigan (1979) and Lubulwa (1986). This is important, because the sum purchase of cars and petrol is highly variable, since the two commodities are fundamentally different. The former is an investment in durable equipment and is largely unrelated to usage. It is subject to huge quality variation – the purchase of a car can entail expenditure anywhere in a wide range. It is also a 'lumpy' variable, because most households will have zero purchases, while a few have very large purchases within a survey year. In contrast, expenditure on petrol is very directly related to usage and therefore the demand for infrastructure is less subject to quality variation and is usually purchased in a regular way. It seems better to treat these items separately. Thus, a more detailed (item by item) analyses covering a number of years, and allowing the estimation of price effects based on individual data would be more interesting and left for further study.[71]

7. CONCLUSIONS

It is seen that the DSL Engel function turns out to be the best function on the basis of the distance function criterion and the non-nested hypothesis testing procedures. This function has the theoretically pleasing feature that it can automatically satisfy the adding-up criterion when the GLS estimation method is used [see Powell (1969) for proof], although it is not relevant for the current study. It can also satisfy the property of thresholds but does not attain the saturation level, which is quite expected for the expenditure on the transport and communication item.[72]

---

[71] Kayser (2000) and Bjorner (1999) studied petrol (gasoline) demand and car choice and car ownership, using household information, while Labeaga and Lopez (1997) studied petrol consumption for Spanish Panel data.

[72] See more about how to choose an appropriate functional form in Verbeek (2000).

For the first time, it is shown in this study that 'transport and communication' is a necessary item in Australia. This might have happened due to more scientific interpretation of the estimated income elasticity together with other factors such as the uses of the more appropriate DSL functional form, data sets and the structural change in the economy. We have also estimated the per capita increase in demand for transport and communication at various levels of per capita total expenditure and per capita total expenditure inequalities. This observation is very important for long-term transport planning in Australia, because it accurately assesses the distributional effects. This gives insights of the household expenditure pattern, which is important in forecasting transport demand. Thus, the estimates of total expenditure elasticity and the increased consumer demand due to changes in total expenditure and their inequalities have a tremendous value in evaluating the social impact of transport and its related components.

Overall, the present analysis demonstrates that transport and communication is a necessary item in Australia on the basis of two criteria viz.:

. its elasticity is not significantly greater than unity; and
. there is an increasing percentage change in demand with a decrease in the Lorenz ratio, which is a property for necessary goods as emphasized by Iyengar (1960b).

CHAPTER 11

DEMAND FOR ALCOHOL IN AUSTRALIA

Alcohol is an important part of Australian life and culture (NEACA 2001). More than half of Australian road fatalities are caused due to drink driving. Hence, it is useful to know the expenditure behaviour of Australian families on alcohol items. By reading this chapter, the readers will get an overview of expenditure patterns of some broadly defined alcohol items in Australia, using data from major Household Expenditure Surveys. We have fitted several alternative Engel functions and chose the best Engel function to estimate total expenditure elasticities for various alcohol items. It shows that beer has the lowest elasticity, whereas the elasticities for wine and spirits were much higher, placing them in the 'luxury' category. The readers will also learn how to calculate the elasticity index of various alcohol items including the contributions of different alcohol items to the total alcohol elasticity index. The percentage changes in demand due to changes in total expenditure and total expenditure inequalities were also calculated. It shows that the per capita changes in demand for beer and wine are inaccurate unless income distribution is considered. This technique can also be used to determine the level of consumption demand for various alcohol items.[73]

1. INTRODUCTION

Alcohol is a part of Australian life and culture. It is frequently associated with celebrations in Australia. It is consumed in religious and cultural ceremonies, social and business functions and also in recreational activities. There are many types of alcohol beverages: beers, wines and spirits, which have different characteristics of colour, taste and smell. Their effects, prices and market characteristics also vary. Makela et al. (1981) wrote a report for the International Study of Alcohol Control Experiences in collaboration with the World Health Organization Regional Office for Europe, which states that:

> ... because of the multiplicity of uses of alcohol and patterns of drinking, it may be misleading to treat aggregate consumption of alcohol as a unified variable.

Unfortunately, many authors, including Podder (1971), Williams (1976a, 1976b, 1977), McRae (1980), Morris and Wigan (1977, 1978, 1879), Bewley (1982), Haque

---

[73] This is a revised version of a paper published earlier in *Drug and Alcohol Review* [see Haque (1990b)].

(1984), Australian Bureau of Statistics (1999) and Heale et al. (2000) have used alcohol and tobacco as a single household consumption item for their demand analyses in Australia. In fact, they estimated total expenditure (income) elasticity for all alcohol and tobacco to give the percentage change in expenditure of this broad item due to a 1% change in household total expenditure (income). The estimate of total expenditure (income) elasticity of alcohol is very helpful for taxation policies, planning and forecasting purposes. It also helps to know the overall impact on the health status of the people of a community, because consumption of alcohol has an enormous effect on health.

Engel (1857) first formulated the empirical laws and established the relationship between income and expenditure on food. This kind of study has been done subsequently for other consumption items in different countries of the world. For example, Blake and Nied (1997) have studied the demand for alcohol in the UK, while Makela (1999) studied the differences in drinking habits and alcohol problems between various socio-demographic groups in the USA. The present chapter gives an overview of expenditure patterns of some broad individual alcohol items in Australia, using the HES data.

The basic aims of the present analysis are as follows. A comparison of the alternative Engel functions will be made to find a best functional form for each broad individual alcohol item. Engel elasticity will then be estimated for each individual 'alcohol item' on the basis of the best fitting functional form. An elasticity index will also be estimated to show how much the elasticity of a commodity deviates from unity over the whole income range. The contributions of sub-items to the inequality measure of 'all alcohol' have been considered by analysing the elasticity index of that broad group with respect to its sub-items. The percentage change in demand with respect to the percentage changes in total expenditure (income) and total expenditure (income) inequality will also be estimated to determine an appropriate level of consumption for various alcohol items.

This chapter is organized as follows. Expenditure patterns of alcohol items are discussed in Section 2. Section 3 deals with the models of Engel functions for various alcohol items, while elasticity estimates for different alcohol items are provided in Section 4. Section 5 provides the measurement of the elasticity index for various alcohol items. Estimation of change in consumer demand due to a change in income and income inequality is presented in Section 6. Some important discussions about this analysis are presented in the final section.

2. EXPENDITURE PATTERNS OF ALCOHOL ITEMS

Various Australian HES data are used for this analysis. Expenditure patterns of alcohol items will be examined to see whether there are any differences of expenditure patterns among various cities, household compositions and ethnic groups. More importantly, we investigate whether low-income households have different expenditure patterns of alcohol from those of high-income households.

The percentage expenditures on all alcohol and tobacco with respect to total household expenditure at different capital cities are presented in Table 9.1. These estimates are based on a number of Australian HES data, which were collected during the period 1967-68 to 1998-99. It is clear that the percentage expenditure on all alcohol and tobacco with respect to total household expenditure decreased consistently over the period 1967-68 to 1998-99 in all capital cities. On the whole, people living in Australian cities spend about 4% of their total expenditure on 'alcohol and tobacco'. But there are some variations, it looks like people who live in big cities like Sydney, Melbourne, Brisbane and Adelaide spend a little less than 4% on 'alcohol and tobacco', while people living in other relatively smaller cities spend about 5% of their total expenditure on this item. A large proportion of ethnic people who don't or consume less compared to Australian people may explain for such differences, because most migrants live in big cities like Sydney or Melbourne. This might also happen due to the fact that in small cities where there is not much recreational and/or amusement facilities, people usually consume alcohol as an amusement. The relative percentage expenditure on alcohol and tobacco in Australian cities decreased from 5.89% in 1974-75 to 4.10% in 1998-99 probably due to Government's higher excise and taxation policy on this item over the years.

Table 11.1 provides the percentages of total expenditure on alcohol items for various household compositions from 1974-75 to 1998-99. This table shows that the percentages of total expenditure on alcohol items have significantly reduced over time for all types of households. This might be due to government taxation policy to reduce alcohol consumption as well as highly publicized road safety campaigns that discourage people to 'drink and drive' in order to reduce the road toll. More importantly, it is observed from this table that households without children spend more on alcohol items than those households who have children. It is also noticed that the percentage of total expenditure on alcohol for households with children decreases as the number of children increases. This is expected because households with more children are required to spend their moneys on other essential items rather than on alcohol.

Table11.1. Percentages of total expenditure on alcohol for various household compositions: 1974-75 to 1998 to 1999

Household compositions					
Year	One adult only	One adult with children	Two adults	Two adults one child	Two adults two children	Two adults with three or more children
1974 -75	6.04	3.58	6.42	5.48	5.43	4.81
1975-76	5.57	4.48	6.32	6.25	5.16	5.30
1984	5.35	4.17	4.96	4.70	3.95	3.58
1988-89	5.52	3.59	4.69	4.10	3.72	2.88
1993-94	4.93	3.73	4.58	4.01	3.05	3.19
1998-99	4.71	4.05	4.44	3.81	3.07	3.12

Source: The Australian Household Expenditure Surveys: 1974-75 to 1998-1999

Table 11.2. *Percentage of total expenditure of alcohol items by household income quintile groups in Australia: 1993-1994 and 1998-1999*

Years	Gross Income Quintiles					
	Lowest 20%	2nd quintile	3rd quintile	4th quintile	Highest 20%	All households
1993-94	4.64	5.08	4.83	4.36	3.90	4.43
1998-99	4.04	4.69	4.44	4.39	4.54	4.46

Source: The 1993-1994 and 1998-1999 Australian HES data conducted by the ABS.

The percentages of total expenditure on alcohol of various income quintiles are presented in Table 11.2. This table shows that percentage of total expenditure on alcohol generally decreased when households moved to higher and higher income quintile groups in 1993-1994. In 1998-1999 the percentage of total expenditure of alcohol was still decreasing for households up to the 4th income quintile, but the households who belong to the highest quintiles spent a higher percentage of total expenditure on alcohol compared to the 4th and lower quintile groups with the exception of the 2nd quintile group. This might be due to the fact that there are older households who are also rich who spend more money on alcohol than other income quintile groups, following the fact that Australia is an ageing society, as seen in Table 11.3.

11.3. *Average per capita expenditure of alcohol for various ethnic households by reference person's age over 65 and under 65 years: 1988-1989*[*]

Age of reference person	Ethnic background (place of birth)				
	Australia	ESC	NESC		
			All	Asia & Africa	Europe
Under 65 years	9.28 (4.58)	9.72 (4.51)	6.81 (3.72)	5.15 (2.93)	7.54 (4.02)
Over 65 years	11.43 (6.09)	8.44 (4.26)	8.95 (4.25)	4.10 (1.62)	9.85 (4.93)

[*] Percentage expenditure on alcohol and tobacco with respect to total expenditure are presented in parentheses.

Source: The Australian 1988-1989 HES Unit Record Tape supplied by the ABS.

It is clear from Table 11.3 that older households spend more money on alcohol than those households whose reference person's age is less than 65 years except households from Asia and Africa, and English speaking backgrounds. Australian and NESC households spend significantly more money on alcohol when their reference person's age is over 65 years compared to less than 65 years with the exception of the Asian and African born people. In general Asian and African background households spend less money on alcohol compared to other ethnic groups. More importantly, they spend a significantly less percentage of total expenditure on alcohol when they are over 65 compared to less than 65 years old. This is probably due to lack of money because of their poor economic situation at an old age together with the religious belief of those who do not drink alcohol at all (i.e., Muslims), mainly coming from Asia and Africa.

These observations are important and useful but not rigorous. In the subsequent sections, we shall estimate total expenditure elasticity, elasticity index and the effects of total expenditure and its inequalities on the demand for various alcohol beverages.

3. MODELS OF ENGEL FUNCTION

An extensive literature on alcohol expenditure and demand, and specifically on the determinants of alcohol expenditure and income elasticity, has indicated that like other commodities, the expenditure of alcohol is responsive to changes in income. The elasticity is historically conditional, because there is considerable variation by time and place. Income elasticity estimated from the HES data can be viewed as related to the pattern of alcohol consumption. Thus, it may be considered as a specific indicator of the structure and culture of a society at a particular point in time.[74]

For the purpose of estimating the elasticity, one needs to specify the form of the Engel function. Allen and Bowley (1935) used the linear Engel function for the analyses of British family budget data. The importance of this type of analysis is now widely accepted [Bewley (1982), Haque (1984), Working (1943), Wold and Jureen (1953), Stone (1954), Prais and Houthakker (1955), Liviatan (1961, Leser (1963), Giles and Hampton (1985), Dunnsire and Baldwin (1999) and Stanford (2000)].

The choice of the mathematical function for the relationship between expenditure on a particular item and total expenditure (income) is a matter for careful deliberation, because the calculated Engel elasticity depends appreciably on the algebraic equation used. Nine alternative functional forms [as mentioned earlier in Chapter 8, including (i) to (vii) of Section 2.1 of Chapter 3 and Share semi-log (SSL) and Share semi-log inverse (SSLI)] were considered before selecting the best one. The functional form should be simple and should satisfy other economic properties as mentioned earlier.

We have fitted nine different Engel functions as stated above, using the Weighted Least Squares (WLS) method in order to find a best functional form from these nine commonly used alternative Engel functions. We then estimated total

---

[74] Some authors performed the trend analysis, using the time series data. For example, Osmond and Anderson (1998) analysed the trend and cyclical effects for the Australian wine industries for the period 1850 to 2000.

expenditure (income) elasticities for various alcohol items based on the selected best Engel function, using the 1975-1976 HES data described in Chapter 3.

3.1 Choice of Best Functional Form Among Various Alternatives

In general, the adjusted coefficient of determination $\overline{R}^2$ is used for this purpose. But there are two problems associated with it. First, there is no justification for comparing $\overline{R}^2$ for curve types having (Y) as regressand and those having (log Y) as regressand in the process of least squares estimation, because to err in (log Y) by an amount ε is to err in (Y) by an amount $e^{\varepsilon}\ 7\varepsilon$. Second, Cramer (1964), Prais and Houthakker (1955) and Prais and Aitchison (1954) have pointed out that the sample correlation obtained from grouped data is not a satisfactory index of the correlation coefficient in the population, and is therefore of little statistical interest. Because of the above difficulties in using $\overline{R}^2$ as the selection criterion, we have used the distance function D^2-criterion defined earlier in Equation (3.4) in Chapter 3.[75]

Table 11.4. The D^2-statistic for different Engel curves fitted to various alcohol items in Australia, 1975 to 1976.

	Functional forms									
Item	*L*	*SL*	*HYP*	*DL*	*LI*	*SSL*	*SSLI*	*LLI*	*DSL*	*Best form*
Beer	0.098	0.066	0.089	0.11	0.064	0.108	0.093	0.063	0.058	DSL
Wine	0.016	0.038	0.068	0.004	0.039	0.017	0.005	0.003	0.003	DSL
Spirits	0.015	0.017	0.022	0.018	0.016	0.016	0.017	0.016	0.014	DSL
All alcohol	0.014	0.019	0.031	0.016	0.014	0.014	0.016	0.017	0.013	DSL

Source: The 1975-1976 Australian HES data based on the 12 weekly per capita income groups supplied by the ABS.

It should be noted that if such a criterion is used to rank the various functional forms, then D^2 and R_b^2 would give the same rankings for the same dependent variable. This property was also observed by Buse (1973), who defined R_b^2 when the equation is estimated by the generalized least squares (GLS) method as

[75] Discrimination among the various functional forms can also be done by the non-nested hypothesis testing procedure, and performing a parametric test on the power parameters of the Box-Cox Engel function developed by Haque (1984). The non-nested hypothesis testing procedure is not applicable for the present study because when we applied the MacKinnon et al. (1983) P_E test we observe that in many cases the log of negative values appear in the formula. This effectively prevents the selection of an appropriate functional form. The parametric test on the power parameters of the Box-Cox Engel function is also not considered here because all the nine functional forms cannot be nested under one super-model.

$R_b^2 = 1 - D^2 / WTSS$, where WTSS is the weighed total sum of squares divided by (g-1). It should be noted here that the ordinary R^2 for heteroscedasticity adjusted data is an *ad hoc* statistic, which is the simple correlation between the unweighted Y and $\hat{Y}$. Buse's R_b^2 is based on generalized sums of squares and is an appropriate measure of goodness of fit for all circumstances. Buse's R_b^2 is directly related to our distance function, D^2-criterion. Thus, our D^2 is better than the conventional R^2 as a criterion for choosing the best functional form from several alternatives. Moreover, D^2 does not involve any extra problems when comparing Engel function with Y and log Y as regressand.

The weighted least squares (WLS) method is used to estimate all nine functions, taking the proportion of the estimated population in each per capita income class as weights. All the nine Engel functions were fitted to each alcohol consumption expenditure item separately. In all, 36 regressions were fitted.

The estimates of the D^2-statistic of various Engel functions for each alcohol items are presented in Table 11.4, which demonstrates that the double semi-log Engel function (DSL) is the best fit for each of the individual alcohol items and for all defined alcohols. The log log-inverse function (LLI) occupied second position. The hyperbolic function (HYP) gave the poorest fit. Thus, the double semi-log (DSL) Engel function is considered as the best function among nine different Engel functions for each individual alcohol item in Australia as judged by the distance function D^2-criterion. This function also has the theoretically pleasing feature that it satisfies the adding up criterion and allows for saturation.

Earlier, Haque (1984) chose this double semi-log Engel function for the 'all alcohol and tobacco' item on the basis of the D^2-criterion and non-nested hypothesis testing procedure. The results of this section suggest that the double semi-log Engel function is the most appropriate function for each individual alcohol items for the Australian 1975-1976 HES data.

We have also used the non-nested hypotheses testing procedure due to Mackinnon, White and Davidson (1983), which has already been discussed earlier in Chapter 3. From the non-nested hypothesis testing procedure it becomes clear that DSL, LLI and LSI are accepted against all other forms taking each of them as H_1. The DSL function is accepted against all other functions. Thus, it is seen from the above analyses that the DSL function turns out to be the best Engel function among the nine alternative commonly used Engel functions studied in this analyses on the grounds of goodness of fit and non-nested hypothesis testing procedure for various alcohol items. Thus, the elasticity estimates for various alcohol items are estimated based on this DSL Engel function for the reminder of this chapter.

4. ESTIMATION OF ELASTICITY

Only the double semi-log Engel function is used to estimate total expenditure elasticity, because this function performed better than other functions for most of the items considered in this chapter on the basis of the goodness of fit and non-nested hypothesis testing procedure as shown in the previous section. The total expenditure elasticities were estimated at the mean values of the total expenditure and family sizes for various alcohol items are estimated, using Equation (10.1) given in Chapter 10. These elasticity estimates for married couple and sole parent households with children are presented in Table 11.5, and elasticity estimates for various household compositions are also provided in Table 11.6 using our new method described in Chapter 7, which is based on the implicit Engel function derived from the concentration Equation (7.12) of Chapter 7.

It is clear from Table 11.5 that alcohol is a necessary item for both sole parent and married couple households with children. However, it is seen from Table 11.6 that alcohol is a necessary item for those households who have children, and it turns out to be a luxury item for households without children on the basis that its elasticity is greater than 1. This provides a more accurate picture about the alcohol expenditure, since it considers the distribution of income among Australian households.

*Table 11.5. Total expenditure elasticity for 'all alcohol' for various household compositions at mean values: 1988 to 1989 HES data**

Household compositions		
Married couples with children		Sole parents with children
With 1 child	0.86 (0.29) [403]	0.42 (0.35) [120]
With 2 children	0.43 (0.32) [711]	0.41 (0.26) [57]
With 3 or more Children	0.39 (0.22) [402]	0.37 (0.21) [19]

* Estimated standard errors are presented in parentheses, and the number of households on which these estimates are based are given in brackets [ ].

Source: The Australian 1988-1989 HES Unit Record Tape supplied by the ABS.

Elasticity estimates of various alcohol items are provided in Table 11.7. It is clear from this table that beer appears as a necessary item on the basis that its elasticity is less than 1, while elasticities for wine and spirits are significantly higher than unity, and hence placing them as luxuries. The elasticity estimate for all alcohol is 1.13, but this is not significantly greater than unity, and hence all alcohol is deemed to be a necessary item in Australia.

We also have estimated elasticities for various alcohol items at different income levels, using our new method based on the concentration curves described in Chapter 7, which are presented in Table 11.8. It is clear from this table that wine and sprits are undoubtedly luxury items in Australia at all income levels. While elasticity of beer indicates that it is a necessary item for almost all households at different income levels except those households whose weekly incomes are less than $70. The combined effect of all of these alcohol items is considered to be a necessary good for Australian households at almost all income levels except those whose weekly income is less than $100.

Table11.6. Total expenditure elasticity for 'all alcohol' for various household compositions at mean values: 1974-75HES data[*]

Household compositions	Total expenditure food elasticity
Head Only	1.6015 (1.6645)
Two adults no children	1.0224 (1.0508)
Three or more adults no children	1.1121 (1.0984)
Head with children	1.0170 (1.1603)
Two adults with one child	0.7074 (1.0820)
Two adults two children	1.4770 (1.2773)
Two adults & three or more children	0.5345 (0.4462)
Three or more adults with children	0.9573 (1.0825)
Total of all households	1.0203 (1.0708)

* Total expenditure elasticities at median values are presented in parentheses ( ).

Source: The 1974-1975 Australian HES data for various household compositions at different household income levels collected by the ABS.

Table 11.7. Elasticity estimates for various alcohol items

Alcohol items	Elasticity estimates at mean values[*]
Beer	0.93 (0.06)
Wine	2.77 (0.12)
Spirits	2.04 (0.18)
All alcohol	1.13 (0.09)

* Standard errors are presented in parentheses.

Source: The 1975-1976 Australian HES data based on the 12 weekly per capita income groups supplied by the ABS.

4.1 Consistent Estimates of Engel Elasticity

We have estimated the parameters of the double semi-log Engel function (a single equation model), using the weighted least squares method, taking total expenditure rather than income as one of the explanatory variables, producing inconsistent estimates of regression coefficients due to simultaneity of the model as pointed by Summers (1959)[76]. Hence, our Engel elasticity estimates presented in the previous sub-section are not consistent.

[76] Andrikopoulos, Brox and Carvalho (1997) also analysed the demand for domestic and imported alcoholic beverages for Ontario, using a dynamic simultaneous equation approach.

Table11.8. Total expenditure elasticities of different alcohol items at various per capita income levels

Weekly per cpita income levels in Australian $	Alcohol commodity groups			
	Beer	Wine	Sprits	All Alcohol*
A$ 30	1.7628	2.2064	2.3733	1.4035
A$ 50	1.4730	2.1511	2.0706	1.2810
A$ 70	1.2353	2.0975	1.8177	1.1795
A$ 100	0.9936	2.0310	1.5543	1.0751
A$ 130	0.8244	1.9722	1.3636	1.0006
A$ 160	0.6965	1.9147	1.2130	0.09431
A$ 190	0.6296	1.8757	1.1300	0.9121
A$ 220	0.5888	1.8459	1.0770	0.8928
A$ 250	0.5619	1.8212	1.0399	0.8797
A$ 280	0.5442	1.8007	1.0140	0.8708
A4$ 310	0.5391	1.7936	1.0062	0.8681
A$ 750	0.5178	1.7387	0.9668	0.8560
Mean	1.1787	2.0832	1.7568	1.1552
Median	1.2817	2.1087	1.8675	1.1994

* All alcohol contains all alcohol items and tobacco

Source: The 1975-1976 Australian HES data based on twelve weekly per capita income groups (these groups are given in Footnote 22) supplied by the ABS.

In order to obtain consistent estimates of the Engel elasticities, we have used the instrumental variable approach.[77] In this study, we have used three instrumental variables to form an instrumental matrix Q for the data matrix X of the same order. The three instrumental variables are measured family income, log of family income and log of family size. It is noted that the latter variable serves as an instrument for itself. The instrumental variable estimates of coefficients $\left(\tilde{\beta}\right)$ for different variables can be obtained by using the Equation (3.5) of Chapter 3. It can be shown that the instrumental variable parameter estimates obtained from formula (3.5) of chapter 3 are consistent, because there exists a high correlation between total expenditure (X) and income (I), and log of total expenditure (log X) and log of income (log I) as shown before. The consistent elasticity estimates for various alcohol items are presented in Table 11.9.

[77] Liviatan (1961) also used this method in order to get consistent estimates of the parameters.

Table 11.9: Consistent elasticity estimates of various alcohol items

Alcohol items	Consistent elasticity estimates at mean values*
Beer	0.84 (0.12)
Wine	2.86 (0.19)
Spirits	2.01 (0.28)
All alcohol	1.03 (0.15)

Asymptotic standard errors are presented in parentheses.

Source: The 1975-1976 Australian HES data based on the 12 weekly per capita income groups supplied by the ABS.

The elasticity estimates presented in Table 11.9 are consistent estimates of total expenditure elasticities for various alcohol items. The classification of each item still remains unaltered as in Table 11.7. Beer is found to be a necessary item, while wine and spirits are luxuries in Australia. The elasticity estimate for the total alcohol item is not significantly greater than unity and hence it becomes a necessary item, probably because of a larger share of expenditure on beer.

5. ESTIMATION OF THE ELASTICITY INDEX

It should be noted that the elasticity estimates presented in the previous section are computed from a specified function at some representative value (usually the mean). But this representative value is arbitrary. Hence, there is no unique measure of elasticity. On the other hand, an elasticity index is a single measure of elasticity or inelasticity of a commodity. However, it should be used with caution. The magnitude of the elasticity index indicates how much the elasticity of the ith commodity deviates from unity over the full range of total expenditure (income). It is thus hoped that these estimates will describe the real picture of the quantitative nature of alcohol consumption in Australia, because it incorporates the effect of total expenditure (income) distribution along with the rise of total expenditure (income).

The procedures of estimating the elasticity index are provided earlier in Chapter 9. The elasticity indices are computed for the various Australian alcohol items, using the Kakwani and Podder (1976) Lorenz curve, which is described earlier in Chapter 8. The ordinary least squares (OLS) method is used to estimate Equation (8.1) of Chapter 8 after taking the logarithms on both sides. Table 11.10 presents the estimated parameters of the Lorenz equation (8.1) together with the values of the coefficient of determination (R^2) between the actual and estimated values of V for all the commodities. It is noted that R^2 is generally very high for all the commodities. It is mentioned here that the original and estimated values of V are very close, up to two decimal places for the entire range of the expenditure. This shows that Equation (8.1) fits well for the Australian data.

Concentration indices and elasticity indices are also given in Table 11.10. It is seen from this table that wine and spirits are highly unevenly distributed among individuals in Australia. While, consumption of beer is more or less equally distributed. Elasticity indices for both per capita total expenditure and income for various alcohol items are also given in Table 11.10.

Table 11.10. Estimates of the Lorenz function and the elasticity index of the various alcohol items in Australia: 1975-1976

Alcohol items	α_i	β_i	γ_i	R^2	Concentration index	Elasticity index	
						Total expenditure	Income
Beer	0.3224	1.0824	1.1724	0.9728	0.2692	0.0272	-0.0726
Wine	0.4781	1.0038	0.9406	0.9978	0.4634	0.2214	0.1216
Spirits	0.5162	1.1901	1.2386	0.9675	0.3964	0.1544	0.0546
All alcohol	0.2773	1.0129	0.9656	0.9966	0.2643	0.0789	-0.0775

Source: The 1975-1976 Australian HES data based on the 12 weekly per capita income groups supplied by the ABS.

Table 11.11. Decomposition of the elasticity index of all alcohol with respect to its individual items

Commodity items	Per capita expenditure on each item	Percentage expenditure on each iem	Elasticity idex	Contribution to the total elasticity index	Percentage contribution
Beer	1.41	66.82	0.0272	0.018175	23
Wine	0.30	14.22	0.2214	0.031483	40
Spirits	0.40	18.96	0.1544	0.029274	37
All alcohol	2.11	100.0	0.0789	0.078900	100

Source: The 1975-1976 Australian HES data based on the 12 weekly per capita income groups supplied by the ABS.

The estimates of elasticity indices for wine and spirits show that these items are highly elastic, which means that if household income is increased by 1%, a household is likely to increase expenditure on these items by more than 1%. Beer appears to have very small elasticity. The total of 'all alcohol' item is also less elastic probably because of a large share of expenditure on beer.

The contribution of each item to the elasticity index of the 'all alcohol' item is presented in Table 11.11. If the elasticity index of 'all alcohol' is taken to be 100, the contributions of beer, wine and spirits are 23, 40 and 37 respectively. Wine contributes the highest amount of inequality of consumption, while beer contributes the lowest inequality to the total alcohol consumption in Australia. Therefore, for any future projection, disaggregation of the group is important for future production estimates. These findings will also assist in setting an optimal tax on various alcohol items, which can provide better estimates of optimal tax on alcohol than the estimates provided by Kenkel (1996).

6. ESTIMATING THE CHANGE IN CONSUMER DEMAND

We now estimate the increase in consumer demand for various alcohol items due to the rise in total expenditure and changes in total expenditure inequalities in Australia. The new co-ordinate system of the Lorenz curve introduced by Kakwani and Podder (1976), given in Chapter 8 is also used for this purpose. More details about the general formulation and estimation of the increase in consumer demand from the Lorenz curve can be found in Haque (1984).[78]

We have estimated the increase in consumer demand with respect to various percentage increases in per capita total expenditure and various percentage changes of the Lorenz ratio by changing only two parameters (one for the total expenditure and another for total expenditure inequality) of the Lorenz equation. There was no effect from other parameters on the changes in consumer demand. The percentage changes in demand estimates based on various changes of level of total expenditure and total expenditure inequalities for various alcohol items are presented in Table 11.12.

Table 11.12 shows that the percentage change in demand is effectively increased by an increase in per capita total expenditure, but also increases with the decrease of the Lorenz ratio for beer and wine. These figures however more or less remain unaltered with the various degrees of reduction of Lorenz ratios for spirits as well as for the total of the 'all alcohol' item.

Earlier, Iyengar (1960b) used Indian data and showed that the percentage change in demand would rise for necessary goods but fall for luxury goods as the Lorenz ratio decreased. Our results do not corroborate with his results. For example, the percentage change in demand for wine rises due to a decrease in the Lorenz ratio, although the elasticity estimate of this item shows that it is a luxury item. These are the findings, which are in direct contradiction to Iyengar's results. This difference might be explained in terms of differences in consumption patterns between the developing and developed countries. Most of the poor people in developing countries spend any extra money on necessary items, whereas in developed countries, if the poor section of the population gets extra money, it is spent on luxury items like wine rather than on food.

In another direction, the percentage increases in demand for a commodity due to changes in per capita total expenditure are directly linked with its elasticity. For example, the elasticity of beer is 1.02 and its demand rises only 55.29% for a 50% rise in per capita total expenditure. But the demand rises as much as 116.06% for a similar rise in per capita income for wine, whose elasticity is 1.92. It should be noted

---

[78] Wilson, Juniper and Lock-shin (2001) showed how to determine the inequality of alcohol consumption using the Theil Index.

that these estimates are based on a simple relationship of per capita income for wine, whose elasticity is 1.92. It should be noted that these estimates are based on a simple relationship of per capita expenditure on each alcohol item and per capita total family expenditure for 12 per capita family income groups.

On the other hand, if the per capita total expenditure increases by 20% and the Lorenz ratio decreases by 10%, then the per capita increases in demand for beer and wine are 29.04% and 44.7% respectively. However, if one does not consider the effect of change in the Lorenz ratio, then the percentage increase in demand for the above items would be 24.6% and 40.5% respectively. In general, this investigation shows that the estimation of demand for beer and wine would be underestimated if the effects of income distribution were not considered. However, income distribution has no effect on the estimation of demand for spirits and 'all alcohol' items.

Table 11.12. Percentage increase (or decrease) in demand

Commodity group	Percentage increase in per capita expenditure	Percentage changes in Lorenz ratio (100β)						Best functional form chosen by the D^2 criterion	Corresponding elasticity of the best function
		-10	-5	0	5	10	20		
Beer	0	-4.7	-2.28	0.000	2.186	4.273	8.141		
	5	1.75	4.17	6.489	8.70	10.8	14.73		
	10	7.96	10.409	12.75	14.9	17.1	21.06	DSL	1.02
	20	19.7	22.238	24.6156	26.882	29.0	33.04		
	50	50.4	52.916	55.2905	57.546	59.6836	63.61		
Wine	0	-2.9	-1.4686	0.00000	1.4146	2.77300	5.311		
	5	6.08	7.7768	9.41640	10.995	12.5114	15.35		
	10	15.6	17.490	19.3097	21.063	22.7456	25.89	DSL	1.92
	20	36.0	38.333	40.5438	42.672	44.7164	48.54		
	50	108.	112.44	116.063	119.55	122.202	129.1		
Spirits	0	0.01	0.0093	0.00000	-0.0093	-0.0187	-0.037		
	5	7.69	7.6850	7.67520	7.6654	7.65560	7.636		
	10	15.4	15.360	15.3504	15.340	15.3299	15.31	DSL	1.47
	20	30.7	30.712	30.7008	30.689	30.6784	30.65		
	50	76.8	76.766	76.7520	76.738	76.7240	76.69		
All alcohol	0	0.01	0.0082	0.00000	-0.0082	-0.0163	-0.032		
	5	6.73	6.7203	6.71180	6.7032	6.69460	6.677		
	10	13.4	13.432	13.4325	13.414	13.4060	13.38	DSL	1.31
	20	26.9	26.856	26.8471	26.837	26.8275	26.80		
	50	67.1	67.130	67.1177	67.105	67.0932	67.06		

* It should be noted that the effect of the family size is not incorporated with these estimates, because the theory of the concentration curve is not yet developed for more than one variable.

Source: The 1975-1976 Australian HES data based on the 12 weekly per capita income groups supplied by the ABS.

7. DISCUSSION

There are many problems in estimating the demand for alcohol in Australia using the 1975-1976 HES data, mainly because these data are taken from a general survey rather than a specially designed survey. The estimated total expenditure elasticities are affected because the grouped per capita income is used rather than the per capita total expenditure data. Consequently, the estimated coefficients of the Engel function have lost their large sample properties and the elasticity estimates have lost a considerable degree of efficiency. A bias is introduced in estimating the coefficients of the double semi-log function when using the arithmetic means as proxies for the within group geometric means for the log X and log S variables. Moreover, the quality elasticities of the commodities have not been estimated, since these data were not collected. More importantly, our estimates of expenditure elasticities might be affected by other economic and demographic factors, which have not been considered in our calculations. For example, price has a significant effect on alcohol consumption, which was shown by Manning, Blumberg and Moulton (1995). They studied the differential response of price on alcohol consumption, which is ignored in the present analyses. Thus, a thorough analysis for the demand of alcohol items based on wide ranging factors that affect alcohol consumption should be undertaken for future studies.

The following conclusions are drawn from the present analyses. The percentage of expenditure on alcohol beverages has decreased over the years, particularly in all capital cities in Australia.

The double semi-log Engel function turned out to be the best function for each individual alcohol item on the basis of the distance function D^2-criterion. This function has the theoretically pleasing feature that it can satisfy other economic criteria. This function can also easily be estimated through the WLS method, using standard available computer software. It is observed that, on the basis of elasticity parameters, beer is classified as a necessary item in Australia, while wine and spirits are luxuries. All alcohol also turns out to be a necessary item, probably because of a large contribution of expenditure on beer, which is a necessary item.

The estimates of the concentration indices of various alcohol items show that beer is more or less evenly distributed among individuals in Australia, but wine and spirits are very unequally distributed. Decomposition of the elasticity index of all alcohol with respect to its individual sub-items showed that beer, wine and spirits contributed 23%, 40% and 37% respectively. These observations are important because the disaggregation of the 'all alcohol' item is essential, particularly for successful future production and policy purposes.

We have also estimated the percentage changes of consumer demand for various alcohol items due to percentage changes in total expenditure and total expenditure inequalities. This showed that the demand for beer and wine might be increased with the decrease of the Lorenz ratio, but there was no effect of income distribution on spirits and all alcohol items. These findings are very helpful for production and policy decisions. This is the first detailed study on the demand for alcohol items in Australia, and is hoped that the findings will be of interest to those people concerned with consumer behaviour. The results on total expenditure elasticities should interest market research investigators, while the elasticity indices and their effects on consumer demand are important in connection with production planning, health, and road safety policy-making purposes. This is because the effect of alcohol consumption has wide ranging implications in health, road safety, criminal violence and other aspects of life, which can be seen from the studies of Bradley, Badrinath, Bush, Boyd-Wickizer and Anawalt (1998), Federal Office of Road Safety (1996, 1997), McLeod and Stockwell (1999), Norstrom (1998), Peach, Bath and Farish (1998), and Rogers et al (2000).

CHAPTER 12

CONSUMERS' EQUIVALENCE SCALES: A REVIEW

A recent review of literature on the measurement of consumers' equivalence scale is presented in this chapter. The estimate of income elasticity based on per capita data is not appropriate, because the needs of the members of the household according to the ages and sexes vary. Thus to find a consumer unit scale, that is exactly how many effective consumers are there in the household, is important to accurately estimate income elasticity, which has a wide range of policy implications. Some of the techniques, which are used to estimate equivalence scales, are presented here, even though none of them can be considered as accurate. More importantly, the readers will find a proposed solution to Forsyth's (1960) identification problem, as well as how the extension of Barten's (1964) procedure can be used to solve Forsyth's problem. Additionally, a few functional forms, which are important for the estimation of 'equivalence scales', are also presented here.

1. INTRODUCTION

The material well being of the household (HH) depends on its composition in addition to income and other factors. The word 'household composition' means how the HH is formed, i.e., what are the ages and sexes of the members of the HH and above all how many people there are in the HH. The ages and sexes of the members of the HH are of considerable importance in the consumer demand analysis, because their needs vary with these characteristics. The cost per person of maintaining a certain standard of living varies due to changes in these characteristics. For example, the cost of maintaining a newly born child is a certain fraction of a cost of maintaining an adult. This is how the notion of *consumer unit scale* emerges, which can determine exactly how many effective number of consumers are there in the HH. In fact, these are the weighting factors that allow comparisons of economic well being among HHs of different types.

The consumer unit scale comprises two components. First, *the income scale* measures the relative income required by HHs of different composition to maintain the same level of satisfaction. Second, the *specific scale* measures the relative consumption expenditures on the specific item of consumption required by different HH types.

189

The HH need analysis also incorporates another important concept, which is popularly known as *economies/diseconomies of scale*. A HH is said to enjoy income economies/diseconomies of scale if it enjoys a higher/lower standard of living than a relatively smaller HH with the same level of per consumer unit income. Like the consumer unit scale, Prais and Houthakker (1955) introduced the idea of 'income' and 'specific' economies/diseconomies of scale in the HH consumption analysis. Prais and Houthakker (1955), Forsyth (1960), Singh (1972, 1973), Woodbury (1944), Iyenger, Jain and Srinivasan (1969), Coondoo (1970), Valenzuela (1996) and Easton (1998), etc., treated the concepts of consumer unit scales and consumer economies/diseconomies of scale separately.

However, later authors such as Barten (1964), Bojer (1977), Deaton and Muellbauer (1980), Gorman (1976), Lazear and Michael (1980), Lee (1982), Muellbauer (1980), Nelson (1986a, 1986b, 1988), Kakwani (1980b), Tsakloglou (1991), Chatterjee and Michelini (1998), Michelini (1998a, 1998b, 1999), Pashardes (1995b), Murthi (1994) and Phipps (1998), etc., amalgamated the two different concepts of consumer unit scales and consumer economies/diseconomies of scale into one single concept, which is known as HH *equivalence scales*. These authors tried to equate income and various specific commodities needed by different HH types in order to maintain a certain level of satisfaction with respect to a reference HH. Thus, Grootaert (1983) defined an equivalence scale as an index, which indicates at reference prices, the cost differential for that a HH may incur due to HH size and composition in order to reach the indifference curve of the reference HH.

Such equivalence scales have many practical applications in a broad range of areas involving the measurement of income inequality and poverty among HHs, in the design of tax policies, as well as in setting the standards for public welfare payments and for many other purposes.

Economists and statisticians made many attempts to estimate consumer equivalence scales during the last hundred years, yet none of them can be considered as a complete success despite their humble approach in establishing a theoretical basis. Moreover, there is no single natural measure of consumer equivalence scales. In this review we examine the available literatures in measuring equivalence scales. The approach is essentially an empirical one in the sense that the estimation of a system is formulated using the actual data. In view of data limitations, one makes use of restrictions, which in part are of theoretical nature. These restrictions reduce the dimensionality of the estimation problem and assist in dealing with certain shortcomings of the available data.

Empirical application requires the specification of the functional form of the demand equations. The choice of the functional form depends on the preferences, aims and the vested interests of the researchers as to which approach he/she will pursue and one is still far from a consensus on the issue of the ideal functional form. In the past a large number of research have been devoted to the specification and estimation of equivalence scales. At present, it is virtually impossible to quote and summarize all the contributions in this field. Therefore in this review the emphasis will be more on the essence of the approach, its possibilities and limitations.

The present state of art prevents estimating a universally acceptable unique set of equivalence scales. Detailed theoretical and empirical aspects of estimation of consumer equivalence scales will be discussed in this chapter. There are four main approaches to the construction of such scales. First, the determination of consumer unit scales for nutritional needs of different age and sex compositions will be discussed. An excellent review of the literature in this area can be found in Visaria (1980) together with further references therein. In this approach, needs are usually based on physiological definitions of poverty, which vary considerably over time and across regions. Moreover, economists such as Atkinson (1975) argued against this concept on the grounds that 'needs' are social rather than physiological concepts. The second approach is based on the use of survey questionnaires, which are directly asked to the HHs about their needs. Kapteyn and Van Praag (1976), Goedhart et al. (1977), Piachaud (1979, 1981) and Van Pragg and Van Der' Sar (1987) were the major exponents in this area. However, economists are suspicious about the validity of collecting such data on the grounds of unconvincing theory. The third approach relies upon haphazard 'public opinion' organized by political pressure groups by asking people what should be the minimum survival needs of a person and/or a child. No such study has been established yet. But actual surveys of expenditure do inform the public from time to time and help to establish public opinion. Fourth, the estimation of the measurement of equivalence scales is based on the observed expenditure of HHs. A huge amount of work has been done on the basis of survey expenditure data including the pioneering contributions of Engel (1883, 1895), Rothbarth (1943), Nicholson (1949), Prais and Houthakker (1955), Forsyth (1960), Barten (1964), Cramer (1973a), Muellbauer (1974, 1975, 1976, 1977, 1980), Bojer (1977) and Kakwani (1977c), etc.[79] From the above discussions, it seems reasonable to estimate consumer equivalence scales based on the last method rather than any other methods. Hence, from now on this review concentrates on only works based on the last approach.

This chapter is organised as follows. Consumer's equivalence scales based on observed Household Expenditure Survey data is provided in Section 2. Section 3 is concerned with the utility theory and consumers' equivalence scales, while the translation model is presented in Section 4. The estimation of consumers' equivalence scales based on the Extended Linear Expenditure System is given in Section 5. Section 6 is concerned with different types of functional forms, which are often used to estimate equivalence scales. Some concluding remarks are provided in the final section.

---

[79] These works are based on consumer demand analysis. There is however another class of separate literature on the cost of an additional person (child) in the HH, which is familiar to demographers [see Lindert (1978, 1980), and Espenshade (1972, 1984) for further references].

2. THEORY OF CONSUMER EQUIVALENCE SCALES BASED ON OBSERVED HOUSEHOLD EXPENDITURE SURVEY DATA

2.1 The Engel Model

The importance of estimating consumer equivalence scales was realized from the beginning of the Engel curve analysis. This is because HH size and compositions are important determinants of consumption items other than income. The measurement of HH size is a big problem in an Engel curve analysis. One of the simplest measures of HH size can be obtained by counting the number of individuals in the HH and in that case the Engel relationship can be expressed as

$$e_{ij} = p_i f_i (E_j, S_j) \tag{12.1}$$

where e_{ij}, E_j and S_j are the expenditure on the ith commodity, total expenditure (TE) and HH size of the jth HH respectively; p_i is the price of the ith commodity and is assumed to be constant across sample HHs; and f_i is the special Engel function for commodity i.

However there exists a strong positive correlation between household TE and size [see Cramer (1973a, p. 147)]. In order to avoid this problem, the per capita model is

$$e_{ij} / S_j = p_i f_i (E_j / S_j) \tag{12.2}$$

This per capita model is widely used in practice, but has the disadvantage that in a randomly selected sample E_j / S_j tends to be negatively correlated with the number of children in the HH. As a result, economies of scale prevail and hence for HHs with the same per capita expenditure, the larger ones would enjoy a higher standard of living, in that they would have larger expenditure per person on luxuries. Hence, HH size measured by counting the number of individuals cannot be acceptable at least for the social welfare context. For these reasons, from the very beginning Engel (1895) himself expressed each HH in terms of total number of children (quet after the name of a famous Belgian Statistician Quetelet), taking the newly born child = 1. Thus, Equation (12.2) can be treated as Engel's original curve that he deflated by a general equivalence scale (S_j), which can reflect HH needs. Later researchers such as Prais and Houthakker (1955), Singh (1972, 1973), and Singh and Nagar (1973) have considered the adult male as a standard member of the family and tried to attach different weights to individuals of different age and sex of the HHs. This procedure can be described as follows.

Suppose l^{th} type of age-sex member in the jth HH is denoted by b_{jl} then total number of consumer units in the jth HH is given by

$$S_j = \sum_l \lambda_{jl}\, b_{jl} \tag{12.3}$$

where λ_{jl} is the relative weight for the lth age-sex type of members of the jth HH compared to the HHs' adult male whose weight is set to unity. These weights are known as *equivalent adult scales*.

Later Sydenstricker and King (1921) introduced the idea of using specific scales one for each commodity. They even tried to estimate these specific scales with the parameters of the Engel curves. This concept was totally ignored until Friedman (1952), Prais (1953b), Prais and Hounthakker (1955), etc., explored the issue for further investigation.[80] In their approach, the formulation of a general Engel function can be expressed as

$$e_i / S_i = p_i f_i (E / S_i), \text{ for all i,} \tag{12.4}$$

$$\text{where}\quad S_i = \sum_l \lambda_{li}\, b_{li} \quad \text{for all i.}$$

Here we omit the subscript j for HH; and λ_{li} is the specific consumer unit scale for the lth type of age-sex number of the HH for good i.[81]

The welfare measurement of the Engel model is usually based on the proportion of a household's TE spent on food. It has two propositions, viz., (i) the proportion of expenditure on food decreases as TE of the HH increases, and (ii) the average propensity of food consumption is lower for smaller HHs than larger HHs at the same level of TE. These two propositions do not guarantee the same level of welfare for those HHs with the same food share but different HH compositions [Vide., Nicholson(1976)]. Nicholson (1976) argued that the food share approach overstated the level of income required to maintain a certain level of material well-being for those HHs serving an extra person (like a child) compared with those not having that person. Deaton and Muellbauer (1986) showed mathematically that the true equivalence scale must be less than or equal to the Engel scale. However, if that extra person has substantial impact on all other expenditure items such as transport, clothing and housing, etc., then it is difficult to establish the direction of the bias for the Engel scales. Finally, it should be mentioned that this is a single equation model, and Tsakloglou (1991) showed under certain conditions how Engle's model can be

---

[80] An excellent review of the literature on economic consumer unit scales can be found in Woodbury (1944) and Prais and Houthakker (1955).
[81] Allen (1942) indicated that it might be possible to construct adult equivalent scales for HHs consisting of parents and children, but not possible if an extra adult is added to the HH, Hence he concluded that the device of scale of equivalence is unnecessary and possibly misleading.

used to estimate the consumers' equivalence scales for different HHs compared to a reference HH in order to maintain the same level of satisfaction for all types of HH.

2.2 The Rothbarth Model

The Rothbarth model is also a single equation model. Under certain conditions this model can also estimate the need of a different HH composition to maintain a constant level of well being compared to a reference HH [see Tsakloglou (1991)]. According to this model all the consumption goods and services can be divided into two groups, viz., (i) goods and services consumed only by adults (known as 'adult goods'), and (ii) those which are consumed jointly by adults and children (known as 'other goods'). Here the measurement of the HH welfare is determined based on the level of expenditure of 'adult goods'. The proposition here is that HHs with the same number of adults are assumed to enjoy the same level of material well-being if they spend the same amount of money on adult goods irrespective of their sizes and TEs. So the whole basis of the Rothbarth model lies on the assumption that there exists a set of 'adult goods', which are demographically separable from children.

However, Deaton, Ruiz-Castillo and Thomas (1989) showed that this separability, which is necessary for Rothbarth's method, is far from sufficient for its validity. They proved that demographic separability is consistent with a number of preference structures and that only one can be considered to be consistent with the Rothbarth approach. Rothbarth (1943) himself used almost all luxury goods including savings as an adult good. Later authors such as Nicholson (1949) estimated income differentials (or the cost of a child) rather than income scales by fixing them at zero for children's specific coefficient for certain commodities like adult's clothing, tobacco and drinks, etc. In principle Nicholson's approach is sound and it is one of the valid techniques available to estimate the consumers' equivalence scales. Cramer (1973a) applied this technique to the British Household Expenditure Survey (HES) data using the double logarithmic Engel function and found the empirical results are disappointing especially for drinks and tobacco. This is probably because the commodities concerned are liable to huge variations as well as the presence of observational errors in those commodities.

Later, Barten (1964), Gorman (1976), Pollak and Wales (1981), and Li and Victoria (2001), etc., indicated that children made goods, which are shared with them relatively more expensive than pure adult goods [this proposition was not accepted by Muellbauer (1977)]. In that case, a HH compensated for the costs associated with the addition of a child will consume more on 'adult goods' than before the child's arrival. The Rothbarth model will pay compensation only to the point where consumption of a pure adult good is unchanged.

Hence, Rothbarth's equivalence scale is too low. Gronau (1985) pointed out that if parents derive utilities from the consumption of their off-springs then their marginal propensity to spend on adult goods is likely to reduce by the addition of a child. If the Engel slopes are affected by this and ignored, then the Rothbarth equivalence scales will be very small, since with the reduced propensity to spend, larger compensation must be paid to restore any given level of adult expenditure.

This suggests that this model would be appropriate with circumspection when the presence of child is likely to cause a substitute for adult goods. Sen (1984) pointed out that Rothbarth model is reasonably good to examine the sex bias.

Deaton and Muellbauer (1986) assumed that all non-food is an adult good and showed mathematically that the Rothbarth scale is less than or equal to the Engel scale. Tsakloglou (1991) tested their underlying assumptions on the same data set (Greek HES conducted in 1981-82), using the same structure of demand equations, so that no difference in the size of the equivalence scales can be attributed to the demand structures. His results show that Engel scales are significantly higher than Rothbarth scales. After Rothbarth's work, a pioneering model formulated by Prais and Houthakker (1955) received considerable attention in estimating consumers' unit scales, which dominated the field in the next two decades. This method is now in order.

2.3 The Prais and Houthakker Model

Prais and Houthakker (1955) incorporated HH composition as a determinant of the consumption pattern and rediscovered the concept of the consumer specific scales originally introduced by Sydnestricker and King (1921). According to the Prais and Houthakker (PH) method, individual age-sex member types are given different weights for different specific items. They have also introduced a concept of an overall 'income scale'. They further generalized their model by incorporating the concepts of income and specific economies/diseconomies of scales. Thus, the fundamental PH model of expenditure per effective consumer unit on commodity i to the standard of living of the HHs is measured by the level of income per consumer unit and can be written as

$$e_i / \{S_i, \theta_i\} = f_i[E / \{S_0, \theta_0\}] \tag{12.5}$$

where e_i, E and S_i are defined earlier in Equation (12.4) and $S_o = \sum \Lambda_l b_l$; Λ_l can be described as λ_l in Equation (12.3) for income. The quantity $\{1 - \theta_i\}$ is the measure of specific economies of scale and $\{1-\theta_0\}$ is the measure of income economies of scale. If there is no economies of scale for a particular commodity i, then $\theta i = 1$, and if there is no economies of scale in the consumption of any commodity then $\theta_0 = 1$. Estimation of specific and income economies of scale can be obtained satisfactorily by the method given in Prais and Houthakkes (1955), if the effective consumer unit scales are provided appropriately. Thus the major problem is to estimate the consumer unit scales, and hence this section is mainly concerned with a simplified PH model that incorporates the consumer unit scale and is given by

$$e_i / S_i = f_i \{E / S_0) \tag{12.6}$$

where all symbols are defined earlier. Among many others, following are the main features of the PH model.

(1) This model analysed the demand for each good separately and without reference to the utility maximization.

(2) This relies on a single equation rather than a complete system approach.

(3) Income scales are the weighted average of the corresponding specific scales, the weights being the budget shares of the commodity concerned by the appropriate equivalent adult scales.

(4) Income and specific effects are in general of an opposite sign due to an increase in HH members.

(5) This is an under identified model.

The identification problem makes it impossible to get a unique set of consumer unit scales. Prais and Houthakker (1955) did not realize the identification problem of their model, because they succeeded in estimating specific scales assuming income scales to be unity for all household type.

It was Forsyth (1960) who first pointed out that the relevant specific scales couldn't be identified when the budget constraint needs to be satisfied. Later, Cramer (1973a) mentioned that

> ...no amount of information about observed Engel curves will render these coefficients determine.

Their argument was based on an algebra exercise for a mathematical specification of an Engel curve of Equation (12.6), which is summarized below. The budget constraint asserts that the sum of expenditures on all commodities must equal TE, i.e.,

$$\Sigma e_i = E: \text{ for all HH composition vectors,} \qquad (12.7)$$

If TE varies and HH composition remains unaltered then

$$\Sigma \frac{\partial e_i}{\partial E} = 1 \text{ ; for all HH composition vectors.} \qquad (12.8)$$

Similarly, if HH composition varies and TE kept constant then from Equation (12.7), we can write

$$\sum_l \frac{\partial e_l}{\partial b_l} = 0 \quad \text{for all } l. \qquad (12.9)$$

Putting equations (12.8) and (12.9) in Equation(12.7), it can be shown that

$$\Lambda_l = \sum_l \left\{ \frac{(e_{il} / S_{il})}{(E / S_0)} \right\} \lambda_{li} \qquad (12.10)$$

This shows that income scale Λ_l is the weighted average of the corresponding specific scales λ_i for all i, the weights being the budget shares for all the commodities taken under consideration corrected by the appropriate equivalent unit scales.

Forsyth's argument states as follows. There are, only (N-1) independent Engel functions for any HH of a given composition if the budget constraint, i.e. Equation (12.7) holds good. Because if consumption of a HH at a fixed level of E is compared with another HH who may have an additional age-sex member type, there will be only (N-1) independent comparisons of the respective Engel functions from which (N+1) parameters [N for specific scales and 1 for overall income scale] are to be estimated. However, Equation (12.10) can be used to reduce the number of parameters by one. Thus, the system of equations is left for solving N unknowns from (N-1) equations, which is indeterminate. Also it can be shown that Forsyth's specification of the constant elasticity Engel function for solving the consumer unit scales problem suffers from an identification problem too.

2.3.1 A Proposed Solution of the Forsyth's Problem

A generalised Engel function, which satisfies the budget constraint, can be expressed as

$$e_i / S_i = \alpha_i (E / S_0) + \beta_i \phi_i (E / S_0) \qquad (12.11)$$

or
$$e_i = \alpha_i S_i (E / S_0) + \beta_i S_i \phi_i (E / S_0) \qquad (12.12)$$

where α_i and β_i are the parameters of the Engel function and ϕ_i (E / So) is such that the budget constraint holds good, i.e., Equation (12.7) implies that

$$\sum_i \alpha_i S_i = So$$

and $\sum_i \beta_i S_i = 0 \qquad \Biggr\}$ (12.13)

Differentiating (11.13) with respect to b_l, we get

$$\sum \alpha_i \lambda_{il} = \Lambda_l$$

and $\sum \beta_i \lambda_{il} = 0 \qquad \Biggr\}$ (12.14)

Equation (12.14) shows that there are two restrictions on λ_{il} for any one commodity. This shows that a given Engel function, which can satisfy the budget constraint, should have a determinate system of equations involving λ_{il} 's and Λ_l. This is because for any i there are exactly (N-1) independent λ_{il} 's [the residual λ_{il}, and Λi can be determined by Equation (12.14), which can be compared with exactly (N-1) independent Engel functions for consumer expenditure HHs of different type]. This shows that Forsyth's conclusion is not valid in general.

2.3.2   *Illustrations with Linear Functions*[82]

Estimating two sets of coefficients for a linear function, which satisfies the adding-up criterion, can be achieved by an iterative procedure, which is similar to Prais and Houthakker (1955).

Let us suppose that the Engel function is given by the following equation

$$\frac{e_i}{\sum_l \lambda_{li} b_l} = \alpha_i + \beta_i \frac{E}{\sum_l \Lambda_l b_l}\ ;\qquad\qquad \text{or all i ;}$$

or

$$\frac{e_i}{\alpha_i + \beta_i\left[E / \sum_l \Lambda_l\, b_l \right]} = \sum_l \lambda_{li}\, b_l$$

or

$$\frac{e_i}{1 + \gamma_i\left[E / \sum_l \Lambda_l b_l \right]} = \alpha_i \sum_l \lambda_{li}\, b_l$$

where $\gamma_i = \beta_i / \alpha_i$.

Now suppose, we start with an initial value of $\Lambda_l = 1$ for all l, then $\sum_l \Lambda_l b_l = S_o$

(HH size)

$$\text{Therefore } \frac{e_i}{1 + \gamma_i M} = \alpha_i \sum \lambda_{i1} b_1 = \alpha_i \lambda_{i1} b_1 + \cdots\cdots + \alpha_i \lambda_{Li} b_L\ ;$$

---

[82] A similar illustration can be made with the Working (1943) Engel function, which is later generalised and applied by Leser (1963).

where M = E/So can be computed for every HHs. Then try different values of γ_i and for each trial value of γ_i regress $[e_i / (1+\gamma_i M)]$ on b_1, b_2 .... b_L, and choose that γ_i for which the coefficient of determination R^2 will be maximum.

$$\text{Therefore } \hat{\alpha}_i^* = \underset{i}{Max}\, \hat{\alpha}_i \lambda_{il}$$

$$\hat{\lambda}_{il} = \frac{\hat{\alpha}_i \lambda_{il}}{\hat{\alpha}_i^*}$$

This should be done for every i, and $\hat{\Lambda}_1$ to be computed from the relation

$$\hat{\Lambda}_l = \sum_i \hat{\beta}_i \hat{\lambda}_{l_i}\,, \qquad\qquad\qquad \text{for all } l;$$

where $\hat{\beta}_i = \hat{\alpha}_i \hat{\gamma}_i$.

This process will be repeated for each household and for every item until convergence is achieved, although convergence does not guarantee identification of the equation. Singh (1973) also indicated that there is a convergence problem for some of his data analysis.

The above discussions clearly indicate that there is a substantial controversy about the identifiability of the PH model. Under this circumstance, the following are the ways to avoid the identification problem of the PH model and give an indication to estimate both the 'specific and income scales'.

First, identify some items such as adult's clothing for which adult's specific scales are zero, as a-*priori* information to estimate the remaining specific scales and income scale. This approach was originally introduced by Rothbarth (1943) and later used by Nicholson (1949), Henderson (1949), Garganas (1977), Deaton and Muellbauer (1986), Gronau (1985), Bradbury (1989a, 1989b), Deaton Ruiz Castillo and Thomas (1989), and Barnow (1994).

Second, nutritional information on food requirements can be used as a basis for various food scales. Other commodity specific scales can then be estimated conditional upon these food scales. Food scales used for this purpose have very little credibility, because these do not reflect the average pattern of consumption in a society. Despite this problem, Muellbauer (1980) considered this to be 'worth serious consideration' and used this information for British HES data. Earlier Howe (1974) also used this technique to estimate consumer equivalence scales.

The third method is based on a regression of expenditure on HH composition. This means it ignores the effect of standard of living on a certain consumption item say i^{th} item (say, salt) whose Engel elasticity = 0. Under this situation, we can write the following expression.

$$e_i / (\sum_l \lambda_{il} b_l) = \text{Constant} = c_i, \text{ (say)}$$

Therefore, $$e_i = c_1 \lambda_{i1} b_1 + c_1 \lambda_{i2} b_2 + \cdots\cdots + c_1 \lambda_{iL} b_L$$

Now regress e_i on $\{b_1, b_2 \ldots\ldots, b_L)$, and accept $\hat{c}_i = \underset{i}{Max} \, \hat{c}_i \hat{\lambda}_{il}$, which gives

$$\hat{\lambda}_{il} = \hat{c}_i \hat{\lambda}_{i1} / \hat{c}_i \qquad\qquad (12.15)$$

Other specific scales can also be estimated whose elasticities are approximately = 0. This method is generally satisfactory for necessary goods, but it has no value for luxury goods. However, using *a-priori* information for some items based on this method, income and specific scales for other items can be estimated. Kemsley (1952) and Quenouille (1950) and others applied this method for their analysis. The beauty of this approach is that its estimated coefficients can be examined through the statistical tests.

Despite the problems associated with the PH model researchers around the world still estimate consumers' equivalence scales, using their method, and incorporating price information. Later, authors estimated consumers' equivalence scales based on the utility theory, which is described below.

3. UTILITY THEORY AND CONSUMERS' EQUIVALENCE SCALES

Consumers' equivalence scales can be constructed for different HH compositions through the utility functions. For example, suppose the utility function of a selected standard HH is given by

$$U = U\,(Q, S, Z) \qquad\qquad (12.16)$$

where Q is a vector of commodities consumed by the HH, S is the vector of the HH compositions of each age and sex category, and Z is a vector of other relevant covariates such as seasons, regions, education and occupation, etc. Associated with this utility function, there is a cost function (C), which gives the minimum expenditure. Under this situation if E is required to attend U at prices P for a given S and Z then the following relation holds.

$$C\,(U, P, S, Z) = E \qquad\qquad (12.17)$$

If U^0 and P^0 are some reference utility level and prices then in order to maintain the same level of satisfaction, then the additional cost of a certain HH type S^h with Z^h covariates compared to a reference HH type S° with Z° covariates, can be expressed as

$$M^h = C\,(U^0, P^0, S^h, Z^h)\,/\,C\,(U^0, P^0, S^0, Z^0) \qquad (12.18)$$

This ratio is popularly known as the equivalence scale.[83] In order to avoid identification problem of the separate influence of S and Z, we have to assume that S and Z are independent since both S and Z differ across HHs. Equations (12.16) to (12.18) involve direct utilities and are unobservable, but they can generate a corresponding system of demand functions which can relate observable expenditures on goods to total expenditure, prices and HH compositions. For example, Hicksian's compensated demand functions can be written as

$$p_i q_i \;=\; \frac{\partial\,C\,(U, P, S, Z)}{\partial \log p_i} \qquad (12.19)$$

and Marshallian demand functions can be obtained by substituting v (E, P, S, Z) for direct utility U (Q, S, Z), i.e.,

$$p_i q_i = \frac{\partial\,C\,[\,v(E, P, S, Z),\, P, S, Z\,]}{\partial \log p_i} = f\,(E, P, S, Z) \qquad (12.20)$$

This approach is criticised by Pollak and Wales (1979, 1981), Fisher (1987), Fisher and Shell (1971) etc., [see also Deaton (1982) and Deaton and Muellbauer (1980, 1986) for a critique of Pollak and Wales]. They argued that this method is not appropriate for welfare comparisons, because the addition of an extra person leads the HH to change their consumption as well as their utility indifference curves. They refer the preferences of the HHs as 'conditional' and 'unconditional' depending on the given HH composition variables or not; and the associated preferences are called 'conditional' and 'unconditional' equivalence scales respectively. The 'conditional' equivalence scales can be estimated from the conditional demand systems, using some identifying assumptions. Blundell and Lewbel (1990) showed how these assumptions vary across demand models and forms of the HH compositions that give different sets of equivalence scales [see also Whiteford (1984) for different sets of equivalence scales based on different models]. On the contrary, Pollak and Wales (1981) argued that 'unconditional' equivalence scales are appropriate for welfare comparisons and should be considered in the longrun, because HHs are the decision makers about their labor supply, inter temporal consumption patterns, inter-generational transfers, as well as compositions of HHs.

However, such a broad concept of welfare may not be useful for most practical policy implementations. In this context, Deaton and Muellbauer (1986) favoured the narrow concept of welfare, which assumes that the overall welfare function is separable into a number of sub-utility functions. This sub-utility function can then

---

[83] Deaton and Muellbauer (1980, 1986) provided a generalized version for the estimation of an equivalence scale based on a utility function.

take care of most of the variables mentioned in the preceding paragraph. Some of the very popular models, which are used to estimate equivalence scales based on utility theory are given as follows. Each of these models are assumed to have a fixed structure of preferences, which remains constant across HHs, although allowance is made to vary some parametric changes in the formulation of demand functions.

3.1 The Barten Model

Barten (1964) was the first who to use the utility theory to establish the relationship between commodity demand, income and HH compositions, etc. He argued that quantities consumed of the bundle of goods and services should be taken as 'standard of living'. This is because a HH is said to have higher level of utility if it consumes higher quantity of one or more goods and services for a given identical preferences and market prices. He showed how his theory could be used to analyse the different needs of different HH compositions for various goods and services. He defined the HH utility as

$$U = U\left[\frac{q_i}{s_i}\right], \qquad i = 1, 2, \ldots\ldots n; \qquad (12.21)$$

where q_i is the quantity of the ith commodity of the HH and s_i is its specific scales, which takes into account the effect of the ith HH age-sex type (b_l) on the utility derived by the HH from a unit of the ith commodity, which can be expressed as

$$s_i = s_i(b_l), \quad i = 1, 2, \ldots, N; \text{ and } l = 1, 2, \ldots, L$$

Now for a given age-sex type, TE and market prices (p_i), the HH maximizes the utility function (12.21) subject to the budget constraint

$$E = \sum_i p_i^* \left(\frac{q_i}{s_i}\right) \qquad (12.22)$$

where $p_i^* = p_i s_i$ is the shadow price. Under the equilibrium conditions, the commodity demand functions can be written as

$$q_i = s_i q_i\left(p_i^*, E\right) \qquad (12.23)$$

From Equation (12.23), it is possible to derive the elasticity of demand with respect to HH composition for the jth HH, and it is given by

$$\frac{b_i \partial q_i}{q_i \partial b_i} = \frac{b_i \partial S_i}{S_i \partial b_i} + \sum_j \frac{p_j \partial q_i b_i \partial S_j}{q_i \partial p_j S_j \partial b_j} \qquad (12.23a)$$

This shows that the overall effect is the weighted sum of the specific effects, weights being the price elasticities of demand for commodity i. It can also be seen from the overall effect that a change in the HH composition can be translated into a pseudo-price change.

3.1.1 Barten's Solution to Forsyth's Problem[84]

Barren (1964) reformulated the equivalence scales in the traditional Engel curve as (12.6), i.e.,

$$\frac{e_i}{S_i} = f_i\left(\frac{E}{S_0}\right), \quad i = 1, 1, 2, 3, \dots, N. \qquad (12.24)$$

where S_0 and S_i correspond to the effective number of consumer units of HH with respect to overall 'income' and 'specific' scales respectively, and are defined by

$$S_k = S_k(b_1, b_2, \dots, b_L), \quad k = 0, 1, 2, \dots, N; \qquad (12.25)$$

where bi (i=1, 2 ....., L) is the number of persons of the ith age-sex type in the HH. The partial derivative of e_i with respect to b_l is given by

$$\frac{\partial e_i}{\partial b_l} = \left(\frac{e_i}{S_i}\right)\left\{\frac{\partial S_i}{\partial b_l}\right\} - \left(\frac{e_i \eta_i}{S_0}\right)\left\{\frac{\partial S_0}{\partial b_l}\right\} \qquad (12.26)$$

where η_i is the partial income elasticity with respect to e_i. Now multiplying (12.26) by $\left(\frac{b_l}{e_i}\right)$ we have

$$f_{il} = g_{il} - \eta_i g_{0l}; \quad i = 1, 2, \dots, N; \ \& \ l = 1, 2, \dots, L; \qquad (1.27)$$

where f_{il}, g_{il} and g_{0l} are (partial) elasticities of e_i, S_i and S_0 with respect to b_l respectively.

---

[84] In his original paper Barten (1964) used qi, the quantity consumed of the commodity i, instead of ei, the expenditure made on the ith commodity.

Multiplying (12.27) by W_i = share of the expenditure on the ith commodity and summing over i, we have

$$\sum w_i f_{il} = \sum W_i g_{il} - \sum W_i \eta_i g_{ol} \qquad (12.28)$$

However, by equations (12.8) and (12.9) for the budget constraint, it is implied that

$$\sum_i W_i f_{il} = 0; \text{ for all } l \qquad (12.29)$$

$$\text{and} \quad \sum W_i \eta_i = 1; \qquad (12.30)$$

where $W_i = \left(e_i \Big/ E \right)$

Thus from Equation (11.28), we have

$$g_{ol} = \sum_i W_i g_{il} \text{ for all } l \qquad (12.31)$$

i.e., the income scale g_{ol} is the weighted average of the corresponding specific scales g_{il} for any l; the weights being equal to the share of the expenditure for the ith commodity.

Therefore, Equation (12.27) can be written as

$$f_{il} = g_{il} - \eta_i \sum_i W_i g_{il} ; \qquad (12.32)$$

The system of Equation (12.32) involving g_{il} unknowns can be written in matrix notation as

$$F = [I - \eta W'] G; \qquad (12.33)$$

where $F = [f_{il}]$ and $G = [g_{il}]$ are NxL matrices, $\eta = [\eta_i]$ and $W = [W_i]$ are Nx1; and I is the NxN identity matrix.

It can be shown that the matrix $[I - \eta W']$ is singular because of (12.30), and hence G cannot be solved uniquely for a given set of estimates of [F] and [η]. Muellbauer (1980) pointed out that this result is valid not only in the neighborhood of a given point, but also extends to the wider set of points for which the matrix [I − $\eta W'$] is continuous and of rank N-1.

At this stage Barten suggested to delete a row of F, the corresponding row and column of $[I- \eta W']$, and the corresponding row of G in order to reduce the matrix $[I - \eta W']$ of full rank. The deleted row of G can be estimated by using the estimates of other rows and restrictions. Thus Barten concluded:

> Forsyth's objection against the traditional method is not very difficult to overcome.

However, Barten's above solution to Forsyth's problem is dubious. This is because, if the kth row of G has been deleted, the solution of (N - I) elements of any column of G from the reduced system of equations is identical to that of (12.33). This implies that Barten assumes g_{kl} to be zero for all l (for a particular k).

Clearly the solution of g_{kl} ($i \neq k$) and $g_{kl} = 0$ satisfies the k equations.

Now from Equation (12.29) we can write

$$f_{kl} = -(1 / W_k) \sum_{i \neq k} W_i f_{il} \text{ for all } l \qquad (12.34)$$

Further from (12.27) we can write

$$\hat{f}_{il} = g_{il} - \eta_i \sum_{j} W_j g_{jl}; \quad i, j \neq k \quad \text{for all } l \qquad (12.35)$$

where $\hat{g}_{il}$ are solutions obtained from the truncated system assuming; $g_{kl} = 0$.
Substituting (12.35) in the right hand side of (12.34), we have

$$f_{kl} = -(1/W_k) \sum_{i \neq k} W_i [\hat{g}_{il} - \eta_i \sum_{j \neq k} W_j \hat{g}_{jl}]$$

$$= \frac{-\sum_{i \neq k} W_i g_{il}}{W_k} + \frac{-\sum_{i \neq k} W_i \eta_i \sum_{j \neq k} W_j \hat{g}_{jl}}{W_k}$$

$$= -(\hat{g}_{ol} / W_k) + (\hat{g}_{ol} / W_k) - (W_k \eta_k \hat{g}_{ol} / W_k) = -\eta_k \hat{g}_{ol} \quad \text{for all } l.$$

Hence $\hat{g}_{il}$ ($i \neq k$) and $g_{kl} \neq 0$ satisfy the kth equation for all l. Therefore, Barten's solution to Equation (12.33) is satisfied by all the row vectors except one which is null. If a row vector of G is null then there is no way of revising the values of its entities without changing the values of the rest of the g_{il}'s. Muellbauer (1980) also pointed out that even after deleting one row and column in $[I - \eta W']$, the remaining matrix is still singular since

$$\sum_{i=2}^{n} W_i \, \eta_i \;=\; 1 \text{ if } \eta_i = 0$$

Earlier this point was also made by Singh and Nagar (1978). This implies that Barten's procedure cannot give the unique solution and hence we cannot identify g_{il}'s and g_{ol}'s from his formulation of the demand system.

3.1.2 Extension of Barten's Procedure for a Solution of Forsyth's Problem

Coondoo (1972) extended Barten's analysis to solve Forsyth's problem. He used the restriction given in (12.31) in order to derive another restriction. He argued that the g_{il}'s remain unaltered in response to a partial change in E. However, the g_{ol}'s may change as a result of budget reallocations arising from such partial changes in E. But from (12.27) we have

$$\frac{\partial g_{ol}}{\partial E} = 0$$

i.e. income scale is invariant with respect to changes in E. Moreover in order to satisfy (12.27) and (12.31), we have

$$\sum \frac{\partial e_i}{\partial E} g_{il} = g_{ol} \text{ for all } l \qquad (12.36)$$

which must be true. Equation (12.36) can also be expressed as

$$\sum W_i \eta_i g_{il} = g_{ol}, \quad \text{for all } l$$

or

$$\sum W_i \eta_i g_{il} - g_{ol} = 0$$

or

$$\sum W_i \eta_i g_{il} - \sum W_i g_{il} = 0$$

or

$$\sum W_i [\eta_i - 1] g_{il} = 0 \quad \text{for all } l \qquad (12.37)$$

Thus, for some i if $W_i \eta_i \neq W_i$, we have an independent restrictions on the g_{il}'s in (12.37). In such case (12.27) together with (12.37) yields a set of N independent equations for solving g_{il}'s for l, g_{ol} can then be calculated by (12.31). Actually, G can be solved from

$$F = [I - \eta W \hat{\eta}]G \qquad (12.38)$$

where $\hat{\eta}$ is the diagonal matrix with η_i being the ith diagonal element.

Obviously, $(I - \eta W \hat{\eta})$ is in general non-singular. Therefore the estimated solution of G is unique and is given by

$$\hat{G} = [I - \eta W' \hat{\eta}]^{-1} F \qquad (12.39)$$

If we pre-multiply (12.38) by W' it can be shown that G obtained from (12.38) can satisfy the restriction in (12.31), i.e.,

$$W' G = W' \hat{\eta} G = g_0$$

where $g_0 = [g_{0i}]$, a vector of order lxl for income scales since $W'F = 0$ by (12.29).

The solution of Forsyth's problem for a general Engel function, which satisfies the adding up criterion is now illustrated below.

Suppose, the form of the Engel function is expressed as

$$(e_i / S_i) = \alpha_i (E / S_0) + \beta_i \phi(E / S_0) \quad \text{for all i,} \qquad (12.40)$$

or $$e_i = S_i \alpha_i (E / S_0) + S_i \beta_i \phi(E / S_0)$$

where $S_k = \Sigma g_{ki} b_i$, $k = 0, 1, 2 \ ....., \ n$; and α_i and β_i are the parameters of the Engel function, and ϕ (E/S) [$\neq 0$ at least for some E] is such that the adding-up criterion is satisfied.

In order to satisfy the budget restriction, i.e., $\Sigma e_i = E$, we must have

$$\Sigma S_i \alpha_i = S_0$$

and $$\Sigma S_i \beta_i = 0$$

This means $\sum \alpha_i g_{il} = g_{ol}$ (12.41)

                          $\sum \beta_i g_{il} = 0$

    Now for given (12.40) and (12.41), if comparisons of consumer expenditure of HH of different composition types are made, there is a determination system of equations involving g_{il}'s and g_{ol}'s for each l; we have (N-I) independent g_{ii}'s [the remaining g_{ii} and g_{ol} can be estimated from (12.41)] and hence there is exactly (N-1) independent comparisons of Engel functions. The method illustrated in Section 3.1.2 can also be applied to estimate the consumer unit scales for those functions, which satisfy the adding-up restrictions such as the linear function, the Working (1943) function and the double semi-log Engel function introduced by Haque (1989b).

    Muellbauer (1980), Pollak and Wales (1981) and Lewbel (1985), etc., studied the PH model extensively in terms of utility and cost functions. Muellbauer (1974, 1980) showed that the model could only be valid if the HH utility is of Leontief type, and the compensated price elasticities are all zero. He also criticized this model on the grounds that marginal rates of substitution are not defined as well as symmetry and concavity constraints, which are the main basis of the utility theory and are lacking here. Pollak and Wales (1981) and Lewbel (1985) on the other hand incorporated the price effect in the model and showed that this modified PH model can be consistent with the utility theory if the direct utility function is additively separable. However these restrictions are hardly met by the HH consumption behavior and hence jeopardize the entire basis of the PH model. Chavas (1989) however derived the necessary and sufficient conditions in order to make the PH model consistent with consumer theory and also established its validity on theoretical grounds.

    Functions can be used to measure the welfare comparisons between HHs. Deaton and Muellbauer (1986) expressed the Barten model with the vector of demographics B as

$$u = u[q_i/si(B)]; \quad i = 1, 2 \ldots n;$$ (12.42)

where u is the measure of welfare of a reference HH and q_i/s_i (B) is the actual consumption of the reference HH. The quantity $s_i(B) = 1$ if no extra person consumes the good, and it would be 2 if the extra person consumes exactly the same amount as before. The cost of the demand functions can be derived as follows, assuming $q_i = \{Q_i/s_i (B)\}$ as the objective of the utility with effective prices $p_i = p_i\, s_i$ (B)

$$x = c\,[u, p_i s_i(B)]$$ (12.43)

and $$q_i = s_i h_i \, [u, \, p_i s_i(B) \,]$$ (12.44)

There are two main features in these equations viz., (i) scaling up the reference demand by 's_i' corresponding to the needs due to the addition of an extra person in the HH, and (ii) the substitution effects on demand that occurs when an extra person in the HH alters the effective prices of the reference HH goods.

This model is quite general yet it fails to answer questions like what happens if the reference HH does not consume certain goods or a HH with an extra person does not consume the good through substitution effects. Gorman (1976) incorporated these problems by adding fixed costs of extra persons in the Barten's model in the following way

$$x = c \, [u, \, p_i s_i(a)] = \Sigma p_j d_j(B), \quad i = 1, 2, \ldots, n$$ (12.45)

where d's are fixed costs associated with the demographic vector B. It should be noted that for the reference HH all d's are zeros due to the absence of extra persons.

4. THE TRANSLATION MODEL

The demographic translation model was first introduced by Pollak and Wales (1978), which assumes different 'pre-committed' quantities of each good. The direct utility function is thus given by

$$u = U(q_i - k_i), \quad i = 1, 2 \, \ldots \ldots, n$$ (12.46)

where k_i's = 0 for all i for the reference HH. A household requires less than the reference HH to have the same level of welfare if the k_i's are negative.

Now let $$q_i{}^* = q_i - k_i$$

and $$E^* = E - \sum_i p_i k_i$$

Therefore, maximizing the utility function (12.46) subject to $pq^* = E^*$ yields the demand function of the form

$$q_i = k_i + q_i \, (E^*, p)$$ (12.47)

This implies that HHs other than the reference HH first purchase k_i for all i commodities and then allocate the remaining budget money in the same manner as the reference HH. Hence to attain a certain level of satisfaction, the non-reference HHs would require an additional cost of $\Sigma p_i k_i$. Unlike Barten's model, the translation model can handle the case where the reference HH does not purchase a commodity, but other comparable families do. In a way, the translation model is similar to the PH model because the overall effect of an extra person enters through the TE variable. There is no price like substitution effect in the model. This model does not take into account the cost differences among various HH types. As a result, empirical fit of the model is expected to be very poor [see Pollak and Wales (1981)].

Gorman (1976) combined the translation and Barten model into a single expression and replaced the original demand system by

$$q_i = k_i + s_i \, [q_i \, (E^* , p)] \qquad (12.48)$$

Note that the translation model can be obtained from the above equation if $s_i = 1$ for all i. Similarly, the Batten model (scaling model) can be obtained if $k_i = 0$ for all i. This specification can also be obtained from the original demand system by first scaling and then translating.

The 'reverse Gorman' specification can be obtained by first translating and then scaling, which gives the demand equation as

$$q_i = {}^{s_i}[k_i + q_i \, (E^*, p)] \qquad (12.49)$$

which satisfies the first order conditions corresponding to the direct utility function

$$u = U \, (q_i / s_i) - k_i; \quad \text{for all } i=1,2....n$$

Bradbury (1992) generalised the translation model assuming that the demand for a commodity in the HH j has two components namely demographic (b_{ij}) and reference (q^*_{ij}). Therefore the total demand for HH j is given by

$$q_{ij} = b_{ij} + q^*_{ij}$$

The utility function of the HH demand was assumed to be separable and can be expressed as

$$u_j = U \, (u_1, u_2) \qquad (12.50)$$

where $\qquad\qquad u_1 = U \, (b_{1j}, b_{2j}, \, ...), \text{ and}$

$$u_2 = U(q^*_{1j}, q^*_{2j} , \, ... \,)$$

The utility function (10.50) should be maximised subject to $\sum_i p_i (b_{ij} + q^*_{ij}) = E$.

According to Gronau (1987) TE, E can be divided into the consumption of an extra person in the HH as

$$E_1 = \Sigma \, p_i \, n_{ij}, \quad \text{and}$$

$$E_2 - \Sigma p_i \, q^*_i$$

The cost of consumption for an extra person enters into the welfare function through u_1, which will vary with family compositions and hence incorporates the factor of economies of scales. The utility function u_2 incorporates the costs of children to the extent their consumption is allocated to n_{ij} rather than the q_i^*.

Bojer (1977) first indicated that the measurement of welfare using the Barten type functions rests on the assumptions: (i) that there is a one to one correspondence between the utility level of one HH member (head) and the utility level of all remaining members; (ii) that the distribution among the members within HH is equitable; and (iii) an increase in income of any member of the HH will benefit all the members of the HH; which might not be necessarily true. He incorporated all these problems and showed how the Barten-type function can be derived from a simple model of distribution for decision-making and joint consumption of the HH.

He pointed out that there is no general valid equivalent scale except one set of scales for every level of income. The theory is analogous to that of constant utility price indices and the usual index formulae apply when consumer unit numbers are known. However, such consumer unit numbers are generally not known and hence he used a method of approximating the true equivalence scales, using budget percentages of foodstuffs of different HHs, which has often been taken as an index of welfare. He argued that such approximation is necessary, because Muellbauer (1975) indicated that consumer unit scales couldn't be identified from HES data.

5. THE EXTENDED LINEAR EXPENDITURE SYSTEM (ELES)

The Barten and Translation models need price variation for identification reasons. Prices are assumed to be constant in a single year HES data. Lluch (1973) extended the Linear Expenditure System (LES) in such a way that there is enough restrictions to estimate the Barten parameters without price variations. Kakwani (1977c), Officials in Social Welfare Policy Secretariat (1981), and Binh and Whiteford (1990) used this method for the Australian HES data to estimate the consumer equivalence scales, while Griffiths and Valenzuela (1996) estimated equivalence scales for Australian household consumption goods based on the Bayesian approach.

The usual linear expenditure demand equation can be expressed as

$$e_{il} = \alpha_{il} + \beta_i (e_l - \alpha_i) \tag{12.51}$$

where $e_{il} = p_i q_{il}$ is the expenditure on the ith commodity for the lth type HH;
$\alpha_{il} = p_i c_i s_{il}$ is the subsistence expenditure on the ith commodity for the t-type HH;
$\alpha = \Sigma \alpha_{il}$ is the subsistence expenditure of the l-type HH;
β_i = the marginal budget share of the ith good, $\beta_0 > 0$ and Σ bi= 1;
e_l = total expenditure of the l-th HH;
p_i and c_i = prices and subsistence amount of the ith good respectively, p_i, c_{io}; i=1,2
...... n; and q_{il} and s_{il} = quantity consumed and equivalence scales of the ith good for the l-type HH respectively.

In the absence of price variation, the demand Equation (12.51) has been extended to identify the specific scales (s_{il}) by introducing the linear aggregate macro-consumption function as given below

$$e_l = \beta l_i + (1 - \beta)\alpha_i \tag{12.52}$$

where l_i = net income of the l-type HH , and β = common marginal propensity to consume.

The (n+l) equations given in (12.51) and (12.52) define the ELES which is formed to incorporate HH compositions. There are two noticeable points in the ELES model, viz., (i) there is no allowance for subsistence savings, and (ii) there is no direct demographic effects on savings, which is not necessarily true, because there is enough justification that HHs' saving has often been planned to spend for the satisfaction of the HH member in some future time. Hence, the estimates of the consumers' equivalence scales obtained from the ELES model should be treated with caution.

6. FUNCTIONAL FORMS

The specification of functional forms is an integral part of demand analysis. It is very important, because the estimated *consumers' equivalence scale* depends on the functional form used. Only a few functional forms are presented here, which can be used to estimate consumer equivalence scales.

6.1 The Extended Working-Leser Function

Engel estimates of equivalence scales rest on the assumption that the HH welfare depends on the HH food share of expenditures. Therefore money needed for the maintenance of an extra person of a HH would be to restore the previous food share of the HH. This requires an Engel function for food. The extended Working (1943), Leser (1963) function given below is widely used for this purpose

$$W_f = \alpha - \beta \log (E/S) + \Sigma \gamma_i s_l + \varepsilon \tag{12.53}$$

where W_f is the food share, s_l is the number of persons in the category l, S is the total number of persons in the HH, E is the TE, α, β, γ are the parameters and ε is a disturbance term.

Converting Engel curve estimates into equivalence scales is given as follows. Suppose W_{fo} is a fixed food share that we wish to maintain for two HHs with budgets E^* and E^o (reference HH). This implies that an additional $(E^* - E^o)$ expenditure is required for the HH to maintain the same food share. In this case the equivalence scale is given by

$$M = E^*/E^o$$

For the Engel curve described in (12.53), E^* is the expenditure required by HH, h to maintain the same level of satisfaction as the reference HH, h = 0 with E^o and S_{lo}, (i = 1.2....L). When food share is equal E is defined by

$$\alpha - \beta \log(E^* / S^h) + \sum_l \gamma_l S_l^h = \alpha - \beta \log (E^0 / S^0) + \sum_l \gamma_l S_l^0$$

Taking anti-logs and rearranging terms, this equation can be expressed as

$$M^h = [E^* / E^0] = [S^h / S^0] \exp \sum_l (\gamma_l / \beta)(S_l^h - S_l^0) \qquad (12.54)$$

This can be evaluated at the mean food expenditure by the estimates of equation (12.53). Bosch-Domenech (1991), Deaton and Muellbauer (1986), Espenshade (1984), etc., used this function for the estimation of equivalence scales.

Tsakloglou (1991) also used the extended Working-Leser Engel function with the following form

$$W_f = \alpha o + \alpha_1 \log E + \alpha_2 (\text{Little Child}) + \alpha_3 (\text{Big Child}) \qquad (12.55)$$

Deaton, Ruiz-Castillo and Thomas (1989) also used this kind of Engel function, but more flexible in the sense that demographic separability can be examined only at particular configurations of the explanatory variables. They used the following form for good i

$$W_i = \alpha_l + \beta_{il} \log(E / S) + \eta_{il} \log S + \sum_l \gamma_{il}(S_l / S) + \delta_i Z + \varepsilon \qquad (12.56)$$

The main difference between (12.53) and (12.56) is the introduction of new terms log S and Z. Hence, the sign of γ_i shows how the demand pattern changes with HH scales. If $\eta_i = 0$, the demand for good i is unaltered due to the scaling HH resources and numbers. The Z variables are the determinants of HH behavior. The equivalentce scales based on Engel function (12.56) are given by

$$M_{il} = [(\eta_i - \beta_i) + \gamma_{il} - \sum_l \gamma_{il}(S_j / S)]/(\beta_i + W_i) \qquad (12.57)$$

Estimates of the ratios are obtained by replacing the estimated parameters and replacing W_i and (S_j / S) by their values at the sample mean of the data.

Muellbauer (1980) used the two types of the Working-Leser function for his analysis.

For the reference HH at reference prices $p_i s_i = 0$, for all i; he used the function

$$W_i = \alpha_i + \beta_i \log E \text{ for all i} \qquad (12.58)$$

with $\Sigma\alpha_i = 1$ and $\Sigma\beta_i = 0$ to satisfy the adding up criterion.

The demand equation for a non-reference HH at a non-reference price is given by

$$W_i = \{p_i s_i/c_o) [\alpha_i + \beta_i \log (E /c_o)] + \varepsilon_i \qquad (12.59)$$

where c_o is the cost of living index which applies simultaneously for comparisons across HHs and prices. Thus, c_o is defined relatively to a reference HH at reference prices, which have been normalized at unity and is given by

$$c_0 = \frac{\sum p_i S_i(B)\beta_i(u)}{\sum \beta_i(u)}$$

Earlier, Muellbauer (1977) introduced two other demand functions, which are given below.

6.1.1 The PIGL Demand System

In budget share, the PIGL demand function is given by

$$W_i = (\alpha\beta / E)^{\gamma} \frac{(\alpha_i p_i / \alpha - \beta_i)}{(\beta^{\gamma} - \alpha^{\gamma})} + \frac{\beta^{\gamma}\beta_i - \alpha^{\gamma}(\alpha_i p_i / \alpha)}{(\beta^{\gamma} - \alpha^{\gamma})} \qquad (12.60)$$

6.1.2 The PIGLOG Function
The PIGLOG function is given by

$$W_i = \frac{\log E - \log \alpha}{\log \beta - \log \alpha}(\beta_i - \alpha_i p_i / \alpha) + \alpha_i p_i / \alpha \qquad (12.61)$$

Another way of expressing (12.61) for HH, l is that

$$W_{il} = u_l \beta_i - (1 - u_l)\alpha_i p_i / \alpha \qquad (12.62)$$

This shows that budget shares are a weighted average of those of 'rich' (β_i) and the 'poor' $(\alpha_i pi)/\alpha$; using the utility level as weight.
The u_h should fall within the range $(0,1)$;

where $u_h = \{\log E_h - \log\alpha\}/\{\log\beta - \log\alpha\}$

6.2 The Bojer Demand Function

Bojer (1977) estimated the following demand function by the Ordinary Least Squares (OLS) method

$$p_i q_i = \alpha + \beta E + \sum_{l=1}^{3}\gamma_l b_l + \sum_{k=1}^{7}\gamma_k D_k \qquad (12.63)$$

where D_k, $k = 1,2, \ldots, 7$; are seven dummy variables for the residential area, occupational status of the head of the HH, and seasonal variation.
Household members are divided into 3 groups: children (aged 0-16 years), adults (aged 17-69 years) and elderly (aged 70 years and over).
The total expenditure corresponding to a budget percentage for foodstuffs can be written as

$$E(v,b_1,b_2) = [(\sum \gamma_l b_l + \alpha)/(V - \beta)] \qquad (12.64)$$

assuming $b_3 = 0$.
Comparing the income of a HH with b_1 adults and b_2 children to that of a one-adult HH and he found that $(v-\beta)$ cancels out. The equivalent income scales are independent of (v). Therefore,

$$E(v,b_1,b_2)/E(v,1,0) = (\gamma_1 b_1 + \gamma_2 b_2 + \alpha)/(\gamma_1 + \alpha)$$
$$(12.65)$$
$$= 1 + (\gamma_1 b_{1*})/(\gamma_1 + \alpha) + (\gamma_2 b_2)/(\gamma_1 + \alpha)$$

where $b_1{}^*$ is the number of adults minus 1. Each adult adds a scale-value of $\gamma_1 / (\gamma_1 + \alpha)$, and each child adds a scale-value of $[\gamma_2 / (\gamma_1 + \alpha)]$ to the HH.

6.3 The Pollak-Wales Demand Functions

Pollak and Wales (1981) estimated the generalised CES demand functions (pooled and unpooled) along with other five functions [see the specification of these functions in Pollak and Wales (1981), p. 1549], which incorporated demographic variables into complete demand systems. Their comparisons are based on the following generalised such as CES demand system into which they incorporated single demographic variables, the number of children in the HH for the British Household Expenditure Survey data.

$$W_i = \alpha_i p_i / E + \frac{\beta_i^\gamma p_i^{1-\gamma}}{\sum \beta_i^\gamma p_i^{1-\gamma}} (1 - \sum \alpha_i p_i / E); \quad \sum \beta_i = 0; \qquad (12.66)$$

where E is the total expenditure on the included categories and W_i is the share of total expenditure devoted to the ith category; α's, β's and γ are parameters. The parameter γ is the elasticity of "substitution between 'supernumerary quantities', $(q_i - \alpha_i)$ with three goods; the generalised CES function has six independent parameters.

They observed that the pooled specification for the demographic variables has no effect on consumption behavior; where as an unpooled specification affects all demand system parameters. Using the likelihood values they found that the two Gorman demand functions, viz., scaling and the modified Prais and Houthakker models dominated over others.

6.4 The Linear Demand System

The linear function

$$e_i = \alpha_i + \beta_i E + \gamma_i T_i + \varepsilon_i \qquad (12.67)$$

where e_i is expenditure on commodity i, E is the total expenditure and T_i is the vector of test variables; $\alpha_i, \beta_i, and \gamma_i$ are the parameters to be estimated. The equivalence scales are to be estimated for households on the basis of 'reference taste' taken to be zero.

The demand function for each of the commodity provides the identifying information for the ELES, Engel and generalised translation models. Equivalence scales are calculated at a specified single income level.

The subsistence expenditure of the reference HH in the ELES model,

$$\alpha_l = \sum_i \alpha_{il} = \sum_i p_i c_i S_{il}$$

The ELES also assumes β_i parameters are identical across different HH types.

Comparing (12.51) and (12.67), the subsistence expenditure of the reference HH is given by

$$e_i^* = -\alpha_{sr} / \beta_s$$

where α_{sr} and β_s are the estimated parameters for the savings for the reference HH. Similarly, the subsistence expenditure of the comparison h-HH type is given by: $-\alpha_{sr} / \beta_s$.

Therefore, the ELES equivalence scale (at the subsistence expenditure level) is given by

$$M^h \text{ (ELES)} = \alpha_{sh} / \alpha_{sr} \qquad (12.68)$$

Similarly, the specific scale for the ith item of the h-HH type other than savings is given by

$$M_{ih}(ELES) = \frac{\alpha_{ih} - \alpha_{sh}(\beta_i / \beta_s)}{\alpha_{ir} - \alpha_{sr}(\beta_i / \beta_s)} \qquad (12.69)$$

The Engel model states that HHs, are equally well-off if the proportion of their TE spent on food is equal, i.e.

$$e_{ih} / E_h = e_{ir} / E_r$$

where e_{ih} and e_{ir} are the expenditure on the ith commodity made by the h-HH type and r-HH type respectively, whereas E_h and E_r are the TE of the h-HH type and r-HH type respectively.

Substituting the expected food expenditures given by (12.67) and assuming that the reference HH has TE, E*, these food ratios would be equal if

$$M^h[Engel] = \alpha_{fh} / [(\alpha_{fr} + E^*(\beta_{fr} - \beta_{fh})] \qquad (12.70)$$

If the βth parameters are defined to be equal across HHs then

$$M^h[Engel] = \alpha_{fh} / \alpha_{fr}. \tag{12.71}$$

which is independent of TE level.

6.5 Further Considerations on Functional Forms

Theil (1965) proposed a number of log-linear specifications, which subsequently became famous as the 'Rotterdam System'. Such models have no restrictive structuring of the estimating equation, because the estimated coefficients are constants. However, these constant coefficients should be taken seriously, because Barten (1977) considered a 'constant in applied econometrics as a magnitude which varied less than the variables it linked'. Usually, the estimated demand models have large residuals. This is not necessarily reflected in R^2 (the coefficient of determination) when the expenditure or the quantity purchased for a particular item is taken as the dependent variable. Not all the variations in observed demand can be examined by the variations of TE or prices. One should look at the demand system as an attempt to see the impact of changes in TE and prices rather than to explain changes in demand exhaustively.

Usually, intertemporal homoscedasticity is assumed for most demand models, which might not be true, and worth further investigation. It is clear in the case of LES that for a long period, the dependent variables are expenditures in current prices, which might introduce heteroscedasticity as a function of the general price level. One way to deal with such a problem is to take budget shares for goods as dependent variables. But other methods should be explored for further research.

To compare the empirical performance of various functional forms, one can use the following statistic for their judgments.

. The average information inaccuracy measure due to Parks (1969).
. Testing the co-efficient of certain terms of the models is one way to measure the performance of different models. Theil (1967) compared the performance of the Rotherdam System, the Indirect Addilog System and the LES, with or without linear trends in the b_i's and γ_i's and also a naive model implying no changes from year to year.
. The coefficient of determination (R^2) and/or the distance function, D^2-criterion can also be used to choose the functional form.
. The likelihood functions should be maximised for various alternatives in order to select an appropriate model from various alternatives [see Deaton (1974)].
. The non-nested hypothesis testing procedure can also be used to find a best functional form, when they belong to separate families. Such a test is applied on a pair wise basis. Haque (1989b) used this test to choose a suitable functional form for his Engel curve analysis.

Lancaster and Ray (1998) estimated equivalence scales based on alternative models, using the Unit Record Data obtained from the Australian HES. Donaldson and Pendakur (1999) estimated income-dependent equivalence scales from equivalent-income functions. On the other hand, Betti (1999) estimated equivalence scales based on a non-parametric approach, and Pendakur (1999) provided semi parametric estimates and tests for base-independent equivalence scales. Lastly, a number of authors such as Coulter, Cowell and Jenkins (1992b) and Matalgliati and Michelini (1999) estimated equivalence scales based on the extent of inequality and poverty. More importantly, Lancaster, Ray and Maria (1999) provided a cross-country study of equivalence scales and expenditure inequality on Unit Record Household Budget Data.

7. CONCLUSION

The essence of consumers' equivalence scales is to provide an income level and specific scales for different goods and services for various family types, so that they can maintain the same level of living even if they differ by HH compositions. Such scales can assist to design tax policies, public welfare payments, and also help to measure income inequality and poverty for different HHs more accurately. Consumer demand analysis can also be performed more accurately if such scales are incorporated in the demand functions. In that sense, the current chapter helps to understand the underlying theory on consumers' equivalence scales as well as their applications to real data for policy-making purposes. Although this is a review work, it has considerable usefulness. At the same time, this review is mainly based on the consumer demand model that concentrates on one side of the market only. It ignores two important factors viz., (i) HH production and dynamic aspects of consumption, which most HHs face; and (ii) consumption capital that influences HH demand.

In practice, consumer demand analysis has been done without any valid reasons of its potential uses. However, in this review, it has become clear how such system can be used to construct consumers' equivalence scales, as an empirical basis for forecasting and planning the composition of the demand bundle, for the construction of certain price indices, and for the design of an optimal tax structure, etc.

The specification of functional forms and the choice of a best functional form from various alternatives have also been discussed. We thus recommend choosing a simpler functional form such as the Working-Leser functional form. Construction of consumer equivalence scales will then be estimated from the chosen functional form.

Many models are mentioned in this review to estimate consumers' equivalence scales. It is now up to the individual investigators to choose which model and for what purpose the equivalence scales would be constructed. Gorman's (1976) combined translation and Barten's model is worth trying. The modified PH model should always be kept in mind as an alternative model. The Rothbarth technique is a good way to estimate consumers' equivalence scales and should be used when the PH or Barten models would be used to estimate equivalence scales. Properties of various demand models and their links with each other are worth investigations in relation to the estimation of consumers' equivalence scales.

CHAPTER 13

CONCLUSIONS

In this chapter we have summarised the main findings and made some concluding remarks about the contributions of the book. Here we mainly discussed the merits and demerits of various methods of estimating income elasticity. We also discuss the usefulness of income elasticity for making economic and social policies for the development of the society. It is argued here that income elasticity can be used to measure economic development in terms of economic growth and other social changes.

1. INTRODUCTION

The book is basically concerned with the estimation of income elasticity by different approaches. The Australian HES data are used to estimate income elasticity. In order to estimate income elasticity, one needs to specify and estimate Engel relationships. As such, the specification and estimation of Engel relationships constitute the central theme. The merits and demerits of these methods of computing Engel elasticity are given in Section 2. Section 3 is concerned with the use of Engel elasticity. Estimation of the change in consumer demand with respect to changes in income and income inequalities is discussed in this section. Finally, a few concluding remarks of the book are given in Section 4.

2. METHODS OF COMPUTING ENGEL ELASTICITY

In this book, we have computed Engel elasticity for various consumption items by different approaches. The merits and demerits of each of these methods are discussed here. In general, econometricians apply the Generalised Least Squares (GLS) method to estimate Engel elasticity for a limited number of Engel relationships from grouped data. They then select a best Engel functional form from a number of alternative functions, which are under investigation on the basis of some economic and statistical criteria and they estimate income elasticity based on that best functional form. Unfortunately, in most cases no single relationship satisfies all the economic and statistical criteria. For example, in our study different functional forms turned out to be the best functional form for different consumption items, even though the double semi-log functional (DSL) form is found to be suitable for most of the Australian household consumption items. This is a new

221

Engel function we have introduced in order to estimate Engel elasticity, which has the pleasing ability to satisfy a number of economic and statistical criterion.

The GLS method is widely applied to estimate linear functions and the functions, which are non-linear in variables but linear in parameters. But there are still many problems associated with the latter type of Engel functions when estimated by the GLS method. For example in order to get unbiased estimates of logarithmic/inverse Engel functions, the GLS method needs the within group geometric/harmonic means which are not available from official publications. In general, most investigators use the reported within group arithmetic means as proxies for the within group geometric/harmonic means, and hence an unbiased estimate of Engel elasticity cannot be achieved when the logarithmic/inverse relationships are estimated by the GLS method. Kakwani (1977b) attempted to estimate the within group geometric/harmonic means based on concentration curves for Indonesian data and used these within group geometric/harmonic means to estimate income elasticity for various consumption items. He found that the differences of elasticity estimates based on the estimated within group geometric/harmonic means, and using arithmetic means as proxies for geometric/harmonic for logarithmic/inverse relations are significant. We have also estimated within group geometric/harmonic means based on concentration curves and observed that the estimated within group geometric means exceed the observed arithmetic means for about 50% of the per capita income classes for every item, which is contradictory to the familiar inequality A.M $\geq$ G.M. Thus, the method of estimating within group geometric/harmonic means based on a concentration curve is subject to criticism. Our results indicate that the differences between the elasticity estimates based on the within group geometric/harmonic means and using arithmetic means as proxies for geometric/harmonic means are not negligible.

The concept of the average elasticity of a variable elasticity Engel function is also considered and extended for multivariate Engel functions in Chapter 4. Empirical results show that the elasticity for the hyperbolic functional form computed at average values are frequently below 1 for some known luxury items, while the average elasticity of this function is able to classify the item correctly. Thus, the average elasticity of a variable elasticity Engel function is more reliable in classifying various consumption items.

It is recognized that total expenditure rather than income is a satisfactory index of the true economic position of the households. However, Summers (1959) shows that estimating a single relationship with total expenditure as one of the independent variables using the Ordinary Least Squares (OLS) method produces inconsistent estimates of Engel parameters due to the simultaneity of the model. Later, Liviatan (1961) used the instrumental variable approach and showed that consistent estimates of Engel parameters could be obtained if recorded household income could be used as an instrument for household total expenditure. We also use the instrumental variable approach to obtain consistent estimates of Engel parameters for multivariate Engel relationships, which have not been applied previously. The difference between the elasticity estimates obtained by the GLS method, taking total expenditure as one of the independent variables, and the Generalised Instrumental Variable (GIV) approach, is referred to as the bias due to inconsistency. These biases are not significant except for a limited number of consumption items. Thus,

Prais's (1953a) remark that specifying the correct model and introducing more accurate data might ignore the amount of bias introduced by the simultaneity of the model might be acceptable.

So far, we have discussed only the problems of using the GLS method to the commonly used Engel functions for grouped data. In this regard, a number of alternative approaches are introduced to overcome the problems of the GLS method for a number of multivariate Engel relationships. Using the Box-Cox transformation, a general Engel function, which encompasses most of the commonly used Engel functions as a sub-set of a broad class of functions, is established for Australian HES data. It is shown in Chapter 5 that for most of the commodities the commonly used Engel functions are not appropriate, although the double log Engel function is not significantly different from the Box-Cox function for five out of ten consumption items. The elasticity estimates obtained from the Box-Cox Engel function do not vary substantially from those of the widely used functional forms for various consumption items. The Box-Cox Engel function yields high standard errors for the estimated elasticity probably due to the need of estimation of power parameters. The conditional standard errors are however small and close to those of various widely used simple functional forms. Also, elasticity estimates obtained from the Box-Cox Engel function satisfy some *a priori* beliefs, which are not generally satisfied by other commonly used Engel functions. Thus, we come to the crucial conclusion that the more flexible Box-Cox Engel function is the most appropriate function for the Australian HES data.

A new method of estimating Engel elasticity is presented in Chapter 7, which is based on two types of concentration curves, namely concentration curves for income and expenditure for a particular item. The elasticity estimates based on this new Engel curve is better than the commonly used Engel functions in two respects, viz., goodness of fit and the adding up criterion. This method is based on grouped data and is free from the problem of estimating unbiased income elasticity due to the use of inappropriate grouped arithmetic means for non-linear Engel functions. Specification of the concentration curve is a big problem, but the greatest disadvantage of this method is that one cannot incorporate the effect of more than one variable in specifying a concentration curve. However, it is important to note that if the data are classified according to income for different family composition then the effects of family composition and economies of scale could be incorporated by computing income elasticity for different compositions and then these elasticities could be combined to find an overall income elasticity of demand for the whole population.

The demand for food and alcohol in Australia is presented in chapters 9 and 11 respectively, where the measurement and estimation of elasticity indices are discussed. It is argued here that the elasticity index is a better measure to classify an item i.e., whether the item is elastic or inelastic, than its elasticity measure. Because, the elasticity index is a unique measure, while elasticity depends on particular values at which it is calculated. More importantly, it is demonstrated how the contributions of sub-items to the inequality measure of a broad group say 'all food' or 'all alcohol and tobacco' can be measured by decomposing the elasticity index of that broad group with respect to its sub-items. It is thus hoped that the empirical findings of the study will help health planners for any future course of action.

3. USES OF INCOME ELASTICITY

The income elasticity is commonly used in demand forecasting. Demand forecasting using income elasticity has a number of problems, because a demand forecast should be made with a new set of prices and a new size distribution of income. The distribution of income may be assumed to be invariant over time, but the assumption of constancy of relative prices is not justifiable. Aggregation is another problem in demand forecasting. The demand function derived from the HES data may be valid for the average household. Hence, the aggregate demand is found by aggregating the demand function over all the households. For prediction purposes, the change in both aggregate income and its distribution among households should be taken into consideration if the marginal propensity to consume varied from household to household. However, if the double-logarithmic functional form is used, the problem of aggregation could be avoided by assuming a proportional change in income of each household. In that case the aggregate demand for a particular item could be calculated in the following way.

Let D be the demand of a particular item and β be the income elasticity and if the change in income/overall expenditure is assumed to be the same for all households, say α per cent, then the prediction for aggregate demand is given by

$$D^* = D(1+\alpha)^\beta \tag{13.1}$$

We have already shown that the double logarithmic Engel function is not appropriate for all the commodities. In fact, frequently, a variable elasticity Engel function fits best to the HES data. On the other hand no theoretical income distribution fits well to real data. Therefore, an alternative method of estimating the increase in consumer demand from HES data is presented in Chapter 8. This method relaxes earlier assumptions about the constant elasticity Engel function and the Paretian or Lognormality income distribution. Thus, in Chapter 8, we consider the effects of changes in income and income inequalities on the future levels of consumption of different commodities. Any planned governmental investment leads to an increase in real income and expenditure of households. As a consequence, the demand for different consumption items will increase. Unless necessary steps are taken in advance to meet the increased demand for consumption, an inflationary pressure is likely to build up in certain sections of the economy. Therefore, it is of considerable importance to forecast aggregate demand for different items for proper production planning. Thus, income elasticity and the demand function derived from cross sectional data are of great importance for production planning, policy making and for prediction purposes.

Apart from the above mentioned uses, HES data can be used in making social policies, showing how poverty may affect certain sections of the population, what proportion of households live in various states of poverty and how these proportions change through time. Econometric investigations are of great interest to academics in understanding the demand structure of consumers and income elasticity.

4. CONCLUDING REMARKS

As far as the method of estimating income elasticity is concerned, the GLS method should be used to estimate the double semi-log Engel function if the complete cross-classification data are available. The Box-Cox Engel function should be used to estimate the income elasticity for different items, particularly for those items where there is any doubt about the commonly used Engel functions. This is because the Box-Cox Engel function is the most appropriate function for Australian HES data, even though it yields high standard errors of the estimated elasticity and needs a large number of observations. If data are available for only a small number of broad income groups, the GLS method should not be used to estimate income elasticity. In that case, the new method of computing income elasticity presented in Chapter 7 should be used. In order to take into account the effect of family size, family composition elasticity for separate types of families can be calculated and then the elasticity for the whole population can be obtained from these family composition elasticities, provided family composition data are available. The income elasticity index is a useful and unique measure to identify whether an item is an elastic or inelastic commodity. So, the income elasticity could be estimated where there is any doubt whether the item is an elastic or inelastic commodity. The increase in consumer demand over time can be estimated by our alternative method for demand projection. It is thus hoped that our method gives a better result than the existing methods for demand projections. Thus, we recommend our method to estimate the increase in consumer demand with two directional changes, namely changes in income and changes in income inequalities of the households. However, all these conclusions are conditional upon the particular model specification adopted in this book and need not hold universally.

The investigations, which were undertaken as a contribution to our knowledge of an important sector of the economic system, did not have any special practical aims in mind. However, it is hoped that some of the findings will be of interest to many whose concern with consumers' behaviour is not purely academic. Thus, much of the material presented here in estimating income elasticity should be of interest from the market research standpoint, while the increased consumer demand is important in connection with proper production planning and policy making.

The present book should be regarded only as indicative of the type of problem that may be solved by an econometric analysis for the HES data. The results presented in this book are thus in the nature of a series of pieces of research, which are based on previous research, but attempt to add a brick here and there and end with the hope that in doing so no weak points are left in the structure.

REFERENCES

Abounoori, E., and Mcloughan, P. (2000). Measuring the Gini Coefficient: An Empirical
    Assessment of Non-parametric and Parametric Methods. Mimeo. Department of Finance and
    Accounting, University of Liverpool. Liverpool.
Agrawal, N. (1989). *Projection as a Tax on Consumers: Who Bears the Burden?* Impact Research
    Center, University of Melbourne. Carlton.
Aguirre-Torres V., and Gallant, A. R. (1983). The null and non-null asymptotic distribution of the
    Cox test for multivariate non-linear regression: Alternatives and a new distribution-free Cox test.
    Journal of Econometrics, 21, 5-33.
Aigner, D. J., and Goldberger, A. S. (1970), Estimation of Pareto's law from grouped observations.
    Journal of the American Statistical Association, 65, 712-723.
Aitchinson, J., and Brown, J. A. C. (1954). On criteria for description of income distribution.
    Metroeconomica, 6, 88-107.
Aitchison, J., and Brown, J. A. C. (1957). *The Log Normal Distribution*, Cambridge University Press.
    Cambridge.
Aitken, A. C. (1934). On least squares and linear combination of observations. *Proceeding of the
    Royal Society of Edinburgh*, 55, 42-48.
Allen, R. G. D. (1942). Expenditure patterns of families of different sizes. In O. Lange, F. McIntyre
    and T. Yntema (eds). *Studies in Mathematical Economics and Econometrics*. Chicago University
    Press. Chicago.
Allen, R. G. D., and Bowley A. L. (1935). *Family Expenditure*. Staples. London.
Allingham, M. G. (1972). The measurement of inequality. *Journal of Economic Theory*, 5, 163-169.
Alperovich, G., Deutsch, J., and Machnes, Y. (1999). The demand for car ownership: Evidence from
    Israeli data. *International Journal of Transport Economics*, 26, 351-375.
Amoroso, L. (1925). Ricerche intorno alla curva dei redditi. *Annali di Mathematica pura ed
    applicata*. Series 4-21, 123-159.
Anderson, H. M., and Vahid, F. (1997). On the correspondence between individual and aggregate
    food consumption function: Evidence from the USA and the Netherlands. *Journal of Applied
    Econometrics*, 12, 477-507.
Anderson, K. and Osmond, R. (1998). *Trends and Cycles in the Australian Wine Industry: 1850 to
    2000*. Centre for Economic Studies, University of Adelaide. Adelaide.
Andrikopoulos, A., Brox, J., and Carvalho, E. (1997). The demand for domestic and imported
    alcoholic beverages in Ontario, Canada: A dynamic simultaneous equation approach. *Applied
    Economics*, 29, 945-954.
Apps, P. (1997). *Income Distribution, Redistribution and Incentives*, Center for Economic Policy,
    Australian National University. (RePEc:fth:aunaep:379).
    http://netec.mcc.ac.uk/HoPEc/geminiabout.html
Atkinson, A. B., Rainwater, L., and Smeeding, T. (1995). *Income Distribution in European
    Countries*. DAE Working Papers/Department of Applied Economics, University of Cambridge.
    (RePEc: cam: camdae: 9535). http://netec.mcc.ac.uk.HoPEc/geminiabout.html.
Atkinson, A. B. (1975). *The Economics of Inequality*. Clarendon Press. Oxford.
Atkinson, A. B. (1970). On the measurement of inequality. *Journal of Economic Theory*, 2, 244-263.
Atkinson, A. B. (1996). Income distribution in Europe and the United States. *Oxford Review of
    Economic Policy*, 12, 15-28.

228

Atkinson, A., Rainwater, L., et al. (1995). *Income Distribution in the OECD Countries: Evidence from the Luxembourg Income Study*. OECD. Paris.

Attanasio, O. P., and Szekely, M. (1999). *Household Savings and Income Distribution in Mexico*. Inter-American Development Bank. (RePEc:fth:inadeb:390).
    http://netec.mcc.ac.uk/BibEc/data/Papers/fthinadeb390.html

Australian Bureau of Statistics (ABS). (1977). *Australian Household Expenditure Survey: 1974-75*. Income Distribution, Bulletin 7. Canberra.

Australian Bureau of Statistics (ABS). (1984). *Household Expenditure Survey*, Catalogue Nos 6527.0 – 6544.0. Canberra.

Australian Bureau of Statistics (ABS). (1986). *Income Distribution Survey*. Canberra.

Australian Bureau of Statistics (ABS). (1987). *1984 Household Expenditure Survey, Australia: Effects of Government Benefits and Tax on Household Income*, Catalogue No. 6537.0. Canberra.

Australian Bureau of Statistics (ABS). (1988). *Housing Survey*. Canberra.

Australian Bureau of Statistics (ABS). (1988-89). *Australian National Accounts*, Catalogue No. 6533.0. Canberra.

Australian Bureau of Statistics (ABS). (1989). *Survey of Employed Wage and Salary Earners*. Canberra.

Australian Bureau of Statistics (ABS). (1991). *1988-89 HES Data Evaluation: Paper I. An Evaluation of Income Data from the 1988-89 Household Expenditure Survey*, Part A. Canberra.

Australian Bureau of Statistics (ABS). (1995). *Summary of Results 1993-94 Household Expenditure Survey: Australia*. ABS Catalogue No. 6530.0. Canberra.

Australian Bureau of Statistics (ABS). (1996). *Detailed Expenditure Items 1993-94 Household Expenditure Survey: Australia*. Catalogue No. 6535.0. Canberra.

Australian Bureau of Statistics (ABS). (1999). *Apparent Consumption of Foodstuffs and Nutrients*. ABS Catalogue No. 4306. Canberra.

Australian Bureau of Statistics (ABS). (2000a). *Household Expenditure Survey, 1998-99*. ABS Catalogue No. 6530.0. Canberra.

Australian Bureau of Statistics. (ABS). (2000b). *Use of the Internet by Households*. Catalogue No. 8147.0, Canberra.

Australian Bureau of Statistics (ABS). (2000c). *Household Use of Information Technology*. Catalogue No. 8146.0. Canberra.

Australian Bureau of Statistics (ABS). *Household Expenditure Survey, 1974-75*, Bulletins 1-8, Catalogue Nos. 6507.0 – 6514.0. Canberra.

Australian Bureau of Statistics (ABS). *Household Expenditure Survey, 1975-76*, Bulletins 1-4, Catalogue Nos. 6516.0 – 6519.0. Canberra

Australian Bureau of Statistics (ABS). *Household Expenditure Survey, 1988-89*, Catalogue Nos. 6527.0 – 654.0. Canberra.

Australian Institute of Family Studies. (1989). *Families and the Tax Package*. AIFS Bulletin No. 6. AIFS. Melbourne.

Australian Parliament. (1999). *Deregulation of the Australian Dairy Industry*. Canberra: Senate Regional Affairs and Transport Reference Committee. October 1999. (Downloadable at www.affa.gov.au/diap).

Australian Taxation Office. (1988-89). *Taxation Statistics*. Australian Government Publication Press. Canberra.

Backer, G. S. (1962). Investment of human capital: A theoretical analysis. *Journal of Political Economy*, 70, 9-49.

Backer, G. S. (1967). *Human Capital and the Personal Distribution of Income*. University of Michigan Press. Ann Arbor.

Banerjee, A. V., and Duflo, E. (2000a). *Inequality and Growth: What can the Data say?* Working Paper No. 00-09, Department of Economics, MIT. Minnesota.

Banerjee, A. V., and Duflo, E. (2000b). *A Reassessment of the Relationship Between Inequality and Growth*. Unpublished manuscript, Department of Economics, MIT. Minnesota.

Banks, J., Blundell, R., and Lewbel, A. (1994). Quadratic Engel curves, indirect tax reform and welfare measurement. University College London, Discussion Paper, January 1994: 28.

Banks, J., Blundell, R., and Lewbel, A. (1997). Quadratic Engel curves and consumer demand. *The Review of Economics and Statistics*, 79, 527-539.

Barnow, B. S. (1994). Economic studies of expenditures on children and their relationships to child support guidelines. Child Support Guidelines: The Next Generation. US Department of Health and Human Services. USGPO. Washington DC.

Barrett, G., Crossley, T., and Worswick, C. (2000). Consumption and income inequality in Australia. *Economic Record*, 76, 116-38.

Barrett G., Crossley, T., and Worswick, C. (1999). *Consumption and Income Inequality in Australia.* Mimeo: Australian National University. Canberra.

Barten, A. P. (1964). Family composition, prices and expenditure patterns. In P. Hart, G. Mills and J. Whittaker (eds). *Economic Analysis for National Economic Planning.* 16th Symposium of the Colston Society. Butterworth. London.

Barten, A. P. (1965). *Evidence on the Slutsky's Conditions for Demand Equations: Monogram.* Report No. 6504. Netherlands School of Economics, Econometric Institute. Amsterdam.

Barten, A. P. (1977). The systems of consumer demand functions approach: A review. *Econometrica,* 45, 23-51.

Bates, D., and Watts, D. (1988). *Non-linear Regression and its Applications.* Wiley. New York.

Batty, I. Z. (1974). Inequality of poverty in rural India. *Sankhya: The Indian journal of Statistics*, 36, 291-336.

Beatty, T. M. K and LaFrance, J. T. (2001). *Income Elasticity and Functional Form.* Working Paper No. 922, Giannini Foundation of Agricultural Economics, California Agricultural Experiment Station.

Becker, G. S. (1967). *Human Capital and Personal Distribution of Income.* University of Michigan Press. Ann Arbor.

Bell, L., and Richard, F. (1998). *A Working Hard: Hours Worked and Income Dispersion in Germany.*

Benabou, R. (1996). *Inequality and Growth, NBER Macroeconomics Annual 1996* . MIT Press. Cambridge, Mass.

Bensu, J., Kmenta, J., and Shapiro H. (1976). The dynamics of household budget allocation to food expenditures. *The Review of Economics and Statistics,* 58, 129-138.

Bentzel, R. (1970). The social significance of income distribution statistics. *Review of Income and Wealth*, series 16, 253-264

Bergantino, A. (1997). Estimating Engel curves for transport expenditures: Evidence from UK household budget data. *International Journal of Transport Economics*, 24, 279-305.

Berndt, E. R., and Showalter, M. H., and Wooldridge, J. M. (1993). An empirical investigation of the Box-Cox model and a non-linear least squares alternative. *Econometric Reviews*, 12, 5-102.

Betti, G. (1999). A non-parametric approach to equivalence scales. *Statistics in Transition*, 45, 181-194.

Bewley, R. A. (1982). On the functional form of Engel curves: The Australian Household Expenditure Survey 1975-76. *Economic Record*, 58, 82-91.

Bhargava, A. (1991). Estimating short and long run income elasticities of foods and nutrients for rural South India. *Journal of the Royal Statistical society,* Series A, 154, 157-174.

Bhattacharya, N. (1973). *The Average Elasticity of Variable Elasticity Engel Curve.* Technical Report No. Econ/2/73, Research and Training School, Indian Statistical Institute. Calcutta.

Binh, T. N., and Whiteford, P. (1990). Household equivalence scales: New Australian estimates from the 1984 household expenditure survey. *Economic Record,* 66, 221-234.

Bjerke, K. (1961). Some income and wage distribution theories: Summary and comments. *Weltwirtschaftliches (Archiv)*, 86, 46-66.

Birrell, B., and Rapson, V. (1997). More single parents equals more poverty. *News Weekly.* October, p. 8.

Bjorner, T. (1999). Demand for car ownership and use in Denmark: A micro econometric model. *International Journal of Transport Economics*, 26, 377-395.

Blackorby, C., Boyce, R., and Russell R. R. (1978). Estimation of demand systems generated by the Gorman polar form: A generalization of the S-branch utility tree. *Econometrica*, 46, 345-365.

Blake, D., and Nied, A. (1997). The demand for alcohol in the United Kingdom. *Applied Economics*, 29, 1655-1673.

Blinder, A. S. (1974). *Toward an Economic Theory of Income Distribution.* MIT Press. Cambridge: Mass.

Blisard, N., Lin B-H., Cromartie, J., and Ballenger , N. (2002). America's changing appetite: Food consumption and spending to 2020. *Food Review*, 25, 2-9.

Blundell, R., and Lewbel, A. (1990). *The Information Content of Equivalence Scales*. IFS Working Paper, W90/4.

Blundell, R., and Preston, I. (1995). Income expenditure and the living standards of UK Households. *Fiscal Studies*, 16.

Blundell, R. and Preston, I. (1998). Consumption inequality and income uncertainty. *Quarterly Journal of Economics*, 113, 603-640.

Blundell, R., Browning, M., and Crawford, I. (1997). Nonparametric Engel Curves and Revealed Preferences. Consumption Seminar, INSEE.

Blundell, R., and Robin, M. (1999). An iterated least squares estimator for conditionally linear equations models. *Journal of Applied Econometrics*, 14, 209-232.

Bojer, H. (1977). The effect on consumption of household size and composition. *European Economic Review*, 9, 169-193.

Bojer, H. (1998). Equivalence Scales and Intra-household Distribution. Memorandum, Department of Economics, (RePEc:att:osloec:28), Oslo.

Borland, J. (1998). Earnings Inequality in Australia: Changes, Causes and Consequences. Centre for Economic Policy Research Discussion Paper No. 390, Australian National University. Canberra.

Borland, J., and Wilkins, R. (1996). Earnings inequality in Australia. *Economic Record*, 72, 7-23.

Bosch-Domenech, A. (1991). Economics of scale, location, age and sex discrimination in household Demand. *European Economic Review*, 35, 1589-1595.

Bourguignon, F. and Morrison, C. (1990). Income distribution, development and foreign trade: Cross sectional analysis. *European Economic Review*, 34, 1113-1132.

Bourguignon, F., and Morrisson, C. H. (1999). The size distribution of income among world citizens, 1820-1990. Manuscript (June).

Bowles, S. (1969). *Planning Educational Systems for Economic Growth*. Harvard Economic Studies, Vol. 133. Harvard University Press. Cambridge, Mass.

Bowman, M. J. (1945). A graphical analysis of personal income distribution in the United States. *American Economic Review*, 35, 607-628.

Box, G. E. P., and Cox, D. R. (1964). An analysis of transformations. *Journal of the Royal Statistical Society,* Series B, 26, 211-252.

Box, G. E. P., and Tidwell, P. W. (1962). Transformation of the independent variables. *Technometrics*, 4, 531-550.

Boyle, G. E. (1996). A MAIDS model of meat demand. *The Economic and Social Review*, 27, 309-319.

Bradbury, B. (1989a). Adult Goods and the Cost of Children. Social Welfare Research Centre, Discussion Paper No. 13. Sydney.

Bradbury, B. (1989b). Adult Goods and the Cost of Children in Australia. Social Welfare Research Center, University of New South Wales. Kensington.

Bradbury, B. (1992). Measuring the Cost of Children. Discussion Paper No. 32, Social Welfare Research Centre, Sydney

Bradbury, B. (1996). Household Income Sharing, Joint Consumption and the Expenditure Patterns of Australian Retired Couples and Single People. Social Research Policy Center, University of New South Wales. Kensington.

Bradley, K. A., Badrinath, S., Bush, K., Boyd-Wickizer, J., and Anawalt, B. (1998). Medical risks for women who drink alcohol. *Journal of General and Internal Medicine*, 13, 627-639.

Bresciani-turroni, C. (1910). Di un indice misuratone della disugaglianza dei redditi. Studi in Onone di B Brugi, pp. 54-61, Palermo.

Bridge, J. L., (1971). *Applied Econometrics*. North-Holland Publishing Company. London.

Bronfenbrenner, M. (1971). *Income Distribution Theory*. Aldine-Atherton. Chicago.

Brosig, S. (1998). A Model of Food Consumption of Czech Private Households 1991-96. Discussion Paper 9802, Institute of Agricultural Economics. Gottingen.

Brosig, S. (2000). A Model of Household Type Specific Food Demand Behaviour in Hungary. Discussion Paper No. 30, Institute of Agricultural Development in Central and Eastern Europe.

Brown, A., and Deaton, A. (1972). Surveys in applied economics: Models of consumer behaviour. *The Economic Journal*, 82, 1145-1236.

Buchinsky, M. (1995). Quantile regression, the Box-Cox transformation model and US wage structure 1963-1987. *Journal of Econometrics*, 65, 109-154.

Budd, E. C. (1970). Post-war changes in the size distribution of income in the US. *American Economic Review*, 60, 247-260.

Burr, I. W. (1972). Cumulative frequency functions. *Annals of Mathematical Statistics*, 13, 215-235.

Buse, A. (1973). Goodness of fit in generalized least squares. *The American Statistician*, 27, 106-108.

Buse, A. (1994). Evaluating the linearized almost ideal demand system. *American Journal of Agricultural Economics*, 76, 781-93.

Buse, A. (1998). Testing homogeneity in the linearized almost ideal demand system. *American Journal of Agricultural Economics*, 80, 208-220.

Buse, A., and Chan, W. H. (2000). Invariance, price indices and estimation in almost ideal demand systems. *Empirical economics*, Forthcoming, 25, 519-539.

Cai, L. (1998). Analyzing household food expenditure patterns on trips and vacations: A Tobit model. *Journal of Hospitality and Tourism Research*, 22, 338-358.

Carnegie, G. D., and Walker, S. P. (2001). Accounting and Accountability in the Australian Household from the Early Nineteenth Century. ARC Large Research Grant, 2001-2002.

Carrol, R. J., Ruppert, J., and Stefanski, L. A. (1995). *Measurement Error in Non-linear Models*. Chapman and Hall. London

Cass, B. (1986). The economic circumstances of single parent families in Australia: Implications for child maintenance policies and the social security system. In Social Justice Project, Child Support. Research School of Social Science, ANU. Canberra.

Cassel, G. (1899). Grundris einer elementaren preislehre. *Zeitschrift fur die Gesamte. Staatwissenschaft*, 55.

Cassel, G. (1918). *Theoretische Sozialokonomie* (4th edn, 1927). Leipzig. Scholl.

Castles, I. (1987). Government welfare outlays: Who benefits? Who pays? *Australian Statistician: Bulletin of Public Administration*, 14. Canberra.

Castles, I. (1991). Responding to the User Needs. *Journal of the Royal Statistical Society*, Series A, 154, 6-10.

Champernowne, D .G. (1952). The graduation of income distributions. *Econometrica*, 20, 591-615.

Champernowne, D. G. (1953). A model of income distribution. *Economic Journal*, 63, 318-51.

Champernowne, D. G. (1973). *Distribution of Income Between Persons*. Cambridge University Press. Cambridge.

Champernowne, D. G. (1974). A comparison of measures of inequality of income distribution. *Economic Journal*, 84, 787-816.

Chang, H. S. (1977). Functional forms and the demand for meat in the United States. *The Review of Economic and Statistics*, 59, 355-359.

Chatterjee, S., Michelini, C., and Ray, R. (1994). Expenditure patterns and aggregate consumer behaviour: Some experiments with Australian and New Zealand data. *The Economic Record*, 70, 278-91.

Chatterjee, S., and Michelini, C. (1998). Household consumption equivalence scales: Some estimates from New Zealand Household Expenditure and Income Survey. *Australian and New Zealand Journal of Statistics*, 40, 141-50.

Chavas, J. P. (1989). How restrictive is the Prais-Houthakker model. *European Economic Review*, 33, 1363-1372.

Chiswick, B. R. (1968). The average level of schooling and the intra-regional inequality of income: A clarification. *American Economic Review*, 58, 495-501.

Chiswick, B. R. (1971). Earning inequality and economic development. *Quarterly Journal of Economics*, 85, 21-32.

Chiswick, B. R. (1974). *Income Inequality: Regional Analysis with a Human Capital Framework*, National Bureau of Economic Research, New York.

Christine, E. S, Geoffrey, N. S, and Murray, H. H. (1998). Patterns of meat consumption: Some Australian evidence. *Australian Agribusiness Review*, 6.

Clark, A. E., and Oswald, A, J. (1996). A satisfaction and comparison of income. *Journal of Public Economics*, 61, 359-381.

Clark, T., and Taylor, J. (1999). Income inequality: A tale of two cycles? *Fiscal Studies*, 20, 387-408.

Clements, K. W., and Selvanathan, S. (1994). Understanding consumption patterns. *Empirical Economics*, 19, 69-110.

232

Cochran, W. G., and Cox, G. M. (1957). *Experimental Designs* (2nd edn). John Wiley. London.

Conniffe, D. (2001). A New System of Consumer Demand Equations, Paper prepared for Economic Workshop Seminar. NUI. Maynooth.

Coondoo, D. (1970). Economies of Scale in Household Consumption in India. Tech. Report No. Econ/7/70, Research and Training School, Indian Statistical Institute. Calcutta.

Coondoo, D. (1972). On the Effect of the Household Composition on Household Consumption Pattern. Tech. Report No. Econ/13/72, Research and Training School, Indian Statistical Institute. Calcutta.

Costa, M., and Michelini, C. (1999). An Analysis of Distribution of Income and Wealth Among Italian Households. Department of Applied and International Economics, Discussion Paper No. 99.11, Massey University.

Coulter, F. A. E., Cowell, F. A. and Jenkins, S. P. (1992a). Differences in needs and assessment of income distributions. *Bulletin of Economic Research*, 44, 77-124.

Coulter, F. A. E., Cowell, F. A. and Jenkins, S. P. (1992b). Equivalence scale relatives and the extent of inequality and poverty. *Economic Journal*, 102, 1067-1082.

Coulter, F., Cowell, F., and Jenkins, Y. S. (1992). Equivalence scale relatives and the extent of inequality and Poverty. *Economic Journal*, 102, 1067-1082.

Cowell, F. A. (1995). *Measuring Inequality* (2nd edn). Harvester Wheatsheaf. Hemel Hempstead.

Cox, D. R. (1961). Tests of separate families of hypotheses. In *Proceedings of the Fourth Berkley Symposium in Mathematical Statistics and Probability,* 1, 105-123. University of California Press. Berkely.

Cox, D. R. (1962). Further results on tests of separate families of hypotheses. *Journal of the Royal Statistical Society, Series B,* 24, 406-424.

Cramer, H. (1946). *Mathematical Methods of Statistic*. Princeton University Press. Princeton.

Cramer, J. S. (1964). Efficient grouping, regression and correlation in Engel curve analysis, *Journal of the American Statistical Association*, 59, 233-250.

Cramer, J. S. (1973a). *Empirical Econometrics (3rd Print)*. North Holland. Amsterdam.

Cramer, J. S. (1973b). Interaction of income and price in consumer demand. *International Economic Review.* 14, 351-363.

Creedy, J. (1997). Inequality, Mobility and Income distribution Comparisons. Working Paper Series No. 555, Department of Economics, University of Melbourne. Melbourne.

Dalton, H. (1920). The measurement of the inequality of incomes. *Economic Journal*, 30, 348-361.

Dasgupta, I. (2001). Gender biased redistribution and intra-household distribution. *European Economic review*, 45, 1711-1722.

Das-Gupta, P., Sen, A. K., and Starrett, D. (1973). Notes on the measurement of Inequality. *Journal of Economic Theory*, 6, 180-187.

David, L. R., and Wales, T. J. (1996). *Flexible and Semi-flexible Consumer Demands with Quadratic Engel Curves*. Discussion Paper No. 96-30, Department of Economics, The University of British Columbia.

Davidson, R. and Mackinnon, J. G. (1981). Several tests for model specification in the Presence of alternative Hypotheses. *Econometrica*, 49, 781-793.

Davidson, R., and Mackinnon, J. G. (1985). Testing linear and log-linear regressions against Box-Cox Alternatives. *Canadian Journal of Economics*, 18, 499-517.

Davidson, R., and Duclos, J. Y. (1998). Statistical Inference for Stochastic Dominance and for the Measurement of Poverty and Inequality, GREQAM/Universite Aix-Marseille III (RePEc:fth:aixmeq:98a14).
   http://netec.mcc.ac.uk/BibEc/data/papers/fthaixmeq98a14.html

Davidson, R., and Duclos, J. Y. (2000). Statistical inference for stochastic dominance and for the measurement of poverty and inequality, *Econometrica*, 68, 1435-1465.

Dayal, N., Gomulka, J., Milford, L., Sutherland H., and Taylor, R. (2000). *Enhancing Family Resources Survey Income Data with Expenditure Data from the Family Expenditure Survey: Data Comparison*. MU/RN/40, Micro-simulation Unit Publications, Department of Applied Economics, University of Cambridge. Cambridge.

De Gregorio, J., and Lee, J. W. (1998). *Education and Income Distribution: New Evidence from Cross-Country Data*. Mimeo. Centre for Applied Economics, Universidad de Chile.

De Wolff, P., and Van Slijpe, A. R. D. (1972). *The Relationship Between Income, Intelligence, Education and Social Background.* Institute of Actuarial Science and Econometrics, University of Amsterdam.

Deaton, A. S. (1974). The analysis of consumer demand in the United Kingdom: 1900–1970. *Econometrica,* 42, 341-367.

Deaton, A. S. (1978). Specification and testing in applied demand analysis. *The Economic Journal,* 88, 524-536.

Deaton, A. S. (1982). Inequality and needs: Some experimental results for Sri Lanka. *Population and Development Review,* 8, 35-49.

Deaton, A. S. (1997). *The Analysis of Household Surveys: A Microeconomic Approach to Development Policy.* John Hopkins University Press. Baltimore.

Deaton A. S., and Muellbauer, J. (1980). An almost ideal demand system. *The American Economic Review,* 70, 312-326.

Deaton, A. S., and Muellbauer, J. (1986). Measuring child costs in poor countries. *Journal of Political Economy.* 94, 720-744.

Deaton, A. S., and Paxson, C. (1994). Inter-temporal choice and inequality. *Journal of Political Economy,* 102, 437-467.

Deaton, A. S., Ruiz-Castillo, J., and Thomas, D. (1989). The influence of household composition on household expenditure patterns: Theory and Spanish evidence. *Journal of Political Economy,* 97, 179-203.

Deininger, K., and Squire, L. (1996). A new data set measuring income inequality. *World Bank Economic Review,* 10, 565-591.

Deininger, K., and Olinto, P. (2000). Asset Distribution, Inequality and Growth. Working Paper No. 2375, World Bank Development Research Group. Washington DC.

Deltas, G. (2000). *The Small Sample Bias of the Gini Coefficient: Results and Implications for Empirical Research.* University of Illinois. Urbana-Champain. http://www.staff.uiuc.edu/~deltas.

Didukh, G. (2001). *Health and Personal Care Consumption Patterns by Foreign Born and Canadian Born Households: 1984-1996,* MA Project. Department of Economics, Simon Fraser University, Harbour City, Canada.

Diewert, W. E., and Wales, T. J. (1987). Flexible functional forms and global curvature conditions. *Econometrica,* 55, 43-68.

Diewert, W. E., and Wales, T. J. (1988a). Normalized quadratic systems of consumer demand functions. *Journal of Business and Economic statistics,* 6, 303-312.

Diewert, W. E., and Wales, T. J. (1988b). A normalized quadratic semi-flexible functional form. *Journal of Econometrics,* 37, 327-342.

Diewert, W. E., and Wales, T. J. (1993). Linear quadratic spline models for consumer demand unctions. *Canadian Journal of Economics,* 26, 77-106.

Diewert, W. E., and Wales, T. J. (1995). Flexible functional forms and tests of homogeneous separability. *Journal of Econometrics,* 67, 259-302.

Dixon, D., Foster, C. and Gallagher, P. (1985). Social security issues and the tax reform debate. *Economic Journal and policy,* 15, 124-144.

Dolton, P. (2002). Evaluation of economic and social policies. *Journal of the Royal Statistical Society,* Series A, 165, 9 -11.

Donaldson, D., and Pendakur, K. (1999). Equivalent-Income Functions and Income-Dependent Equivalence Scales. Discussion Paper 99-16, Department of Economics, University of British Columbia, (dvdd@interchange.ubc.ca)

Dong, D., Shonkwiler, J., S., Capps, Jr. O. (1998). An estimation of demand functions using cross sectional household data: The problem revisited. *American Journal of Agricultural Economics,* 80, 466-473.

Dougherty, C. R. S. (1971). *Estimates of labour aggregate functions.* Harvard Center for International Affairs, Economic Development Report No. 190, Development Research Group, Cambridge.

Dougherty, C. R. S. (1972). Substitution and the structure of the labour force. *Economic Journal,,* 82.

Department of Social Security (DSS). (2000). *Households Below Average Income: A Statistical Analysis 1994/5 – 1998/99,* Corporate Document Services: Leeds.

Duclos, J. Y., and Makdissi, P. (2000). Welfare, Inequality and Poverty: A Unifying Approach. Working Paper 00-01, Department d'Economique, Universite de Aherbrooke.

234

Dunnsire, M., and Baldwin, S. (1999). Urban-rural comparisons of drink-driving behaviour among late teens: A preliminary investigation. *Alcohol and Alcoholism*, 34, 59-64.

Easton, B. (1998). *Household Equivalence Scales and the Household Survey. Economic and Social trust on New Zealand*. Wellington.

Ebert, U. (1995). Income inequality and differences in household size. *Mathematical Social Sciences*, 30, 37-55.

Edgar, D. (1989). The Cost of Children. In D. Edgar, D. Keane, and P. McDonald (eds). *Child Poverty*. Allen and Unwin. Sydney.

Ellis, D. F. (1976). A Slutsky equation for demand correspondence. *Econometrica*, 44, 825-828.

Elsner, K. (1999). *Analysing Russian Food Expenditure Using Micro Data*. Discussion Paper 23. IAMO. Halle.

Elteto, O., and Frigyes, E. (1968). New inequality measures as efficient for casual analysis and planning. *Econometrica*, 36, 383-396.

Engel, E. (1857). Die- Produktiopns und Consumptions Verhaltnisse des Konigreichs Sachsen. In *Zeitschrift des Statistisehen Bureaus des Koniglich Sachsischen Ministerium des Innern,* 22 (November)

Engel, E. (1883). Ver werth des menschen; I. Teil: Der kostenwerth des menschen. In *Volkswirtschaftlich Zeitfragen,* Vol. 37-38, L. Simon. pp. 1-74, Berlin.

Engel, E. (1895). Die lebenskosten belgisch arbeiter-familien fruher und Jetzt. *International Statistical Institute Bulletin,* 9, 1-124, Rome.

Espenshade, T. J. (1972). The price of children and social-economic theories of fatality. *Population Studies,* 26, 207-221.

Espenshade, T. J. (1984). *Investigating in Children: New Estimates of Parental Expenditure*. Urban Institute Press. Washington.

Evans, G. A and Deaton, A. (1980). Testing linear versus logarithmic regression models. *Review of Economics Studies,* 47, 275-91.

Fagiolo, G. (2001). *Engel Curves Specifications in an Artificial Model of Consumption Dynamics with Socially Evolving Preferences*. Sant'Anna School of Advanced Studies, Laboratory of Economics and Management. Pias.

Fair, R. C. (1971). The optimal distribution of income. *Quarterly Journal of Economics,* 85, 551-579.

Federal Office of Road Safety (FORS). (1996). *Alcohol and Road Fatalities*. Monograph 10. FORS. Canberra.

Federal Office of Road Safety (FORS). (1997). *Alcohol and road Fatalities in Australia 1996.* Monograph 22. FORS. Canberra.

Feller, W. (1966). *An Introduction to Probability Theory and Its Applications*, II. Wiley, New York.

Firebaugh, G. (1999). Empirics of world income inequality. *American Journal of Sociology,* 104, 1597-1630.

Fisher, F. M. (1987). Household equivalence scales and interpersonal comparisons. *Review of Economic Studies,* 54, 519-524.

Fisher, F. M., and Shell, K. (1971). Taste and quality change in the pure theory of the true cost of living index. In Z. Griliches (ed.). *Price Indices and Quality Change: Studies in New Methods of Measurement*. Harvard University Press. Cambridge.

Fisk, P. R. (1961). The graduation of income distributions. *Econometrica*, 29, 171-185.

Flemming, J., and Micklewright, J. (1999). *Income Distribution: Economic Systems and Transitions*. Available for download as a pdf file from http://www.unicef-icdc.org

Flores, N., and Carson, R. (1995). *The Relationship Between the Income Elasticities of Demand and Willingness to Pay*. Manuscript. University of California. San Diego.

Florio, M. (2001). The great divestiture: An evaluation of the welfare impact of British privatizations 1979-1997. Mimeo. DEPA. University of Milan.

Forbes, K. J. (2000). A reassessment of the relationship between inequality and Growth. *American Economic Review*, 90, 869-887.

Forsyth, F. G. (1960). The relationship between family size and family expenditure. *Journal of the Royal Statistical Society*, 123, 367-397.

Fousekis, P., and Revell, B, J. (2001). Meat demand in the UK: A differential approach. *Journal of Agricultural and Applied Economics*, 32, 11-19.

Friedman, M. (1952). A method of comparing incomes of families differing in composition. *Studies of Income and Wealth*, Vol. 15. National Bureau of Economic Research. New York.

Friedman, M. (1953). Choice, chance and personal distribution of income, *Journal of political Economy*, 61, 277-290.

Friedman, M. (1957). *A Theory of Consumption Function*. Princeton University Press. Princeton.

Frohberg, K., and Winter, E. (2001). Functional Forms in Complete Demand Systems - Do they matter for Policy Analysis? Internal Working Paper, IAMO. Halle, Germany.

Fry, J. M., Fry, T. R. L., and McLaren, K. R. (1996a*)*. *Compositional Data Analysis and Zeros in Micro Data*. General Paper No. G-120. March 1996. The Centre of Policy Studies, Monash University, Clayton.

Fry, J. M., Fry, T. R. L., and McLaren, K. R. (1996b). The stochastic specification of demand share equations: Restricting budget shares to the unit simplex. *Journal of Econometrics*, 73, 377.

Fry, V. and Pashardes, P. (1992). An Almost Ideal Quadratic Logarithmic Demand System for the Analysis of Microdata. IFS-WP.

Garganas, N. C. (1977). Family composition expenditure patterns and equivalence scales for children. In G. Fiegehen, S. Lansley and A. D. Smith (eds). *Poverty and Progress*. Cambridge University Press. Cambridge.

Garner, T., and Terrell, K. (1998). A Gini decomposition analysis of inequality in the Czech and Slovak Republics during the transition. *Economics of Transition*, 6, 23-46.

Gastwirth, J. L. (1971). A general definition of the Lorenz curve. *Econometrica*, 39, 1037-39.

Geoffrey, D. P. (1998). A growing market: expenditures by Hispanic consumers. *Monthly Labor Review*, 3-21.

Geoffrey, D. P., and Ferraro, D. L. (1996). *Do Expenditure Explain Income: A Study of Income Imputation*. US Bureau of Labor Statistics, Division of Price and Index Number Research. Washington DC.

Georgescu-Roegen, N. (1936). The pure theory of consumer's behaviour. *Quarterly Journal of Economics*, 50, 545-593.

Gibrat, R. (1931). *Les inegalites economiques*. Sirely. Paris.

Giles, D. E. A., and Hampton P. (1985). An Engel curve analysis of household expenditure in New Zealand. *Economic Record*, 61, 450-462.

Gini, C. (1921). Measurement of inequality of incomes. *Economic Journal*, 31, 124-126.

Glyn, A., and Miliband, D. (1994). *Paying for Inequality*. Rivers Oram Press. London.

Godfrey, L. G., McAleer, M., and McKenzie, C. R. (1988). Variable addition and Lagrange multiplier tests for linear and logarithmic regression models. *Review of Economics and Statistics*, 70, 492-503.

Goedhart, T., Halberstad, V., Kapteyn, A., and Van Praag B. (1977). The poverty line: Concept and Measurement. *Journal of Human Resources*, 12, 503-520.

Goldfeld, S. M., and Quandt, R.E. (1972). *Non-linear Methods in Econometrics*. North Holland. Amsterdam.

Gong, Xiaodong, Soest, Arthur van, Zhang, Ping (2001). Sexual and household consumption: A semi-parametric analysis of Engel curves in rural China. IZA. Forschungsinstitut Zur Zukunft der Arbeit – Diskussionspapiere, 40, 212.

Goodman, A., Johnson, P., and Webb, S. (1997). *Inequality in the UK*. Oxford University Press. Oxford.

Goodman, A., and Webb, S. (1995). The distribution of UK household expenditure, 1979-92. *Fiscal Studies*, 16, 55-80.

Goreux L. M. (1960). Income and food consumption. *Monthly Bulletin of Agricultural Economics and Statistics*, 9, 1-13.

Gorman, W. M. (1976). Tricks with utility functions. In M. Artis and A. R. Nobay (eds). *Essays in Economic Analysis*. Cambridge University Press. Cambridge.

Gottschalk, P., and Smeeding, T. M. (2000). Empirical evidence on income inequality in industrialized countries. In A. B. Atkinson and F. Bourguignon (eds). *Handbook of Income Distribution*. Elsevier Science.

Griffiths, W., and Valenzuela, R. (1996). Bayesian estimation of some Australian ELES: Based equivalence scales. In M. McAleer, Miller, P. W., and Ong, C. (eds). *Proceedings of the Econometric Society: Australian Meeting 1996*, Vol. 4 (Microeconometrics). University of Western Australia. Perth.

236

Gronau, R. (1985). The Allocation of Goods Within the Household and Estimation of Equivalence Scales: How to Separate the Men from the Boys. Manuscript. Department of Economics, Hebrew University. Jerusalem.

Gronau, R. (1987). The Intra-family Allocation of Goods: How to Separate the men from the boys? Economic Research Center/NORC, Discussion Paper No. 873.

Grootaert, C. (1983). The conceptual basis of measurements of household welfare and their implied data requirements. *Review of Income and Wealth*, 29, 1-21.

Haitovsky, J. (2001). Grouped observations. In N. L. Smelser and P. B. Baltes (eds). *International Encyclopedia of the Social and Behavioral Sciences*. Elsevier. Oxford.

Hamilton, L. R., and Wyckoff, J. (1991). Modelling charitable giving using a Box-Cox standard Tobit model. *Review of Economics and Statistics*, 73, 460-470.

Hanrahan, K. F. (2002). A fully regular model of Irish meat demand. Paper presented at the AES Annual Conference 2002. The University of Wales, Aberystwyth.

Hansen, J., Formby, J. and Smith, J. (1996). The income elasticity of demand for housing: Evidence from concentration curves. *Journal of Urban Economics*, 39, 173-92.

Haque, M. O. (1984). *The Analysis of Australian Family Budget*. Unpublished Ph.D. Thesis. Faculty of Economics, The University of Sydney. Sydney.

Haque, M. O. (1988). Estimation of Engel elasticities from the Box-Cox Engel function. *Metroeconomica*, 39, 317-335.

Haque, M. O. (1989a). Estimation of Engel elasticities from concentration curves. *Journal of Economic Development*, 14, 93-114.

Haque, M. O. (1989b). Functional forms for Engel curves. *Indian Journal of Quantitative Economic*, 5, 13-34.

Haque, M. O. (1990a). Use of appropriate grouped means and average elasticity of variable elasticity Engel functions. *Indian Journal of Quantitative Economic*, 6, 23-53.

Haque, M. O. (1990b). The demand for alcohol in Australia. *Drug and Alcohol Review*, 9, 43-52.

Haque, M. O. (1991a). Estimation of transport demand in Australia: Using household expenditure survey data. *The International Journal of Transport Economics*, 18, 81-102.

Haque, M. O. (1991b). Estimating increase in consumer demand from Household Expenditure Survey Data. *Sankhya: Indian Journal of Statistics*, Series B, 53, 134-149.

Haque, M. O. (1991c). *The Expenditure Pattern of Australian Families*: A *Monogram For Measuring Living Standards*. Australian Institute of Family Studies. Melbourne.

Haque, M. O. (1992). Aggregate Expenditure Elasticity for Transport and Communication in Australia. *Transportation: An International Journal Devoted to the Improvement of Transport, Planning and Practice*, 19, 43-57.

Haque, M. O. (1993). Problems in estimating non-linear Engel parameters in the absence of appropriate grouped means and average elasticity of variable elasticity Engel functions. *Journal of Applied Statistics*, 20, 481-494.

Haque, M. O. (1994). On the measurements of consumers' equivalence scales: A review. *Indian Journal of Quantitative Economics*, 9, 35-69.

Haque, M. O. (1995). Some basic observations on ABS Household Expenditure data. *Indian Journal of Quantitative Economics*, 10, 125-142

Haque, M. O. (1996). Expenditure pattern of sole parent families in Australia. *Indian Journal of Quantitative Economics*, 11, 107-131.

Haque, M. O. (2000). Expenditure pattern of Australian families. *Indian Journal of Quantitative Economics*, 15, 49-80.

Haque, M. O. (2001). Health related expenditure patterns of older persons: Selected migrant groups in Australian. *Indian Journal of Quantitative Economics*, 16, 27-48.

Haque, M. O. and Ironmonger, D. S. (2001). Consumption Inequality: Share of Household Products. ARC Large Research Grant. 2001-2003. Melbourne.

Harding, A. (1984). *Who Benefits? The Australian Welfare State and Redistribution*. SWRC Reports and Proceedings No. 45, Welfare Research Center, University of New South Wales. Kensington

Harding, A. (1995). The impact to health, education and housing outlays upon income distribution in Australia in the 1990s. *Australian Economic Review*, 28, 71-86.

Harding, A. (1997). The suffering middle: Trends in income inequality in Australia, 1982 to 1993-94. *Australian Economic Review*, 30, 341-358.

237

Hardy, G. H., Littlewood, J. E., and Polya, G. (1929). Some simple inequalities satisfied by convex functions. *Messenger of Mathematics*, 26, 145-53.

Hardy, G. H., Littlewood, J. E. and Polya, G. (1934). *Inequalities*. Cambridge University Press. Cambridge.

Hausman, J., Newey, W., and Powell, J. (1995). Non-linear errors in variables estimations of some Engel curves. *Journal of Econometrics*, 65, 205-33.

Hayakawa, M. (1951). The application of Pareto's law of income to Japanese data. *Econometrica*, 19, 174-183

Heale, P., Stockwell, T., Dietze, P., Chikritzhs, T., and Catalono, P. (2000). *Patterns of Alcohol Consumption in Australia: 1998*. National Alcohol Indicators Bulletin No. 3.

Heitjan, D. F. (1889). Inference from grouped continuous data: A review. *Statistical Science*, 4, 164-183.

Henderson, A. M. (1949). The cost of children, Part I. *Population Studies*, 3, 130-150.

Henderson, A. M. (1950). The cost of children, Part II. *Population Studies*, 4, 267-298.

Henderson, R. F., Harcourt, A., and Happer, R. V. A. (1970). *People in Poverty: A Melbourne Survey*. Cheshire. Melbourne.

Hicks, J. R., and Allen, R. G. D. (1934). A reconsideration of the theory of value. *Economica*, N. S. 1, 52-76; 196-219

Hilderbrand, H. and Kneip, A. (1990). Modelling aggregate Consumption Expenditure and Income Distribution Effects. Discussion Paper series A, University of Bonn, Germany (RePEc:bon:bonsfa:510), http://www.wipol.uni-bonn.de/adressen.tlml

Hinkley, D. V., and Runger, G. (1984). The analysis of transformed data (with discussion). *Journal of the American Statistical Association,* 79, 302-328.

Hoa, T. V. (1986). The heterogeneity of the consumer's preference over time: A system-wide analysis of discrete panel data. *Economics Letters*, 20, 297-300.

Hoa, T. V., Ironmonger, D.S., and Manning, I. (1983). Energy consumption in Australia: Evidence from a Generalised Working Model. *Economics Letters*, 12, 382-389.

Hofsten, E. V. (1952). *Price Indexes and Quality Changes,* Stockholm.

Houghton, S. (1988). Income differentials and housing costs in cities and suburban areas. *Urban Policy and Research,* 6, 161-180

Houthakker, H. S. (1957). An international comparison of household expenditure patterns: Commemorating the centenary of Engel's law. *Econometrica*, 25, 532-551.

Houthakker, H. S. (1961). The present state of consumption theory: A survey article. *Econometrica,* 29, 704-740.

Houthakker, H. S. (1965). New evidence on demand elasticities. *Econometrica*, 33, 277-288.

Howe, H. J. (1974). *Estimation of the Linear and Quadratic Expenditure System: A Cross Section Case for Columbia*. Unpublished Ph. D. Dissertation, University of Pennsylvania.

Huang, K. S., and Lin, B-H. (2000). *Estimation of Food Demand and Nutrient Elasticities from Household Survey data*. Research Service Technical Bulletin No. 1887, United States Department of Agriculture.

Hui-Shung, C., and Bettington, N. (2001). Demand for Wine in Australia: Systems versus Single Equation Approach. Working Paper Series No. 2001-5, Graduate School of Agricultural and Resource Economics. University of New England. Armidale.

Hurst, W., Gregory, E., and Gussman, T. (1997). *Alcoholic Beverage Taxation and Control Policies*. Brewers' Association of Canada.

Husen, T. (1968). Ability, opportunity and career: A 26 year follow-up. *Education Research*, 10, 170-179.

Hymans, S. H., and Shapiro, H. T. (1976). The allocation of household income of food consumption. *Journal of Econometrics*, 4, 167-188.

Iyengar, N. S. (1960a). On a Method of Computing Engel Elasticities from Concentration Curves. *Econometrica,* 28, 882-891.

Iyengar, N. S. (1960b). On a problem of estimating increase in corner demand. *Sankhya: The Indian Journal of Statistics,* 22, 379-390.

Iyengar, N. S. (1964a). A consistent method of estimating the Engel curve from grouped survey data. *Econometrics,* 32, 591-618.

Iyengar, N. S. (1964b). Contributions to analyse of consumer expenditure. Unpublished Ph.D. Dissertation. Indian Statistical Institute. Calcutta.

238

Iyengar, N. S. (1967). Some estimates of Engel elasticities based on national sample survey data. *Journal of the Royal Statistical Society:* Series A (general), 130, 84-101.

Iyengar, N. S. and Jain, L. R. (1969). Projections of consumption rural/urban: 1970-71 and 1975-76. *Economic and Political Weekly*, 8, 129-143.

Iyengar, N. S. and Jain, L. R. (1973). Projections of household expenditures in India, 1971-75. *Indian Journal of Agricultural Economics*, 28, 56-70.

Iyenger, N. S., Jain, L. R., and Srinivasan. (1969). *Economics of Scale in Household Consumption.* presented at the 7th Indian Econometric Conference. Poona, India.

Jain, L. R. (1976). An empirical evaluation of the system of indirect Addi-log Engel curves. Discussion Paper No. 80 (mimeo, revised version). Indian Statistical Institute. New Delhi.

Jain, L. R., and Tendulkar, D. S. (1973). Analysis of occupational differences in consumer expenditure patterns in India. *Sankhya: The Indian Journal of Statistics*, Series B, 35, 239-267.

Jain, S. (1975). *Size Distribution of Income: A Compilation Data*. World Bank. Washington DC.

Joanna, G. (1994). *Grossing Up: A note on calculating household weights from family Composition totals.* MU/RN/ 4, Micro-simulation Unit Publications, Department of Applied Economics, University of Cambridge. Cambridge.

Johnson, P. (1996). The assessment: inequality. *Oxford Review of Economic Policy*, 12, 1-14.

Johnston, J. (1972). *Econometric Methods* (2nd edn). McGraw Hill. Tokyo.

Jones, A., and Mazzi, M. G. (1996). Tobacco consumption and taxation in Italy: An application of QUAIDS model. *Applied Economics*, 28, 595-603.

Jones, A. M., and Yen, S. T. (2000). A Box-Cox double-hurdle model. *The Manchester School*, 68, 203-221.

Jones, J. (2000). Wine at the cross-roads. *Australian Farm Journal*, 8-18.

Kakwani, N. C. (1974). A note on the efficient estimation of the new measures of income inequality. *Econometrica*, 42, 597-600.

Kakwani, N. C. (1976). On the estimation of income inequality measures from grouped observations. *Review of Economic Studies*, 43, 483-492.

Kakwani, N. C. (1977a). Application of Lorenz curve in economic analysis. *Econometrica*, 45, 719-727.

Kakwani, N. C. (1977b). On the estimation of Engel elasticities from grouped observations with applications to Indonesian data. *Journal of Econometrics*, 6, 1-17.

Kakwani, N. C. (1977c). On the estimation of consumer unit scale. *Review of Economics and Statistics*, 59, 507-510.

Kakwani, N. C. (1978). A new method of estimating Engel elasticities. *Journal of Econometrics*, 8, 103-110.

Kakwani, N. C. (1980a). On a class of poverty measure. *Econometrics*, 48, 437-466.

Kakwani, N. C. (1980b). *Income Inequality and Poverty: Methods of Estimation and Policy Applications.* Oxford University Press. Oxford.

Kakwani, N. C. (1986). *Analysing Redistribution Policies: A Study Using Australian Data.* Cambridge University Press, Cambridge.

Kakwani, N. C., and Podder, N. (1973). On the estimation of the Lorenz curves from grouped observations. *International Economic Review*, 14, 278-292.

Kakwani, N. C., and Podder, N. (1976). Efficient estimation of Lorenz curve and associated inequality measures from grouped observations. *Econometrics*, 4, 937-148.

Kalwij, A., Alessie, R., and Fontein, P. (1997). *Household Commodity Demand and Demographics in the Netherlands: A Micro-econometric Analysis.* Center for Economic Research and Economics Institute. Tilburg.

Kapteyn, A. and Van Praag, B. (1976). A new approach to the construction of family equivalence scales. *European Economic Review*, 7, 313-335.

Karlsson, T., and Simpura, J. (2001). Changes in Living Conditions and Their Links to Alcohol Consumption and Drinking Patterns in 16 European Countries, 1950 to 2000. *Nordisk alkihol-ochnarkotikatidskrift,* 18 (English supplement).

Kats, A. (1972). On the social welfare function and the parameters of income distribution. *Journal of Economic Theory*, 5, 90-91.

Kayser, H. (2000). Gasoline demand and car choice: estimating gasoline demand using household Information. *Energy Economics*, 22, 331-348.

Keen, M. (1986). Zero expenditure and the Estimation of Engel curves. *Journal of Applied Econometrics*, 1, 277-286.

Kemsley, W. F. F. (1952). Estimates of costs of individuals from family data. *Applied Statistics*, 1, 192-201.

Kendall, M. G., and Stuart, A. (1967). *The Advanced Theory of Statistic,* (2nd edn) Vol. 2. Griffin. London.

Kenkel, D. S. (1996). New estimates of the optimal tax on alcohol. *Economic Inquiry*, 34, 296-319.

Klein, L. (1953). *A Textbook of Econometrics*. Row, Peterson and Company. Evanston.

Klein, L. (1962). *An Introduction to Econometrics*. Pentice-Hall, Englewood. Cliffs.

Kneip, A., and Engel, J. (1995). Estimation of non-linear regression model under shape invariance. *Annals of Statistics*, 23, 551-570.

Koebel, B., Martin F., and Francois, L. (2001). *Imposing and Testing Curvature Conditions on a Box-Cox Function*. Discussion Paper 114, 00/70. Centre for European Economic Research. Mannheim.

Kordos, J. (1985). Towards an integrated system of household surveys in Poland. *Bulletin of International Statistical Institute*, 51, 13-18.

Kravis, I. B. (1960) International differences in the distribution of income. Review of Economics and Statistics, 42, 408-416

Kravis, I. B. (1962). *The Structure of Income: Some Quantitative Essays*. University of Pennsylvania Press, Philadelphia.

Kuznets, S. (1955). Economic growth and income inequality. *American Economic Review*, 45, 1-28.

Kuznets, S. (1963). Quantitative aspects of the economic growth of nations, III: Distribution of income by size. *Economic Development and Cultural Change*, 11, 1-80.

Labeaga, J., and Lopez, A. (1997). A study of petrol consumption using Spanish panel data. *Applied Economics*, 29, 795-802.

LaFrance, J. T., Beatty, T. K. M. (2000). US Income Distribution and Gorman Engel Curves for Food. In *IIFET 2000 Proceedings*, pp. 1-7. International Institute of Fisheries Economics and Trade, Oregon State University, Oregon.

LaFrance, J. T., Beatty, T. K. M., Pope, R. D., and Agnew, K. (2002). Information theoretic measures of income distribution in food demand. *Journal of Econometrics*, 107, 235-257.

Lancaster, G., and Ray, R. (1998). Comparison of alternative models of household equivalence scales: The Australian evidence on Unit Recode Data. *The Economic Record*, 74, 1-14.

Lancaster, G., Ray, R., and Maria, R. V. (1999). A cross country study of equivalence scales and expenditure inequality on Unit Record Household Budget Data. *Review of Income and wealth,* 45, 455-82.

Lange, O. (1962). *Introduction to Econometrics*, Pergamon Press. Oxford.

Lankford, R. H., and Wyckoff, J. H. (1991). Modeling charitable giving using a Box-Cox standard Tobit Model. *Review of Economics and Statistics*, 73, 460-470.

Lariviere, E., Laure, B., and Chalfant, J. (2000). Modelling the demand for alcoholic beverages and advertising specifications. *Agricultural Economics*, 22, pp. 147-162.

Lau, L. J. (1996). Functional Forms in Econometric Model Building. In Z. Griliches and M. D. Intriligator (eds). *Handbook of Econometrics*, Volume III. Elsevier Science Publishers BV. Stanford.

Lawrence, J., and Law. (1986). Functional forms in econometric model building. In Z. Griliches and M. D. Intriligator (eds). *Handbook of Econometrics*, Volume III. Elsevier Science Publishers BV. Stanford.

Lazear, E., and Michael, R. (1980). Family size and the distribution of real per capita income. *American Economic Review*, 70, 91-107.

Lechner, M., and Pfeiffer, F. (eds) (2001). *Econometric Evaluation of Labour Market Policies.* Physica, Heidelberg.

Lee, J. Y., and Brown, M. G. (1986). Food expenditures at home and away from home in the United States: A switching regression analysis. *Review of Economic Statistics*, 68, 142-147.

Lee, M. (1982). *Levels of Living in the Sixties: A Decade of Change*. Ph.D Dissertation, University of Wisconsin. Madison.

Leifman, H. (2001). Homogenisation of alcohol consumption in 15 European countries. *Nordisk akkohol - & narkotikatidskrift*, 18, (English supplement).

240

Leser, C. E. V. (1961). Commodity group expenditure functions for the United Kingdom 1948-1957. *Econometrica*, 29, 24-32.

Leser, C. E. V. (1963). Forms of Engel functions. *Econometrica*, 31, 694-703.

Levedahl, J. W. (1995). A theoretical and empirical evaluation of the functional forms used to estimate the food expenditure equation of food stamp recipients. *American Journal of Agricultural Economics*, 77, 960-968.

Levine, D. B. and Singer, N. M. (1970). The mathematical function between the income density function and the measurement of income inequality. *Econometrica*, 38, 324-330.

Levy, P. (1925). *Calcul des probabilities*. Gauthier-Villars. Paris.

Levy, P. (1937). *Theorie de l'addition des variables aleatoires*. Gauthier-Villars. Paris.

Lewbel, A. (1985). A unified approach to incorporating demographic or other effects into demand systems. *Review of Economic Studies*, 52, 1-18.

Li, G., and Victoria, V. (2001). Testing the Barten Model of Economies of Scale in Household Consumption: Toward Resolving a Paradox of Deaton and Paxson. TX 78712. Department of Economics, University of Texas. Austin.

Lindert, P. H. (1978). Fertility and Scarcity in America. Princeton University press. Princeton.

Lindert, P. H. (1980). Child costs and economic development. In R. A. Easterlin (ed.). *Population and Economic Change in Developing Countries*. University of Chicago Press. Chicago.

Linnet, K. (1988). Testing normality of transformed data. *Applied Statistics*, 37, 180-186.

Liviatan, N. (1961). Errors in variable and Engel curve analysis. *Econometrica*, 29, 336-362.

Lluch, C. (1973). The extended linear expenditure system. *European Economic Review*, 4, 21-32.

Lluch, C., Powell, A. A., and Williams, T. R. A. (1977). *Patterns in Household Demand and Saving*. World Bank. Oxford University Press. Oxford.

Lorenz, M. O. (1905). Methods of measuring the concentration of wealth. *Journal of the American Statistical Association*, 9, 209-219.

Lubulwa, A. S. G. (1986). Brandow demand functions for Australian long distance travel. In *Proceedings of the 11th Australian Transport Research Forum*, 2, 200-218. Darwin.

Lyssiotou, P., Pashardes, P., and Stengos, T. (1999). Testing the rank of Engel curves with endogenous Expenditure. *Economics Letters*, 64, 61-65.

Machado, J. A. F., and Mata, J. (2000). Box-Cox quantile regression and the distribution of firm sizes. *Journal of Applied Econometrics*, 15, 253-274.

Machin, S. (1996). Wage inequality in the UK. *Oxford Review of Economic Policy*, 12, 47-64.

Mackinnon, J. G. (1983). Model specification tests against non-nested alternatives. *Econometric Review*, 2, 85-110.

Mackinnon, J. G., White, H., and Davidson, R. (1983). Tests for model specification in the presence of alternative hypotheses. *Journal of Econometrics*, 21, 53-70.

Mahalanobis, P. C. (1960). A method of fractile graphical analysis. *Econometrica*, 28, 325-351.

Maitra, P., and Ray, R. (1999). The Effects of Transfers on Household Expenditure Patterns and Poverty in South Africa. Working Paper No. 99-16. University of Sydney.

Makela, K., Rfam, R., Single, E., Sulkunen, P., and Walsh, D. (1981). *Alcohol, Society and the State: A Comparative Study of Alcohol Control*. Report of the International Study of Alcohol Control Experiences in collaboration with the World Health Organization Regional Office for Europe. Additive Research Foundation. Toronto.

Makela, P. (1999). *Views into Studies of Differences in Drinking Habits and Alcoholic Problems between Socio-demographic Groups*. Information Access Company. Federal Legal Publications, pp. 633-644.

Maltagliati, M., and Michelini, C. (1999). Equivalence Scales and Consumption Inequality A Study of Household Consumption Patterns in Italy. Discussion Papers No. 99.04. Department of Applied and International Economics, Massey University. dipeco@imiucca.csi.unimi.it

Mamuneas, T. P., Kalaitzidakis, P., and Stengos, T. (2000). A non-linear sensitivity analysis of cross-country growth regressions. *Canadian Journal of Economics*, 33, 604-617.

Mandelbrot, B. (1960). The Pareto-Levy law and the distribution of income. *International Economic Review*, 1, 79-105.

Manning, I. (1984). Can there be a budget based equivalence scale for Australia? *Social Security Journal*, December, 11-19.

Manning, W. G., Blumberg, L., and Moulton, L. H. (1995). The demand for alcohol: The differential response to price. *Journal of Health Economics*, 14, 123-148.

Mario, W. (1995). Non Means-tested Social Security Benefits and the Family Expenditure Survey: Disaggregating the 1991 Data. MU/RN/ 7. Micro-simulation Unit Publications, Department of Applied Economics, University of Cambridge. Cambridge.

Marshall, A. (1890). *Principles of Economics* (8th Edn, 1946). London. Macmillan.

Mazzarino, G. (1986). Fitting of distribution curves to grouped data. *Oxford Bulletin of Economics and Statistics*, 48, 189-200.

McDonald, J. B. (1984). Some generalized functions for the size grouped distribution of income. *Econometrica*, 52, 647-663.

McDonald, P. (1989). Research on the costs of children: Policy implications. Paper presented at the Third Australian Family Research Conference. Ballarat College of Advanced Education. Ballarat.

McDonald, P. (ed.). (1993). *The Australian Living Standards Study: Berwick Report*. Australian Institute of Family Studies. Melbourne

Mcleod, R., and Stockwell, T. (1999). The relationship between alcohol consumption patterns and injury. *Addiction*, 94, 1719-1734.

McRae, I. (1980). An analysis of Australian Household Expenditure Survey Data. Paper presented to the 5th Australian Statistical Conference. University of New South Wales. Kensington.

Meenakshi, J. V., and Ray, R. (1999). Regional differences in India's food expenditure pattern: A completed demand systems approach. *Journal of International Development*, 11, 47-74.

Michelini, C. (1997). New Zealand Household Consumption Patterns 1983-1992: An Application of the Almost-Ideal-Demand-System. Discussion Paper No. 97.06. Department of Applied and International Economics, Massey University. Palmerston North, New Zealand.

Michelini, C. (1998a). New Zealand Household Consumption Equivalence Scales from Quasi UnitRecord Data: An Application of the ELES Model. Discussion Paper No. 98.05. Department of Applied and International Economics, Massey University. Palmerston North, New Zealand.

Michelini, C. (1998b). The Estimation of Some Rank 3 Demand Systems from Quasi-Unit RecordData of New Zealand Household Consumption. Discussion Paper No. 98.12. Department of Applied and International Economics, Massey University. Palmerston North, New Zealand.

Michelini, C. (1999). *New Zealand Household Consumption Equivalence Scales From Quasi-Unit Record Data*. Discussion Paper No. 99.02, April 1999. Department of Applied and International Economics, Massey University. Palmerston North, New Zealand.

Milanovic, B. (1999). *True Income Distribution, 1988 and 1993: First Calculations, Based on Household Surveys Alone*. Country Economics Department, World Bank. (RePEc:fth:Wobaco:2244) http://netec.mcc.ac.uk/BibEc/data/Papers/fthwobaco2244.html

Miles, D., Pereyra, A., and Rossi, M. (2000). Income Elasticity of Environmental Amenities. Departamento Economia Aplicada, Universidad de Vigo. Espana. dmiles@uvigo.es

Mills, J. A. Y., and Zandvakili, S. (1997). Statistical inference via bootstrapping for measures of inequality. *Journal of Applied Econometrics*, 12, 133-150.

Mincer, J. (1958). Investment in human capital and personal income distribution. *Journal of Political Economy*, 66, 281-302.

Minhas, B. S. (1970). Rural poverty, land redistribution and development. *Indian Economic Review*, 5, 97-128.

Mitchell, D., Harding, A., and Gruen, F. (1994). Targeting welfare. *Economic Record*, 70, 315-340.

Mizon, G. E., and Richard, J. F. (1982). *The Encompassing Principle and Its Application to Non-nested Hypotheses*. Unpublished manuscript.

Moore, H. L. (1914). *Economic Cycles: Their Law and Cause*. Macmillan. New York.

Moore, H. L. (1922). Elasticity of demand and flexibility of prices. *Journal of American Statistical Association*, 18, 8-19.

Moore, H. L. (1925-26). Partial elasticity of demand. *Quarterly Journal of Economics*, 40, 393-401.

Moran, J., and Nelson, J. (1995). Advertising and United States alcohol beverage demand: System-wide Estimates. *Applied Economics*, 27, 1225-1237.

Morgan, J. (1962). The anatomy of income distribution. *Review of Economics & Statistics*, 44, 270-283.

Morris, J. M., and Wigan, M. R. (1977). Family expenditure survey data and their reference to transport Planning. *Forum Papers. Third Australian Transport Research Forum*, Ministry of Transport., Victoria. Australia.

Morris, J. M., and Wigan, M. R. (1978). Transport Planning: A family expenditure perspective. Research Report, ARR No. 71. Australian Road Research Board.

242

Morris, J. M., and Wigan, M. R. (1979). A family expenditure perspective on transport planning: Australian evidence in context. *Transport Research*, 13A, 249-285.

Muellbauer, J. (1974). Household composition, Engel curves and welfare compositions between households. *European Economic Review*, 5, 103-122.

Muellbauer, J. (1975). Identification and consumer unit scales. *Econometrica*, 43, 807-889.

Muellbauer, J. (1976). Can we base welfare comparisons across households on behaviour. Mimeo. Presented at SSRC Economic Theory Study Group. Cambridge.

Muellbauer, J. (1977). Testing the Barten model of household composition effects and the cost of children. *Economic Journal,*, 87, 460-487.

Muellbauer, J. (1980). The estimation of the Prais-Houthakker model of equivalence scales. *Econometrica*, 48, 153-176.

Murthi, M. (1994). Engel Equivalence Scales in Sri Lanka: Exactness, Specification, Measurement Error. In R. Blundell, I. Preston and I. Walker (eds). *The Measurement of Household Welfare*. Cambridge University Press. Cambridge.

National Expert Advisory Committee on Alcohol (NEACA). (2001). *National Alcohol Strategy: A Plan for Action 2001 to 2003-2004*. Commonwealth of Australia. Canberra.

National Centre for Social and Economic Modelling (NATSEM). (1998). Changes in the Income of the Aged, IRD Issue No. 9. University of Canberra. Canberra.

National Centre for Social and Economic Modelling (NATSEM). (2000). Regional Income Inequality Increasing While the Middle Disappears. IRD Issue No. 12. University of Canberra. Canberra.

Nelson, J. A. (1986a). Household Demands with Household Public Goods. Mimeo. US Bureau of Labor Statistics.

Nelson, J. A. (1986b). Household Demands and Individual Consumption, Mimeo. US Bureau of Labor Statistics

Nelson, J. A. (1988). Household economics of scale in consumption: Theory and evidence. *Econometrica*, 56, 1301-1314.

Newbery, D. (1970). A theorem on the measurement of inequality. *Journal of Economic* Theory, 2, 264-266.

Newbridge. (1999). Internet Protocol: Internetworking Transport Tutorial. www.webproforum.com. Chicago.

Newell, F., Ham. R., and Coady, C. (1987). Do Australian families spend their money. *Journal of the Home Economics Association of Australia*, 19, 21-27.

Newell, G. (1990). How Australian households balanced the family budgets. *Journal of the Home Economics Association of Australia*, 22, 80-81.

Nicholson, J. L. (1949). Variations in working class family expenditure. *Journal of the Royal Statistical Society,* Series A (General), 112, 359-418.

Nicholson, J. L. (1976). Appraisal of different methods of estimating equivalence scales and their results. *Review of Income and Wealth*, 22, 1-12.

Norstrom, T. (1998). Effects on criminal violence of different beverage types and private and public drinking. *Addiction*, 93, 689-699.

Oczkowski, E. (1994). A hedonic price function for Australian premium table wine. *Australian Journal of Agricultural Economics*, 38, 93-110.

Ogwang, T., and Rao, U. L. G. (1996). A new functional form for approximating the Lorenz curve. *Economics Letters*, 52, 21-29.

Ojha, P. D., and Bhatt, V. V. (1964). Patterns of income distribution in an underdeveloped economy: A case study of India. *American Economic Review*, 54, 711-720.

Ornelas, F. S., Shumway, C. R., and Ozuna, T. Jr. (1994). Using the quadratic Box-Cox for flexible functional form selection and unconditional variance computation. *Journal of Empirical Economics*, 19, 639-45.

Oshima, H. T. (1962). The international comparison of size distribution of family incomes with special reference to Asia. *Review of Economics and Statistics*, 44, 439-445.

Oshima, H. T. (1970). Income inequality and economic growth: The post war experience of Asian Countries. *Malaysian Economic Review*, 15, 7-41.

Osterberg, E. (1995). Do alcohol prices affect consumption and related problems. In H. Holder and G. Edwards (eds). *Alcohol and Public Policy: Evidence and Issues*. Oxford University Press. Oxford.

Page, B. I., and Simmons, J. R. (2000). *What Government Can Do: Dealing with Poverty and Inequality*. University of Chicago Press. Chicago.

Pareto, V. (1897). *Cours De Conomique Politique*. 2, Part I, Chapter 1. Lausanne.

Paris, Q. (1970). An Appraisal of Income Elasticities for Total Food Consumption in Developing Countries. Technical Papers. Development Centre of the Organization for Economic Co-operation and Development. Paris.

Park, J. L., Holcomb, R. B., Raper, K. C., and Capps, Jr. O. (1996). A demand systems analysis of food commodities by US Households segmented by income, *American Journal of Agricultural Economic*, 78, 290-300.

Parks, R. W. (1969). Systems of demand equations: An empirical comparison of alternative functional forms. *Econometrica*, 37, 629-650.

Pashardes, P. (1995a). Equivalence scales in a rank-3 demand system. *Journal of Public Economics*, 58, 143-158.

Pashardes, P. (1995b). Bias in estimating equivalence scales from grouped data. *Journal of Income distribution, Special Issue: Symposium on Equivalence Scales*, 4, 253-264.

Pashardes, P., and Fry V. (1994). Abstention and aggregation in consumer demand. *Oxford Economic Papers*, 46, 502-518.

Pashardes, P., Dickens, R., and Fry, V. (1993). Non-linearities and equivalence scales. *The Economic Journals*, 103, 359-368.

Paukert, F. (1973). Income distribution: A survey of the evidence. *International Labour Review*, 108, 97-125.

Peach, H. G., Bath, N. E., and Farish, S. J. (1998). Comparison of unsafe drinking between a rural and metropolitan area. *Drug and Alcohol Review*, 17, 117-120.

Pena, Y., and Ruiz-Castillo. (1998). Inflation and inequality bias in the presence of bulk purchase for food and drinks. *Journal of Business and Economic Statistics*, 16, 292-303.

Pendakur, K. (1998). Changes in Canadian family income and family consumption inequality between 1978 and 1992. *Review of Income and Wealth*, 44, 259-283.

Pendakur, K. (1999). Semi-parametric estimates and tests of base-independent equivalence scales. *Journal of Econometrics*, 88, 1- 40.

Pendakur, K. (2001). Consumption poverty in Canada 1969 to 1998. *Canadian Public Policy*, 1.

Perali, F. (2001). The Second Engel Law and Economics of Scale: An Empirical Puzzle to be Resolved. Child N. 28/2001. Centre for Household, Income, Labour and Demographic Economics. Department of Economics, University of Verona.

Perkins, J. (1991). Patterns of household expenditure. *National Economic Review*, 14, 40-46.

Persson, T., and Tabellini, G. (1994). Is inequality harmful for growth? *American Economic Review*, 84, 600-621.

Pesaran, M. H. (1974). On the general problem of model selection", *Review of Economic Studies*, 41, 153-171.

Pesaran M. H., and Deaton, A. S. (1978). Testing non-nested non-linear regression models. *Econometrica*, 46, 677-694.

Philippe, A., Caroli, E., and Garcia-Penalosa, C. (1998). Inequality and Economic growth (Part I). In A. Philippe and J. G. Williamson, *Growth, Inequality and Globalization: Theory, History and Policy*. Cambridge University Press. Cambridge.

Philippe, A, Caroli, E., and Garcia-Penalosa, C. (1999). Inequality and economic growth: The perspective of the new growth theories. *Journal of Economic Literature*, 37, 1615-1660.

Phipps, S. (1998). What is the income "cost of child"? Exact equivalence scales for Canadian two-parent families. *Review of Economics and Statistics*, 80, 157-164.

Phlips, L. (1974). *Applied Consumption Analysis*. North Holland Publishing Company. Amsterdam.

Piachaud, D. (1979). *The Cost of a Child: A Modern Minimum*. Child Poverty Action Group. London.

Piachaud, D. (1981). *Children and Poverty*. Poverty Research Series 9. Child Poverty Action Group. London.

Pietra, G. (1948). *Studi di Statistica metodologica*. Giuffre. Milan.

Piketty, T. (1999*)* Attitudes Towards Income Inequality in France: Do People Really Disagree? CEPREMPA Working Papers. (RePEc:cpm:cepmap:9918) http://netec.mcc.ac.uk/BibEc/data/Papers/cpmcepmap9918.html

244

Podder, N. (1971). Patterns of household consumption expenditure in Australia. *Economic Record,* 47, 379-398.

Podder, N. (1972). Distribution of household income in Australia. *Economic Record*, 48, 181-200.

Podder, N., and Kakwani, N. C. (1975). Distribution and redistribution of household income in Australia. *Australian Taxation Committee Commissioned Studies*, 111-152. Government Publishing Services. Canberra.

Podder, N., and Kakwani, N. C. (1976). Distribution of wealth in Australia. *Review of Income and wealth*, 22, 75-91.

Poirier, D. J. (1976). *The Econometrics of Structural Change.* North Holland Publishing Company. Amsterdam.

Poirier, D. J. (1978). The use of the Box-Cox transformation in limited dependent variable models. *Journal of the American Statistical Association*, 73, 284-287.

Pollak, R. A., and Wales, T. J. (1978). Estimation of complete demand systems from household budget data: The linear and quadratic expenditure systems. *American Economic Review*, 68, 91-107.

Pollak, R. A., and Wales, T. J. (1979). Welfare comparisons and equivalence scales. *American Economic Review Papers and Proceedings*, 69, 216-212.

Pollak, R. A., and Wales, T. J. (1981). Demographic variables in demand analysis. *Econometrica*, 49, 1533-1551.

Powell, A. (1969). Atkin estimators as a toll in allocating predetermined aggregates. *Journal of the American Statistical Association*, 64, 913-922.

Powles, J., Hage. B., and Cosgrove, M. (1990). Health related expenditure patterns in selected migrant groups: data from the Australian household expenditure survey, 1984. *Community Health studies*, 14, 1-17.

Pradhan, M., Asep, S., Sudarno, S., and Lant, P. (2000). *Measurement of Poverty in Indoneasia:1996, 1999 and Beyond.* SMERU Working Paper. Jakarta, Indonesia.

Prais, S. J. (1953a). Non-linear estimates of the Engel curves. *Review of Economic Studies*, 20, 87-104.

Prais, S. J. (1953b). The estimation of equivalent adult scales from family budgets. *Economic Journal*, 63, 791-810.

Prais, S. J., and Aitchison, J. (1954). The grouping of observations in regression analysis. *Review of the International Statistical Institute*, 22, 1-22.

Prais, S. J., and Houthakker, H. S. (1955). *The Analysis of Family Budgets.* Cambridge University Press. Cambridge.

Psacharopoulos, G., and Hinchliffe, K. (1972). Further evidence on the elasticity of substitution among different types of educated labor. *Journal of Political Economy*, 80, 786-796.

Pyatt, G. (1975). *On the Interpretation and Disaggregation of Gini Coefficients.* Development Research Centre, World Bank Processed. Washington DC.

Pyatt, G. (1976). On the interpretation and disaggregation of Gini coefficients. *Economic Journal*, 86, 243-255

Quandt, R. (1966). Old and new methods of estimation and Pareto distribution. *Metrica*. 10, 55-82.

Quenouille, M. H. (1950). An application of least squares to family diet surveys. *Econometrica*, 18, 27-44.

Prais, S. J. (1953). The estimation of equivalent adult scales from family budgets. *Economic Journal*, 63, 791-810.

Rae, I. (1980). *An analysis of Australian Household Expenditure Data.* A paper presented to the 5th Australian Statistical Conference. University of New South Wales. Kensington.

Ramsay, J. O., and Silverman, B. W. (2002). *Applied Functional Data Analysis: Methods and Case studies.* Springer-Verlag. New York.

Ramsey, J. B. (1969). Tests for specification errors in classical linear least-squares regression analysis. *Journal of the Royal Statistical Society,* Series B, 31, 350-371.

Ramsey, J. B. (1978). Non-linear estimation and asymptotic approximations. *Econometrica*, 46, 901-929.

Ranadive, K. R. (1965). The equality of incomes in India. *Bulletin of the Oxford Institute of Statistics,* 27, 119-134.

Rnadive, K. R. (1968). Patterns of income distribution in India: 1953/54 - 1959/60. *Bulletin of the Oxford Institute of Statistics*, 30, 110-122.

Rao, V. M. (1969). Two decompositions of concentration ratio. *Journal of the Royal Statistical Society,* Series A, 132, 418-425.

Rasche, R. H., Gaffney, J., Koo, A. Y. C., and Obst, N. (1980). Functional Forms for Estimating the Lorenz Curve. *Econometrica,* 48, 1061-1062.

Ray, A. K. (1973). An Analysis of Consumer Behaviour in Rural Areas of West Bengal. Technical Report No. Eco/9/73. Research and Training School, Indian Statistical Institute. Calcutta.

Reinsdorf, M. (1998). Formula bias and within stratum substitutions bias in the US CPI. *Review of Economic Studies,* 80, 175-187.

Richardson, A. J., and Loeis, J. M. (1997). Estimation of Missing Income Data in Household Travel survey. *21st ATRF Papers of the Australian Transport Research Forum,* 1, 249-266. The Transport Systems Centre. Adelaide.

Rimmer, M., and Powell, A. (1994). Engel Flexibility in Household *Budget Studies: Non-Parametric Evidence versus Standard Functional Forms.* CoPS/IMPACT Paper OP-80, Monash University. Melbourne.

Rogers, B., Korten, E. A., Jorm, A. F., Jacomb, P A., Christensen, H., and Henderson, A. S. (2000). Non-linear relationships in associations of depression and anxiety with alcohol use. *Psychological Medicine,* 30, 421-432.

Rongve, I. (1998). *Estimation of Inequality Indices using Parametric Lorenz Curves.* Department of Economics, University of Regina. (RePEc:fth:regina:77).
http://netec.mcc.ac.uk/BibEc/data/Papers/fthregina77.html

Rothbarth, E. (1943). A note on a method of determining equivalent income for families of different composition. In C. Madge. *War-Time Patterns of Saving and Spending* (Appendix 4). Cambridge University Press. Cambridge.

Rothschild, M., and Stiglitz, J. E. (1973). Some further results on the measurement of inequality. *Journal of Economic Theory,* 6, 188-204.

Roy, A. D. (1950). The distribution of earnings and of individual outputs. *Economic Journal,* 60, 489-505

Roy, J., Chakravarty, I. M., and Laha, R. G. (1960). A Study of Concentration Curves as a Description of consumption patterns. Studies in Consumer Behaviour. Indian Statistical Institute. Calcutta.

Rutherford, R. S. G. (1955). Income distributions: A new model. *Econometrica,* 23, 277-294

Ryan, D. L., and Wales, T. J. (1996). Flexible and Semiflexible Demands with Quadratic Engel Curves. Discussion Paper No. 96-30. Department of Economics, University of British Columbia. Vancouver.

Ryan, D. L., and Wales, T. J. (1999). Flexible and semi-flexible consumer demands with quadratic Engel curves. *Review of Economics and Statistics,* 81, 277-287.

Ryan, D. L. Wales, T. J. and Woodland, A. D. (1982). Engel curves for meat consumption in Australia. *Australian Economic Papers,* 21, 106-122.

Raymond, J. (1987). *Bring Up Children Alone: Policies for Sole Parents.* Issues Paper No. 3. Social Security: Review, Australian Government Publishing Services. Canberra.

Saha, A., Capps, O., Jr., and Byrner, P. J. (1997). Calculating marginal effects in models for zero expenditures in household budgets using a Heckman-type correction. *Applied Economics,* 29, 1311-1316.

Sahn, D., and Stifel, D. (2000). Exploring Alternative Measures of Welfare in the Absence of Expenditure Data. Draft mimeo. Cornell University.

Saint-Paul, G., and Verdier, T. (1996). Inequality, redistribution and growth: A challenge to the conventional political economy approach. *European Economic Review,* 40, 719-728.

Salem, A. B. Z., and Mount, T. D. (1974). A convenient descriptive model of income distribution: The gamma density. *Econometrica,* 42, 115-127.

Saunders, P. (ed.), (1987). Redistribution and the welfare state: Estimating the effects of government benefits and taxes on household income. In *Proceedings of a Workshop held at the University of New South Wales.* 13 May 1987.

Saunders, P. (1992). Poverty, inequality and recession. *Economic Papers,* September, 1-22.

Saunders, P. (1994). *Welfare and Inequality.* Cambridge University Press, Cambridge.

Saunders, P. (1997). Living standards, choice of poverty. *Australian Journal of Labour Economics,* 1, 49-70.

Saunders, P. (1998). *Development of Indicative Budget Standards for Australia.* Social Research Policy Center, University of New South Wales. Kensington.

Schlesselman, J. (1971). Power families: A note on the Box and Cox transformation. *Journal of the Royal Statistical Society,* 33, 307-311.

Schultz, T. P. (1998). Inequality in the distribution of personal income in the world: How it is changing and why? *Journal of Population Economics,* 11, 307-344.

Schultz, T. P. (2000). *Inequality in the Distribution of Personal Income in the World: How It Is Changing and Why.* Yale Economic Growth Center. (RePEc:fth:Yalegr:554).
http://netec.mcc.ac.uk/BibEc/data/Papers/fthyalegr554.html

Schumpeter, J. A. (ed.) (1954). *History of Economic Analysis.* Allen and Unwin. London.

Schutz, R. R. (1951). On the measurement of income inequality. *American Economic Review,* 41, 107-122.

Sen, A. K. (1969). *Collective Choice and Social Welfare.* Holdenday. San Franscisco.

Sen, A. K. (1973). *On Economic Inequality.* Clarendon Press. Oxford.

Sen, A. K. (1984). Family and good: Sex bias in poverty. In A. K. Sen (ed.). *Resources, Values and Development,* Harvard University Press. Cambridge, Mass.

Seneca, J. J., and Taussing, M. K. (1971). Family equivalence scales and personal income tax exemptions for children. *Review of Economics and Statistics,* 53, 253-262.

Shahabi-Azad, S. (2001). Immigrant Expenditure Patterns on Transportation. Working Paper No. 01-01, RIIM. Research on Immigration and Integration in the Metropolis, Vancouver Center of Excellence. Vancouver.

Sheshinski, E. (1972). Relation between a social welfare function and the Gini index of inequality. *Journal of Economic Theory,* 4, 98-100.

Shirras, G. F. (1935). The Pareto law and the distribution of income. *Economic Journal,* 45, 663-681.

Shorrocks, A. F. (1995). Income and Welfare Evaluation of Heterogeneous Income Distributions. Discussion Paper 447, Department of Economics, University of Essex.

Simon, H. A. (1955). On a class of skew distribution functions. *Biometrika,* 42, 425-440. Also in: H. A. Simon (1957). *Models of Man.* Wiley. New York .

Simpura, J., and Karlsson, T. (2001). Trends in drinking patterns among adult population in 15 European countries, 1950 to 1995: A review. *Nordisk alkihol - ochnarkotikatidskrift,* 18 (English supplement).

Singh, B. (1972). On the determination of economies of scale in household: Consumption. *International Economic Review,* 13, 257-270.

Singh, B. (1973). The effects of household composition on its consumption pattern. *Sankhya: The Indian Journal of Statistics,* Series B, 35, 207-226.

Singh, B., and Nagar, A. L. (1973). Determination of consumer unit scales. *Econometrica,* 41, 347-356.

Singh, B., and Nagar, A. L. (1978). Identification and estimation of consumer unit scales. *Econometrica,* 46, 231-233.

Singh, S. K. and Maddala, G. S. (1976). A function for size distribution of income. *Econometrica,* 44, 963-973.

Sinha, R.P. (1966). An analysis of food expenditure in India. *Journal of Farm Economics,* 48, 113-123.

Slesnick, D. (1998). Empirical approaches to the measurement of welfare. *Journal of Economic Literature,* 36, 2108-2165.

Smith, D. E. (1991). Towards an aboriginal household expenditure survey: Conceptual, methodological and cultural considerations. Centre for Aboriginal Economic Policy research. Discussion Paper No. 10/1991. http:// http://www.anu.edu.au /caepr /1991 /1991_10.html

Social Welfare Policy Secretariat. (1981). *Report on Poverty Measurement.* Australian Government Publishing Service. Canberra.

Spahn, P. E. (1974). Simulating Long-term Changes of Income Distribution within an Income Tax Model for West Germany. Unpublished manuscript. Harvard University.

Spanos, A. (1995). On normality and the linear regression model. *Econometric Reviews,* 14, 195-203.

Spitzer, J. J. (1976). The demand for money, the liquidity trap, and functional forms. *International Economic Review,* 17, 220-227.

Spitzer J. J. (1977). A simultaneous equations system of money demand and supply using generalized functional forms. *Journal of Econometrics,,* 5, 117-128.

Stanford, L. (2000). Observations on alcohol beverages consumption. *Australia and New Zealand Wine Industry Journal*, 15, 14-27.

Stark, T. (1972). *The Distribution of Personal Income in the United Kingdom:1949-63*. Cambridge University Press. Cambridge.

Steindl, J. (1965). *Random processes and the Growth of Firms*. Griffin. London.

Stiglitz, J. E. (1969). Distribution of income and wealth among individuals. *Econometrica*, 37, 382 – 397.

Stone, J. R. N. (1954). *The Measurement of Consumers' Expenditure and Behaviour in the United Kingdom 1920-1930*, Vol. 1. Cambridge University Press. Cambridge.

Strauss, J., and Thomas, D. (1998). Health, nutrition and economic development. *Journal of Economic Literature*, 36, 1010-46

Summers, R. (1959). A note on least squares bias in household expenditure analysis. *Econometrica*, 27, 121-126.

Sutherland H., Taylor R., and Gomulka J. (2001). Combining Household Income and Expenditure Data in Policy simulations. Micro-simulation Unit Discussion Paper MU0101, Department of Applied Economics, University of Cambridge. Cambridge.

Sutherland, H. (1996). *Households, Individuals and the re-Distribution of income*, DAE Working Papers, Department of applied economics, university of Cambridge (RePEc:cam:camdae:9614). http://netec.mcc.ac.uk.HoPEc/geminiabout.html

Sydnestricker, E., and King, W. I. (1921). The measurement of the relative economic status of families. *Journal of the American Statistical Association*, 17, 842-857.

Szulc, A. (2000). Economic Transition, Poverty and Inequality: Poland in the 1990's. http://www.worldbank.org/research/transition/inequal.htm.

Taylor R., Gomulka J., and Sutherland, H. (2000). Creating order out of chaos? Identifying homogeneous groups of households across multiple datasets. Paper presented at the 26th General Conference of the International Association for Research in Income and Wealth. University of Cambridge. Cambridge.

Theil, H. (1965). The information approach to demand analysis. *Econometrica,*33, 67-87.

Theil, H. (1967). *Economics and Information Theory*. North-Holland. Amsterdam.

Thesia, I. G., and Blanciforti, L. A. (1994). *Household Income Reporting: An Analysis of US Consumer Expenditure Survey Data*. US Bureau of Labor Statistics, Division of Price and Index Number Research. Washington DC.

Thurow, L. C. (1970). Analyzing the American income distributions. *American Economic Review*, 60, 261-269

Tiffin, A., and Tiffin, R. (1999). Estimation of food demand elasticities for Great Britain: 1972-1994. *Journal of Agricultural Economics*, 50, 140-147.

Timothy, K., Beatty, M., and LaFrance, J. T. (2001). *Income Elasticity and Functional Form*. Working Paper No. 922, Department of Agricultural and Resource Economics, Division of Agriculture and Natural Resources, University of California. Berkeley.

Tinbergen, J. (1975). *Income Distribution: Analysis and Policy*. North Holland. Amsterdam.

Tinmet, G., and Kadekodi, G. (1971). Note on the transformation of variables in simultaneous equations systems. *Journal of Indian Society: Agricultural Statistics*, 23, 163-173.

Tintner, G., and Kadekodi, G. (1971). Note on the transformation of variables in simultaneous equations Systems. *Journal of Indian Society of Agricultural Statistics*, 23, 163-173.

Titmuss, R. M. (1962). *Income Distribution and Social Change*. Allen and Unwin. London.

Tsakloglou, P. (1991). Estimation and comparison of two simple models of equivalence scales for the cost of children. *The Economic Journal*, 101, 343-357.

Tsuji, M. (1972). A note on Professor Stiglitz's distribution of income and wealth. *Econometrica*, 40, 947-949.

Tukey, J. W. (1957). On the comparative anatomy of transformations. *Annals of Mathematical Statistics*, 28, 602-632.

Tukey, J.W., and Moore, P.G. (1954). Answer to query 112. *Biometrics*, 10, 562-568.

United Nations. (1989). *National Household Survey Capability Program: Household Income and Expenditure Surveys: A Technical Study*. New York.

Valenzuela, R. J. (1996). Engel scales for Australia, the Philippines and Thailand: A comparative analysis. *The Australian Economic Review*, 29, 189-98.

248

Van de Ven, J. (2001). Distributional limits and Gini coefficient. Department of Economics (RePEc:fth:melbec:776), Melbourne. http://netec.mcc.ac.uk/BibEc/data/Papers/fthmelbec776.html

Van Praag, B. M. S., and Van Der'sar, N. L. (1987). Empirical uses of subjective measures of well-being: Household cost functions and equivalence scales. *The Journal of Human Resources*, 23, 193-210.

Veeernik, J. (1998). *Household Income Distribution and Redistribution in the Czech Republic: Readjustment to the Market*. Institute of Sociology, Academy of Sciences. Prague.

Verbeek, M. (2000). *A Guide to Modern Econometrics*. John Wiley and Sons. New York.

Vickery, W. (1947). Resource distribution pattern and the classification of families. *Studies in Income and Wealth*, 10. NBER. New York.

Vickery, W. (1949). Some limits to the income elasticity of tax yield. *Review of Economics and Statistics*, 31, 140-145

Visaria, P. (1980). *Demographic factors and the distribution of income: Some issues*. World Bank Reprint No. 129. Washington DC.

Von Bortkiewiez, L. (1930). Die Disparitats masse de einkommensstatistik. *Bulletin de l'Institut International de Statistique*, 25, 189-298.

Warren, N. A. (1986). The distributional impact of changing the tax mix in Australia: Some preliminary Findings. In J. G. Head (ed.). Changing the Tax Mix. Paper presented at a conference organised by the Centre of Policy Studies. Monash University. Clayton.

Warren, N. A. (1991). The effects of Australian taxes and social welfare on the distribution of income in 1975-76, 1984-85 and 1988-89. Paper presented at the Social and Economic Inequality Conference, Centre for Applied Economic Research and Social Policy Research Centre, University of New South Wales. Kensington.

Werner, C. (2000). A Taste of Canada: An Analysis of Food Expenditure Patterns for Canadian-born and Foreign-Born Consumers. Working Paper #00-05, RIIM. Research on Immigration and Integration in the Metropolis, Vancouver Center of Excellence. Vancouver.

Wesson, J. (1972). On the distributions of personal incomes. *Review of Economic Studies*, 39, 77-86.

White, K. J. (1972). Estimation of the liquidity trap with a generalized functional form. *Econometrica*, 40, 193-199.

Whiteford, P. (l984). A family's needs: Equivalence scales and social security. *Social Security Journal*, December, 54-61.

Whiteford, P. (1985). A Family's Needs: Equivalence Scales, Poverty and Social Security. Research Paper No. 27, Department of Social Security. Canberra.

Whiteford, P. (1986). Issues in Assistance for Families: Horizontal and Vertical Equity Considerations. Research Paper No. 29, Department of Social Security. Canberra.

Whiteford, P. (1991). How we spend our money? *Social Policy Research Centre Newsletter No. 37.*

Widjajanti, E., and Li, E. (1996). Food expenditure patterns in urban and rural Indonesia: 1981 to 1993. *Australian Agribusiness Review*, 3, 93-113.

Williams, R. (1976a). Estimation of Household Demand Responses Using Cross-section Data: A System's Interpretation of Podder's Result. Preliminary Working Paper, PS-02. University of Melbourne. Melbourne.

Williams, R. (1976b). Household consumption in Australia: an examination of patterns across socio-economic classes. Unpublished Preliminary Working Paper No. SP-04. University of Melbourne. Melbourne.

Williams, R. (1977). Engel Curves and Demand System: Demographic Effects on Consumption in Australia. Unpublished Preliminary Working Paper SP-07. University of Melbourne. Melbourne.

Williams, R. A. (1978a). Demographic effect on consumption patterns in Australia: A preliminary analysis of the ABS 1974-75 Household Expenditure Survey. Preliminary Working Paper No. SP-11, University of Melbourne. Melbourne.

Williams, R. (1978b). The Use of Disaggregated Cross-section Data in Explaining Shifts in Australian Consumer Demand Patterns Over Time. Preliminary working Paper PS-13. University of Melbourne. Melbourne.

Williams, R. (1978c). Structural Change and Private Consumption: Evidence from the 1974/75 Household Expenditure Survey. General Paper No. G-15. University of Melbourne. Melbourne.

Wilson, D., Juniper, J., and Lock-shin, J. (2001). Determining the inequality of alcohol consumption using the Theil index. In S. Chetty, and B. Collins (ed.). *Bridging Marketing Theory and Practice.* ANZMAC Conference. New Zealand.

Wilson, M. (1995). Earning Distributions from the Family Expenditure Survey and the New Earnings Survey Campared. DAE Working Papers. Department of Applied Economics, University of Cambridge. Cambridge. (RePEc:cam:camdae:9534). http://netec.mcc.ac.uk.HoPEc/geminiabout.html.

Wing-Cheong Yuen. Food Consumption in Rich Countries. Economic Research Centre, Department of Economics, University of Western Australia. Perth.

Wodon, Q., and Yitzhaki, S. (2001a). *The Effect of Group Data on the Estimation of the Gini Income Elasticity.* World Bank. Washington DC.

Wodon, Q., and Yitzhaki, S. (2001b). *Inequality and Social Welfare*, In J. Klugman (ed.). in Poverty Reduction Strategies Sourcebook. World Bank. Washington DC, Forthcoming.

Wold, H. O. A., and Jureen, L. (1953). *Demand Analysis*. Wiley. New York.

Wold, H. O. A., and Whittle, P. (1957). A model explaining the Pareto distribution of wealth. *Econometrica*, 25, 591-595.

Woodbury, R. M. (1944). Economic consumption scales and their uses. *Journal of the American Statistical Association*, 39, 45-56.

Wooldridge, J. M. (1992). Some alternatives to Box-Cox regression model. *International Economic review*, 33, 935-955.

Working, H. (1943). Statistical laws of family expenditure. *Journal of the American Statistical Association,* 38, 43-45.

Wu, Y., Li, E., and Samuel, S. N. (1995). Food consumption in urban China: An empirical analysis. *Applied Economics*, 27, 509-515.

Yao, S., and Zhu, L. (1998). Understanding income inequality in China: A multi-angle perspective. *Economics of Planning*, 31, 133-50.

Yatchew, A. (1999). An elementary nonparametric differencing test of equality of regression functions. *Economics Letters*, 62, 271-78.

Yatchew, A. (1977). An elementary estimator for the partial linear model. *Economics Letters,* 57, 135-143.

Yates, J. (1991). Australia's Owner-Occupied Housing Wealth and its Impact on Income Distribution. In *Social Policy Research Center: Reports and Proceedings No. 92,* University of New South Wales. Kensington.

Yntema, D. W. (1933). Measures of the inequality in the personal distribution of wealth and income. *Journal of the American Statistical Association*, 28, 423-443.

Young, C. (1986). *Selection and Survival Immigrant Mortality in Australia*, Department of Immigration and Ethnic Affairs. Australian Government Publishing Services. Canberra.

Zarembka, P. (1968). Functional form in the demand for money. *Journal of the American Statistical Association*, 43, 502-511.

Zarembka, P. (1972). An econometric analysis of the food consumption function. In *Towards the Theory of Economic Development.* Holden Day. San Francisco.

Zarembka, P. (1974). Transformation of variables in econometrics. In P. Zaremabka (ed.). *Frontiers in Econometrics,* pp. 81-104. Academic Press. New York.

Zellner, A. (1962). An efficient method of estimating seemingly unrelated regressions and rests for aggregation bias. *Journal of the American Statistical Association,* 57, 348-168.

Zweimuller, J. (1998). *Aggregate Demand, Non-linear Engel Curves and R&D Investments.* University of Zurich and CEPR. Zweim@iew.unizch.ch

Zweimuller, J. (2000). Schumpterian entrepreneurs meet Engel's law: The impact of inequality on innovation driven growth. *Journal of Economic Growth*, 5, 185-206.

INDEX

252

256

Advanced Studies in Theoretical and Applied Econometrics

1. J.H.P. Paelinck (ed.): *Qualitative and Quantitative Mathematical Economics*. 1982
    ISBN 90-247-2623-9
2. J.P. Ancot (ed.): *Analysing the Structure of Econometric Models*. 1984
    ISBN 90-247-2894-0
3. A.J. Hughes Hallet (ed.): *Applied Decision Analysis and Economic Behaviour*. 1984
    ISBN 90-247-2968-8
4. J.K. Sengupta: *Information and Efficiency in Economic Decision*. 1985
    ISBN 90-247-3072-4
5. P. Artus and O. Guvenen (eds.), in collaboration with F. Gagey: *International Macroe-conomic Modelling for Policy Decisions*. 1986   ISBN 90-247-3201-8
6. M.J. Vilares: *Structural Change in Macroeconomic Models*. Theory and Estimation.
    1986   ISBN 90-247-3277-8
7. C. Carraro and D. Sartore (eds.): *Development of Control Theory for Economic Anal-ysis*. 1987   ISBN 90-247-3345-6
8. D.P. Broer: *Neoclassical Theory and Empirical Models of Aggregate Firm Behaviour*.
    1987   ISBN 90-247-3412-6
9. A. Italianer: *Theory and Practice of International Trade Linkage Models*. 1986
    ISBN 90-247-3407-X
10. D.A. Kendrick: *Feedback*. A New Framework for Macroeconomic Policy. 1988
    ISBN 90-247-3593-9; Pb: 90-247-3650-1
11. J.K. Sengupta and G.K. Kadekodi (eds.): *Econometrics of Planning and Efficiency*.
    1988   ISBN 90-247-3602-1
12. D.A. Griffith: *Advanced Spatial Statistics*. Special Topics in the Exploration of Quanti-tative Spatial Data Series. 1988   ISBN 90-247-3627-7
13. O. Guvenen (ed.): *International Commodity Market Models and Policy Analysis*. 1988
    ISBN 90-247-3768-0
14. G. Arbia: *Spatial Data Configuration in Statistical Analysis of Regional Economic and Related Problems*. 1989   ISBN 0-7923-0284-2
15. B. Raj (ed.): *Advances in Econometrics and Modelling*. 1989   ISBN 0-7923-0299-0
16. A. Aznar Grasa: *Econometric Model Selection*. A New Approach. 1989
    ISBN 0-7923-0321-0
17. L.R. Klein and J. Marquez (eds.): *Economics in Theory and Practice*. An Eclectic Approach. Essays in Honor of F. G. Adams. 1989   ISBN 0-7923-0410-1
18. D.A. Kendrick: *Models for Analyzing Comparative Advantage*. 1990
    ISBN 0-7923-0528-0
19. P. Artus and Y. Barroux (eds.): *Monetary Policy*. A Theoretical and Econometric Approach. 1990   ISBN 0-7923-0626-0
20. G. Duru and J.H.P. Paelinck (eds.): *Econometrics of Health Care*. 1990
    ISBN 0-7923-0766-6
21. L. Phlips (ed.): *Commodity, Futures and Financial Markets*. 1991
    ISBN 0-7923-1043-8

Advanced Studies in Theoretical and Applied Econometrics

Advanced Studies in Theoretical and Applied Econometrics

42. M.O. Haque: *Income Elasticity and Economic Development.* Methods and Applications. 2005
ISBN 0-387-24292-9

Printed in the United States
99049LV00003B/117/A

CONCORDIA UNIV. LIBRARY

CONCORDIA UNIVERSITY LIBRARIES
MONTREAL